Polygyny

UNIVERSITY PRESS OF FLORIDA

Florida A&M University, Tallahassee
Florida Atlantic University, Boca Raton
Florida Gulf Coast University, Ft. Myers
Florida International University, Miami
Florida State University, Tallahassee
New College of Florida, Sarasota
University of Central Florida, Orlando
University of Florida, Gainesville
University of North Florida, Jacksonville
University of South Florida, Tampa
University of West Florida, Pensacola

Polygyny

What It Means
When African American
Muslim Women
Share Their Husbands

Debra Majeed

University Press of Florida

Gainesville

Tallahassee

Tampa

Boca Raton

Pensacola

Orlando

Miami

Jacksonville

Ft. Myers

Sarasota

This book may be available in an electronic edition.

21 20 19 18 17 16   6 5 4 3 2 1

First cloth printing, 2015
First paperback printing, 2016

Library of Congress Cataloging-in-Publication Data
Majeed, Debra, author.
Polygyny : what it means when African American Muslim women share
their husbands / Debra Majeed.
pages cm
Includes bibliographical references and index.
ISBN 978-0-8130-6077-4 (cloth)
ISBN 978-0-8130-5406-3 (pbk.)
1. Polygyny—United States. 2. African American women—United States. 3. Muslim
women—United States. 4. Man-woman relationships—United States. I. Title.
GN480.35.M35 2015
306.84'23—dc23
2015003596

The University Press of Florida is the scholarly publishing agency for the State
University System of Florida, comprising Florida A&M University, Florida Atlantic
University, Florida Gulf Coast University, Florida International University, Florida State
University, New College of Florida, University of Central Florida, University of Florida,
University of North Florida, University of South Florida, and University of West Florida.

University Press of Florida
15 Northwest 15th Street
Gainesville, FL 32611-2079
http://www.upf.com

Contents

Preface

Are plural marriages in the United States solely the extension of male desire? Do they exploit women? Is criminalizing them just and, if so, for whom? How do Americans make meaning of some family structures while disavowing others? How do African American Muslims explain what they are doing and why when they establish multiple-wife households? What forms of agency or capacity for action do Muslim women exert when they share their husbands? These and other questions have tugged at my consciousness since 2002, much as I once clung to the hem of my mother's skirt until I captured her attention.

At that time, I was a divorced Muslim woman hoping to remarry an African American Muslim man. Though I realized that I could consider potential mates from any cultural group, I believed—as do most of my subjects—that I resonated most with Americans of African ancestry. Intellectually, I was also drawn to consider the influence of religion and ideology in the organization of African American Muslim family life. By then I had read and heard enough about the strains on Muslim women who shared their husbands to be wary of people who spoke highly about the benefits of multiple-wife unions. Like many people, I thought such relationships were merely about sex, male privilege, and female submission—just another variety of female exploitation. I also figured that the women involved must be crazy! As I struggled to support a good friend whose husband was about to take another wife, however, I discovered that my perspective was too simplistic and that in the world of African American (and some other) Muslims this form of plural marriage is much more complex than I realized.

For nearly two decades, my friend and her husband lived monogamously, raised children from former marriages, and built a prosperous business together. Longtime attendees of our local religious community revered them as an ideal married couple. I did too. While I was acquainted with the husband, I loved and adored his wife. Never during their marriage, according to my friend, did her husband ever tell her that he desired to enter into a marriage contract with another woman—until he was about to say "I do." So, yes, I was biased against this household arrangement at the outset. Even so, my friend and I knew that the Qur'an, the single highest authority in Islam, offers conditional permission for men to marry up to four women simultaneously. Neither my friend nor I believed the necessary conditions were present in her situation, however. We were convinced, too, that neither the new wife nor my friend would benefit if her husband contracted a marriage that could not be recognized legally. Yet her husband proceeded with his plans, with the apparent approval of our local religious leaders and some of our friends.

Most of the members of our association of Muslims—those who follow the leadership of Imam W. D. Mohammed, the foremost Muslim leader in the United States until his death in 2008—were publicly silent on the issue of multiple-wife marriage when I first began this study. They consider family formation to be a private matter, off limits to public discussion. In this, they echo the teachings of their leader, who responded this way to criticism of his marriage to a woman fifty years his junior: "You should stay out of private business." I would not reduce this comment made in 2004 to unconditional support for multiple-wife marriage nor to indifference to the impact one's private life can have on one's community. Not only would that conclusion be untrue, but it would also overlook the importance Imam Mohammed placed on marriage and family life throughout his ministry and his concern for the safety and protection of women. Instead, his statement and some reactions to it embody the many paradoxes I encountered and the varied ways in which Muslims translate what they hear, read, and are taught into everyday action.

In 2002 my friend was convinced that she fully understood Islam's perspectives on marriage. In hindsight, she did not. She had yet to realize her own responsibility in her marital decisions. She had yet to fully engage her own agency, choosing docility instead. Her "knowledge" reflected unquestioned assumptions taught to her by her husband and by her local mosque and bequeathed to her by earlier generations that rendered conditional permission as unconditional approval. Hers is a stance also taken by most of our Muslim friends and associates. Thus within months of her husband's marriage, she grudgingly accepted a role consistent with her self-imposed label: "co-wife."[1] I never expected the effect her experience would have on me or the gravitational pull I would feel to educate others and myself about marital multiplicity in Islam.[2]

As my friend struggled to deal with her husband's absences, reduced financial support, and the marital intimacy now extended to another legitimate wife—insofar as Islam views consensual sexual intercourse between a man and a woman—I began to negotiate a marriage of my own. In the process, I wondered what I would do if my husband-to-be took a similar stand. While I was intent on creating a monogamous union, my friend's experience confirmed for me that I should not assume that my husband-to-be shared the same plan. Quickly my journey moved from theoretical and empathic to the status of personal—very personal. When asked whether ours was intended to be a continuously monogamous union for him, my fiancé replied, "I cannot say 'No' to what Allah has said 'Yes.'" That union dissolved after ten years and never included a second wife. But it could have, as I discovered during our first year together. Our exchange confirmed for me the importance of this exploration.

I have become acutely aware that other African American Muslims struggle with similar questions and concerns as they strive to practice their religion, grapple with the benefits and responsibilities of marriage and singleness, and contribute to Muslim community life in a Muslim-minority context. As they do, many come to realize that the absence of a transparent process for handling marriage and divorce issues sentences too many women living polygyny to suffering in silence, sometimes jettisoning them to the margins of their communities. This is especially trying for African American Muslims, who distrust civil authorities due to a legacy of racism and alienation, or for those who believe that the state should not intervene in regulating religious practices such as marriage. Regardless of their positions, most African American and other American Muslims agree on the need for adequate resources to enter into and sustain Muslim marriages in the United States, that is, to ensure justice.

Polygyny is a book about authority and cultural particularities. It also is about limits and possibilities and real and perceived power disparities. About religion and household organization. About African American Muslim women and their right to speak, be heard, and control representations of themselves, their marriages, and their lived realities. *Polygyny* is not a definitive work on the subject of multiple-wife marriage among African American Muslims or even of marital multiplicity in Islam. I do not seek to promote the practice, but I also do not advocate its eradication. What this book does do is use a small sampling of American Muslim life to ask readers to rethink their ideas about what constitutes a family as it encourages Muslim women and men to recognize their agency more fully and to be more cognizant of their responsibilities to one another. I invite readers on the journey on which I embarked, one that compelled me to think more critically about gender inequality, gender responsibility, and gender justice in Muslim family life.

I hope to challenge the presuppositions people might impose on familial systems that differ from their own. I invite readers to acknowledge realities and choices experienced by individuals who are often loathed because of them. The subjects of this work are people who, like all of us, are at times uncomfortable with the ramifications of their decisions. They also live, work, love, struggle, and strive in an era that has witnessed constitutional challenges to traditional views about marriage and family.

The pages that follow consider multiple-wife marriage in Islam as one remedy for and a demographic challenge to the absence of marriageable African American men as well as the high number of female-led households in black America. They offer insights that can expand debates about the regulation and recognition of consenting adult relationships beyond questions related to the legitimacy of same-sex marriage. They also draw attention to other ways multiple-wife marriages coupled with a certain cultural and religious consciousness can constrain or liberate women. The dominant voices in this work are those of my female subjects—some who welcome the practice, some who oppose it, some who acquiesce to it, and still others who locate their negotiating power within it.

I chose to offer a female-focused study for three reasons. First, I want to draw attention to the contradictions and paradoxes that abound for those who live in households led by men married to multiple women.[3] Most popular and academic literature on the subject gravitates between representations, on one hand, of Muslim women as victims who lack agency and, on the other, of Muslim men as the authorities of household formation who take additional wives because they can. Each of these perspectives rests on a single rhetorical flaw—that a conflict exists between Islamic mandates on marriage, gender justice, and what it means to be human. I decided to write a book explaining this presumed conflict and to demonstrate that the manner in which African American Muslims organize their families and the rationales that drive their marital choices are far more complicated, situational, and multilayered than has been explicated.

Second, I set out to acknowledge the centrality of women's experiences in any project on Muslim family life. Two of the ways this female-inclusive exploration augments understandings of what I will explain as polygyny in Islam are in its consideration of women who seek wives for their husbands and in its challenge to mosques and religious leaders who welcome and perform multiple-wife marriages while doing little to provide resources for the maintenance of those unions. Listening to the stories of my subjects and observing their interactions with each other and with their husbands helped me appreciate how sharing a husband with a second, third, or fourth wife is preferable, an expression of faith, for some women, while it is dehumanizing for others. Providing space for Muslim women to articulate their own lived realities is crucial to understanding the relationship between universals and particulars in the way polygyny is practiced within diverse Muslim contexts. (That said, I soon came to appreciate better the astute sentiments of Lepore: "Finding out and writing about people, living or dead, is tricky work. It is necessary to balance intimacy with distance while at the same time being inquisitive to the point of invasiveness.")[4]

Finally, this book draws attention to Qur'anic exegesis that posits husband-sharing as a cultural *jihad*, an internal struggle that "good" Muslim women endure for the maintenance of community life. It questions unexamined adherence to local interpretations of the Qur'an that link cultural preservation with desires to reaffirm traditional Islamic tenets such as the oft-quoted saying of the Prophet "Marriage is half of the religion." In the process, this work invites a holistic reading of the Qur'an, one that resembles the work of Rahman in its promotion of interpretations that "determine the spirit behind the literal force of certain injunctions."[5] Approaches to rereading and retranslating dominant traditional articulations of the word of Allah delivered to the Prophet Muhammad in seventh-century Arabia are gaining visibility in the twenty-first century. As will become evident in the pages that follow, Muslim scholars like Amina Wadud make a strong case for questioning embedded patriarchal assumptions about the manner in which good Muslim women express agency. In addition to exploring their interpretative methods, in this work I challenge abstract and idealized depictions of women who share their husbands.

Acknowledgments

A project of this magnitude seldom reaches fruition without the support and guidance of individuals whose names never appear on the cover. This book is no exception.

My first and primary thanks go to my subjects and those who provided the background and context for this study of multiple-wife marriage. Those who are living or have ever lived polygyny took courageous steps in speaking with me at the level of intimacy I experienced. I owe an enormous debt to the women and men who shared their anger, tears, and excitement with me, fully aware that theirs is a journey I would never choose for myself. I wish you health, happiness, and the peace of G'd.

I am eternally grateful for the generosity, insight, and wisdom of my religious leader and the first Muslim I met, Imam W. D. Mohammed. It was under your leadership that I became Muslim in 1998, and I am humbled to benefit from the legacy that you bequeathed to the world. I pray that Allah (Subhanahu Wa Ta'ala) grants you eternal mercy, grace, and paradise. I pray, as well, that we who continue to benefit from your guidance and teaching use what we learn to help create strong families and a better world.

The imams, scholars, and other religious leaders who opened doors to me, whose names helped me gain access to spaces otherwise closed, and those who critiqued research questions, focus-group approaches, and portions of the manuscript have challenged and directed me in ways that have had a profound influence on my intellectual journey and spiritual life. I am especially indebted to Imam Khalil Akbar, Nadiyah Ahmad, Imam Qasim Ahmed, Imam Plemon El-Amin, Imam A. K. Hasan, Debra Hasan, Dr. Jamillah Karim, Qaedah Karriem, Imam Nasif Majeed, Aminah Muhammad, Laila Muhammad, Maryam Muhammad, Imam Faheed Muwakil, Dorothy Rahman, Imam Mikal Ramadan, Barbara Rasheed, Imam Mikal Saahir, Imam Ronald Shaheed, Judge David Shaheed, and Imam Faheem Shuaibe.

I am similarly grateful to colleagues and mentors Dr. Amina Wadud and Dr.

Aminah McCloud for your direction and insight throughout this project. You continue to be mirrors that help ground me. I humbly acknowledge Dr. Kecia Ali, Dr. Juliane Hammer, Dr. Laury Silvers, and Dr. Carolyn Moxley Rouse for the time and conversation you contributed through reading and commenting on chapters of the manuscript at various stages. I most appreciate your diligence, mercy, and relentless honesty. I am also thankful for Dr. Asifa Quraishi and your patient explanations of legal issues.

To my editor, Sian Hunter, and her marketing team at University Press of Florida, I say thank you for being a consistent source of support. I appreciate Tana Silva, who gently guided me through the copyediting stage.

I extend heartfelt thanks to staff members at my home institution, Beloit College, who assisted my access to materials, technological support, Institutional Review Board approvals, and who gave me encouragement: Denny Broderick, Dr. Greg Buchanan, Eula Buchanan, Cindy Cooley, Drew Gracyalny, Teresa Leopold, Deb Lynch, Sarah Meadus, Chris Nelson, and Sherry Monahan, and Dr. George Williams.

As is the practice on many liberal arts campuses, I took advantage of every opportunity to link my research and teaching. In this regard, the contributions of four former students who served as research assistants proved invaluable. Thank you, Atiera Coleman, Madison Glenn, Caitlin Gunn, and Jennifer Olson.

At the same time that I completed the major portion of the data collection for this project, two colleagues and I decided to form what we call the Paragraph Club. There, we committed to a regular schedule of writing, reflection, and evaluation of each other's work. The questions raised, methodologies considered, and arguments presented and challenged contributed greatly to the completion of this book. Paragraph Club members, Dr. Beatrice McKenzie and Dr. Linda Sturtz, and my womanist scholar mentors, Dr. Katie G. Cannon, Dr. Cheryl Kirk-Duggan, Dr. Cheryl Townsend Gilkes, Dr. Jacquelyn Grant, Dr. Rosetta Ross, Dr. Linda Thomas, and Dr. Emilie Townes, continue to help make me a better scholar and human being. Thank you for trusting, pushing, encouraging, and celebrating what you knew I could do and become.

I was also sustained throughout the development of this book by the community, feedback, and institutional support I received as a Sanger Summer Research Fellow at Beloit College, as a research associate at the Hadassah-Brandeis Institute at Brandeis University, and as a Womanist Scholar at the Interdenominational Theological Center in Atlanta, Georgia.

I am grateful to my family and friends whose love, support, and single-mindedness—"When is the book coming out?"—helped keep the endless mercy of Allah ever before me. The earthly journey of my mother, Martha Elizabeth Craig McGrew Jackson March, ended before the completion of this book. I thank Allah (SWT) for you and for the survival skills and determination you inspired. I pray, too, that we will be reunited in paradise. Finally, special thanks are due my husband, Imam Rabbani Mubashshir, whose kindness, theological challenges, wit, and care helped me to keep my eyes on the prize of completion.

Introduction

Now that I am growing, learning, and doing better in my
deen and in my spirit, I need to be married. I deserve that.
And that's what Allah has deemed fit for me.

Kubayah, a divorcee about to enter polygyny

Attractive and direct when she needs to articulate her position on almost any issue, Kubayah had been divorced for four years when we met following a presentation I gave at an Atlanta *masjid* in 2009. Then the mother of a twenty-nine-year-old son, she described herself as a retired hair stylist and bartender, who currently worked in the transportation industry. At forty-seven, Kubayah had just returned to actively engaging her religion after nearly nine years of introspection and what she called "getting my mind together and changing a couple of things." As the epigraph above indicates, Kubayah perceived marriage as an expected outgrowth of her Muslim identity, particularly when she focused on fulfilling the dictates of G'd as outlined in the teachings of her religion. Hers is a characterization shared by most of the subjects of this book. Moreover, to Kubayah and many other American Muslims, marriage provides one of the surest protections against sexual sin, and it is a powerful means of strengthening the *ummah*. Thus, women like Kubayah who would not otherwise choose to marry often do so to maintain their purity and to extend the reach of Islam.

This introduction opens my study on African American Muslim women who share their husbands. It begins by describing forms of marriage in Islam and two methodological elements central to this work. I then proceed to draw attention to the racial backdrop of the United States, whose institutional and structural racism has led some African American Muslims to contemplate partnering choices beyond monogamy. From the ramifications of a specific geographic region I move to an explication of the cautionary tones that I encountered as I began to explore the dynamics of family life within Imam W. D. Mohammed's community. Before outlining the remainder of the book and identifying its potential audience, I devote attention to the use of storytelling as a way to document the experiences of my subjects.

Three types of marriage dominate the landscape of Muslim life: heterosexual monogamy, multiple-wife marriage, and *mut'a*, or temporary marriage.[1] Because of its plurality of spouses, multiple-wife marriage is often misconstrued as polygamy, which refers to multiple spouses, whether husbands *or* wives.[2] But women are not permitted multiple husbands, and thus polygamy is un-Islamic. In keeping with my goal of sharing the voices of my subjects and their household arrangements as they understand them, I use the term "polygyny" rather than "polygamy" to describe their marital decisions. The occasional use of "polygamy" reflects the vocabulary of the literature.

The historical practice of a husband living with multiple wives is not the preferred form of marriage for Muslims across the globe or for the estimated one to two million African American Muslims who reside in the United States. When the overwhelming majority of African American Muslims marry, they enter into heterosexual, monogamous unions—as do most other Muslim Americans.[3] In fact, I estimate that there are fewer than a thousand African American Muslim polygynous households in the United States. This figure represents about 0.07 percent of all African American Muslims according to the 2010 study "Muslim-American Outreach," a small segment of the estimated 30,000 to 100,000 people living polygyny in the United States.[4]

Neither Kubayah nor any of my other female subjects expressed a desire to have multiple husbands. A few, like Kubayah, did indicate that the urgency they felt to be married prompted them to see polygyny as a viable option. What separates Kubayah from the rest of my interviewees, however, is her willingness to accept as her husband a man already married to two other women. Polygyny "has always been on my mind," she explained. "During the time I spent with him, he got my heart." Still, the geographical location of her co-wives—Saudi Arabia and West Africa—helped to make her acceptance easier. "I will be the American wife," she proclaimed.[5]

Key Methodological Features

Central to this project is an investigation into the rationale African American female Muslims offer as justification for their decisions to share their husbands and the lengths they traverse to keep their marriages intact. I examine the daily reality of Muslim women living polygyny through the lens of Muslim womanism, a "philosophical perspective" that draws attention to the varied conditions of black womanhood as experienced by African American Muslims, and the values of Islam they articulate. This framework, outlined in chapter 1, questions the ways some African American Muslims use the Qur'an to sanction and define their family structures and the obligation of Muslim communities to ensure the health and well-being of families. Womanism is a method most visible within intellectual circles in the United States as an articulation of the experience and agency of African American Christian women. I transform what I learned in those spaces as a Christian minister for the construction of a perspective that enables African American Muslim women to portray themselves in their own situations. Indeed, chapter 2 features dialogical performance as a tool that creates a discussion among twelve informants that did not occur. This tool enables me to invite the reader into the world of women living polygyny with more depth. Drawing a portrait of polygyny and Islam among African American Muslims through the realities of women affords the opportunity to explore an incompletely documented subject, much as a microhistorian might examine an individual life as an "allegory for broader issues affecting the culture as a whole."[6]

While the overwhelming majority of my subjects include both women and men who constitute the "community" of Imam Mohammed, I privilege the experiences and voices of women because theirs are routinely marginalized and misinterpreted, even though they also are posited as the "face" and/or "truth" of Islam. I contend as well that it is easier to discover what men think about polygyny or any other issue because they tend to be the public "voice" within Islam and other monotheistic traditions. This exploration into the private and public spaces African American Muslims inhabit permits the reimaging of authority as inclusive of "the most important focal point" of any multiple-wife marriage: women.[7] The centrality of women with respect to polygyny in this study recognizes their right and responsibility to contribute to rules and regulations drafted by men about female realities and the recognition of communal practices.

A Context Ripe for Polygyny?

Backgrounding this study is the racial context of the United States that has contributed to social, political, and economic disadvantages for black people and pervasively disparaging race and gender images that African Americans encounter in contemporary American life. The collective experiences of African Americans living in the United States inform the manner in which many

African American Muslims approach the question of polygyny. Members of the association of Imam Mohammed are part of the single largest group of African American Muslims.[8] The vast majority of this group came to Islam through the doorway of the nationalistic version of the religion espoused by his father, Elijah Muhammad, the architect and second leader of the original Nation of Islam.[9] Most of them would come to embrace a broader and more accurate view of Islam during W. D. Mohammed's thirty-three-year ministry, which began in 1975 following his father's death.[10] Those who would come to rely upon the teachings of father and son would also witness the family dynamics of two African American Muslim leaders who some are convinced practiced polygyny.[11]

From headquarters in Chicago, Elijah Muhammad and his seventh son, Warith Deen (W. D.) Mohammed, held a socially and historically constructed view of race consciousness, informed by contemporary struggles against antiblack racism and discrimination that they either witnessed or experienced. Both leaders addressed and attracted a following that included descendants of African slaves and U.S. southern migrants and their offspring who yearned for a religious ideology appreciative of a deep and textured understanding of black life. Even though the northern-born son offered a more traditional and racially tolerant form of Islam, institutionalized racism and its legacies proved to be a significant focus of the leadership of both him and his father, a southern migrant. Moreover, their leadership models acknowledged the embedded nature of religion in the texture of everyday life for African Americans. In fact, each promoted his faith as the best response to oppression of blacks, fully cognizant that "to be black and Muslim in the United States of America has always been a challenge."[12] It would surprise few who knew either man that some followers would attempt to emulate the perceived household formations of their religious leaders.

When reflecting upon the challenges that confront black women, political scientist Harris-Perry argues that their "internal, psychological, emotional, and personal experiences are inherently political" because the social world of black women is shaped by outside assumptions of their character and identity.[13] I would extend her claims to include African American Muslims, particularly those with ties to the Nation of Islam. Even as Elijah Muhammad sought to create a separate nation in 1961, African American Muslims have worked to self-design and preserve their identities as Americans, as black people, and as Muslims. With their efforts to secure recognition as citizens, African American Muslims—like other African Americans—have encountered challenges within a society whose laws "were written to legalize white oppression on moral, so-cial, economic and religious grounds."[14]

Within black America, these Muslims have always had to wrestle with as-sumptions about the religiosity of black people that frame black religion in very narrow ways—often restricted to the confines of Christianity—and thus negat-ing the multiplicity of African American religious experience. I appreciate the commentary of Sherman Jackson in his contextualization of black Christianity and black Islam; however, I do lament the invisible status he affords to women as if the label "Blackamerican" describes men only.[15] Among the global body of believers in Islam, African American Muslims routinely confront questions of authenticity due to some of the teachings of Elijah Muhammad and confusion about their ties to and/or affiliation with the contemporary movement led by Minister Louis Farrakhan. Imam W. D. Mohammed would later characterize W. D. Fard, founder of the Nation of Islam, and the ideology he and Elijah Muhammad espoused as "a piece of satire." Even so, Mohammed worked dili-gently to expand upon one of his father's foundational arguments: the need for African American Muslims to do for themselves.

Drawing Attention to Polygyny and Family Life

My ethnographic research from 2003 to 2013 among more than fifteen dis-tinct African American Muslim communities in which current and/or former polygynists and their families reside confirms that the practice of polygyny is becoming more visible if not growing.[16] For example, the title of a well-publicized marriage conference in Atlanta in 2009 was "A Refreshing Look at Polygyny with Qur'anic Insights and a Focus on Justice and Freedom in an Adverse Environment." Apparently, promoters were so uninhibited about announcing their topic that they distributed and hung posters throughout the downtown Atlanta area where the conference was held. By the summer of 2013, YouTube videos with titles such as "Black Muslim Man—Why You Can't Have More than One Wife," "The Benefits of Polygamy for the Black Community," "Polygamy in the African American Ummah," and "Polygamy in Islam: Muslimah Perspective" became easily accessible on the Internet. These uncensored depictions of African American Muslim life vary in their consideration of the difficulty, complexity, and benefits of multiple-wife house-holds. With such grassroots visibility comes whispered speculation about the legality of such unions, the agency and financial protection of the women involved, communal responsibility for the health and maintenance of polygynous families, and the unwanted governmental scrutiny these arrangements can attract.

This attention to polygyny among African Americans is concerning at a time when Western discourses about Islam concentrate on what are perceived to be the abnormalities of Muslim life, especially after the events of September 11, 2001. Such sketches routinely assume links to terrorism and the agency available to Muslim women to structure their public and private spheres. Granted, some of what one might read, see, and hear about Muslim women is accurate. What the bulk of representations about Muslim women and Muslim life do not offer is what this work does: nuanced portrayals of the lived realities of Muslim women as complex subjects and the multilayered voices of their narratives.

Throughout my research on the dynamics of family life within the community of Imam Mohammed, some imams, or spiritual leaders, strongly encouraged me not to proceed with this work. To them and a few of the individuals I approached for interviews, any consideration of a family dynamic practiced by a minority group and whose form and function is contrary to U.S. law could only fuel stereotypes about Muslims and black sexuality. Those who tried to dissuade me were particularly concerned about the high level of media attention and the increase in hate crimes that American Muslims have experienced since 2001. Since then, their concerns have focused on attempts to link multiple-wife marriages with same-sex unions and accusations that Muslims who practice polygyny are somehow antifamily. Rather than "put our business in the streets," I was cautioned to focus instead on an issue that would enhance the daily realities of African American Muslims who live, work, and struggle to survive in this country.

To me, this consideration of polygyny is precisely such an issue. Above all, I intend in this work to encourage self-examination of Muslim American family life and promote closer attention to the welfare of African American communities, American families, and society as a whole. The connection between religion and family formation and the choices that affect the health and well-being of African American Muslims has been underexplored in both popular and academic contexts. This is a subject whose thoughtful consideration can help us better understand how some Americans choose their loyalties, share their truths, and articulate the conflicts they encounter at the meeting of religious command or interpretation, temporal authority, and communal survival.[17]

I also chose to proceed with this book to afford African American Muslim women a public forum to voice their perspectives on polygyny, to portray themselves in the reality and light of their individual experiences. By doing so, I set out to provide these adherents of Islam with serious intellectual space in which they can enable other Americans to "imagine" Muslims as neighbors with similar hopes, challenges, and strengths. I also want to encourage more rigorous dialogue in local mosques and the development of additional resources focused on the creation and maintenance of healthy family life.

In essence, the conditional permissibility of polygyny and the egalitarian nature of the Qur'an suggest that African American and other Muslims would benefit from family-life education for residence in a Muslim-minority context. As with many other Americans, they could be served by expanded premarital counseling for those who choose monogamy or polygyny, as well as gendered dialogues about rights and responsibilities in marriage. Understandably, these are issues that affect all U.S. families, particularly in light of the high rate of divorce in America. Such resources would be helpful regardless of one's race, class, religion, or sexual orientation or one's position on the acceptability of polygyny, but they are crucial to those living it. They also could help address global perceptions and stereotypical representations of Muslim women as silent, submissive, and veiled women who, as prisoners of their faith, require Western liberation.[18] Moreover, a centerpiece of this study that could have broad appeal is consideration of the "authority of experience" that can position African American Muslim women at the table of discussions to decide what happens, when, by whom, and for whose benefit in regard to any issue that involves them.

Equally noteworthy is the weight African American and other Muslims attribute to communal interpretations of religious sources. By drawing attention to the nuances of black life in America, I offer a glimpse into the context that produced the single largest ethnic group of American Muslims. Finally, surveys that examine attitudes about Muslims in the United States and around the world consistently conclude that the voices and experiences of Muslim women need to anchor any discussion about what Muslims believe, how Muslims live, what Muslims value, and what Muslim women want.[19] Such female participation at levels that ascribe authority is more significant when the landscape is the core of the Muslim community—the family.

Disclaimers and Positionality

For American Muslims, marriage and family life form the nucleus of daily life and worship and serve as the social connectors that bind one generation to the next. As such, the future of American Islam depends upon the development

and maintenance of healthy marriages and strong families. It is precisely because of the centrality of family for black people and their historical struggles
to define themselves and organize community life in the United States that I
have chosen to look at polygyny within the households of African American
Muslims. Their explanations and experiences dramatize the parallels and tensions that exist between the lived realities of a minority group and the dominant norms of a democratic society. Two important disclaimers are these: first,
I have made a conscious effort not to universalize the journeys of my subjects as
the experience of all African American Muslims. Nevertheless, I am persuaded
that the common history and experiences they do share with other African
American Muslims have something to teach us. Indeed, these commonalities
are sufficient for their realities to be used as a window into a group that is aptly
situated to educate non-Muslims in the United States and American Muslims
born outside of the country about the complexities of balancing family life,
gender justice, civil rights, and religious freedom. Second, I have worked dili-
gently to balance my initial disapproval of the practice with my commitment
to tell these stories as they were given to me and with my desire to help foster
stronger families for a better future. As a female Muslim, an academic, and an
activist, I felt it was important for me to understand how deeply entrenched are
certain perspectives on gendered agency and marriage and to reflect upon my
personal response to them. I will let others judge my success.

The Path to Storytelling

The research presented here represents an illuminating and challenging journey, one that accompanied Imam Mohammed's declaration to his leaders that
they should talk about polygyny and maintain a national dialogue on marriage
and Islam in America. While his recommendation was unequally incorporated
into the schedules of mosques under his leadership, the mere mention of it
opened numerous doors to me. Thus, over a ten-year period beginning in 2003
I was welcomed at fifteen mosques in thirteen cities—Los Angeles, Atlanta,
Detroit, New York, Chicago, Philadelphia, Indianapolis, Charlotte, Raleigh,
Washington, D.C., Newark, Dallas, and Jacksonville—the major cities in which
a community of Imam W. D. Mohammed is located.[20]

Data collected from focus groups, impromptu group conversations, and
more than four hundred survey responses complement one-on-one interviews
I conducted in person or via e-mail or telephone with forty-one adult Muslims
(eighteen years of age or older) currently or formerly living polygyny. That I

was able to interview only two triads was a disappointment but one that symbolized the different perceptions members of the same "family" may hold of their environment.[21] I presented some of my research as the *taleem* to communities in Indianapolis, Chicago, Atlanta, Charlotte, and Raleigh. Finally, I served along with one triad in facilitating a 2009 conference on multiple-wife marriage, and I delivered a presentation to attendees at the 2010 and 2013 MARIAM (Muslim American Research Institute Advocating Marriage) conferences in Chicago.[22]

The primary objective of *Polygyny* is to document the experience of African American Muslims living polygyny and associated with the leadership of Imam Mohammed. This goal can best be described as a way forward on four levels: to encourage further the thoughtful and important dialogue the imam desired among African American and other Muslims; to dispel myths that a single form of polygyny exists in the United States; to present multiple-wife marriage from the perspectives of Muslim women who react to and live it; and to promote "authority of experience" as a form of Qur'anically approved liberation that Muslims must utilize if healthy family and community life is to be a permanent fixture. By documenting their experiences, I mean to value the realities of African American Muslim women living polygyny by providing space for them, for their stories.

The storytelling approach used throughout this work reflects the fusion of aspects of qualitative and quantitative research methods. That is, I have chosen to serve as the instrument in the collection of data that takes the form of words, pictures, or objectives. I designed the dialogical performance featured in chapter 2 to enable my subjects to become the authors and actors of their own narratives. In reference to quantitative methods, my aim is to explain what I observed, using such tools as questionnaires, focus groups, and brief surveys. I proceeded with the awareness that the extent to which my results may be generalized beyond Imam Mohammed's community to represent all African American Muslims is debatable. The data presented here do, however, constitute a case study of the marital aspirations, expectations, and decision making of a significant American Muslim community.

The Contours of This Book

Chapter 1 situates African American Muslims as a visible segment of American Muslims who live polygyny. I explore the religious and social dynamics they use to justify their household arrangements. I then distinguish Muslim polygyny from the form of multiple-wife marriage adopted by some Mormons, then introduce the central theoretical thread of this book: Muslim womanism. Throughout *Polygyny* I rely heavily on the experiences of African American Muslim women, and present them in various ways. A performance in which twelve participants converse about the practice of polygyny opens chapter 2. This chapter draws attention to the paradoxes and contradictions of living polygyny and acknowledges the benefits available to Muslim women in polygynous households who claim their experiences with polygyny as liberating authority. It also addresses one of the prevailing questions in this book: What options are available to African American Muslim women who desire marriage at the same time that African Americans are portrayed as the single most uncoupled people in the country?

In chapter 3 I explore the Islamic sources African American Muslims consult when organizing their households. As with their coreligionists around the world, African American Muslims revere the Qur'an and the *sunna* as their primary and most authoritative sources for the development of Muslim family life, including polygyny. As citizens of African ancestry in America, however, they read these sources through the prism of their experiences of life in a white-dominated, white-supremacist, Muslim-minority society. I submit that another authority, female experience as textual exegesis, should be examined. Thus, in chapter 3 I consider the Qur'an's position on multiple-wife marriage, drawing specific attention to what Islam says about polygyny and how African American Muslims embody what they hear, read, and witness, as I seek to answer this question: Under what conditions is polygyny a viable form of marriage for African American Muslims?

Chapter 4 focuses on legal considerations of polygyny, drawing particular attention to family law in Islam and directives that the commentary of Imam Mohammed suggest should reflect the proper practice of polygyny in the United States. His position differs from those of many other American Muslim leaders such as the former executive director of the Islamic Society of North America (ISNA), an association of eight organizations in the United States and Canada. Louay M. Safi advises his constituents to obey the law, "particularly when the law is not forcing them to do something against their moral principles."[23] Such divergent perspectives illustrate that African American and immigrant Muslims are divided not only by race and experience but also by their considerations of the American legal system. These differences can add to the tension between African American Muslims and immigrant Muslims.[24] Nevertheless, for members of the association of Imam W. D. Mohammed, the teachings of their leader best reflect the most viable way to apply Islam to their real-world experiences and remain true to their original nature.[25]

Chapter 5 brings Imam Mohammed's teachings to the forefront of this exploration of polygyny. With it, I outline the nine guidelines for living polygyny that Imam Mohammed announced to his community in a series of public forums and private conversations. His directives were not fully followed by his adherents in multiple-wife households. Yet, they do demonstrate the ways in which a twenty-first-century thinker might intentionally coalesce with opponents of polygyny who contend that gender justice is antithetical to the practice while also declaring that those who desire multiple-wife marriage should consider breaking the law.

The experiences of individuals living polygyny vary, sometimes greatly. Indeed, the offspring of polygynous unions and some spouses are vulnerable to injustices such as undeserved moral or emotional pain, deteriorating health, material loss, and/or financial hardship. No exploration of family life in Islam is complete without a broader discussion about the social implications of legalizing marriages that are not monogamous or about Muslim communal resources focused on the stability of family life and the welfare of women and children. That is why in chapter 6 I consider the mental health of living polygyny and its undeniable effects on marital harmony and on the decisions children make about how or whether they will practice Islam once they are on their own. The second major focus of the chapter is consideration of a probate case that seemingly identified Imam Mohammed as a polygynist after his death.

The afterword that follows the chapters serves as an opportunity to offer recommendations for healthy family life in the community of Imam Mohammed and to other American Muslims who strive to negotiate the boundaries of secular and religious law.

Through formal and informal encounters with African American Muslim audiences at *masaajid* across the country, I have attempted to jumpstart a more inclusive conversation about Islam and marriage that is long overdue. Granted, my concerns are not new or profound. Others have made the subject of marriage and relationships and African American Muslims a core component of their communal work.[26] I chose to focus exclusively on polygyny not to suggest that monogamous households are without challenges or to demonize multiple-wife unions. Rather, my intent is to shed additional light on women's time, women's space, and women's culture in a more marginalized environment. I can confirm that for many women living polygyny, the inconsistencies in the practice mitigate against achieving a consistently strong and healthy family life. Without a doubt, this is not a challenge peculiar to African American Muslims. Indeed, all Muslims and other Americans pass on to their children and others their understandings of religion, of marriage, of communal responsibility. Nonetheless, framing multiple-wife marriage among African American Muslims around the experiences of women will, I hope, discourage further undue self-sacrifice among my core subjects and encourage a willingness to demand the resources needed for their individual and communal needs. It should also demonstrate potential links between African American Muslims and other Muslims around the globe whose household formations have led to petitions for the legalization of polygyny.[27]

Writing *Polygyny*

I wrote this book to be useful in the fields of religion, history, and women's studies. I have written with diverse readers in mind to provide a broader context for discussion and examination of American families. This work is sociological because it uses the voices of African American Muslim women to describe their comings and goings in their public and private spaces. Attention to Islam's primary sources, particularly the Qur'an, offers a theological contribution. And this is a womanist work in that it is grounded in the lived realities of African American women. In the end, it is my hope that *Polygyny: What It Means When African American Muslim Women Share Their Husbands* is received as a thoughtful examination of one aspect of African American family formation and a type of marriage into which Kubayah and other Muslims enter.

1

The Road to Understanding Polygyny

> There is pretended monogamy in the West, but there
> is really polygamy without responsibility.
>
> *Ann Besant,* The Life and Teachings of the Prophet Muhammad

It is hot and humid outdoors, but excitement sprinkled with chaos is what dictates the temperature inside this rented home in an upscale St. Petersburg, Florida, neighborhood. Moving day is about a week away. Overstuffed boxes compete for floor space on well-used, once cream–colored carpet. The reflection of the sun on furniture pieces and their glass doors reveals multiple tiny handprints—evidence that any or all of the six children of this household mark their territory.

Early on this Sunday, the voices of two older boys fighting over a piece of toast greet me at the front door, along with Nissa, the thirty-seven-year-old mother of eleven (including five adults from a previous union). After extending the Islamic greeting "As Salaam Alaikum," she returns to the kitchen, which now resembles the natural-disaster area of any family with five children under age twelve. Scraps of food litter the floor. Traces of milk and breadcrumbs transform the kitchen table into a cleaning project. While I observe the family dynamics, I secretly celebrate my own reality at the time—parental care to only two children born to my husband in a former marriage—and wonder how this nationally recognized Muslim activist keeps her cool.

Perhaps this morning she has more reason to keep her cool than any other; today is her fifteenth wedding anniversary, and she will spend the afternoon alone with her husband. And the children? Well, they will also be in good hands. While their parents enjoy this too-infrequent childless private time together, the children will be in the safe care of their father's other wife.

Nissa and her co-wife, Salimah, have shared the same husband, Abdul Hameed, for the past ten years. Salimah, mother of three adult children, lives in a cozy apartment on the other side of town. Together, Abdul Hameed and his wives operate a growing real estate and educational operation. Like other subjects of this book, Nissa and Salimah defy many labels imposed upon female spouses in polygynous households: they are attractive, smart, accomplished women who do not identify themselves as polygynists. They argue that the term more appropriately applies to their husband, who is married to more than one wife. They, in turn, are married monogamously to one husband. Each wife is dedicated to her children and her husband. At every opportunity, Nissa, Salimah, and Abdul Hameed quickly and unashamedly defend their partnering choices. The weekend I spent with this triad convinced me that keeping these households intact is almost as important to them as being good Muslims. In many respects, the two goals are intertwined.

The living situations of these co-wives and their husband are as layered as they are reflective of the wide spectrum of realities experienced by hundreds of African American Muslims who have been and/or are living in polygynist households—as wives, husbands, or children. These individuals are just as representative of Muslim societies as the followers of Islam who maintain monogamous and single-parent households. Similarly, the concerns that often lead to these polygynous unions—lack of marriageable black males, the desire to maintain cultural norms, and commitment to Islamic ideals of family—and the dilemmas that evolve are issues that affect the quality of life in black America.

This is their story of living polygyny.

In this chapter, I begin to situate African American Muslims in the center of a dialogue on multiple-wife marriage. With it, I argue that by examining the relationships of agency, rights, identity, and responsibility, what comes into clear focus is the religious and social rationale that members of the community of Imam W. D. Mohammed employ to justify the gender and marital organizations they maintain. I further contend that by partnering experience as authority and a woman-centered method with praxis, we can foster acknowledgement of and respect for the authoritative potential African American Muslims possess to influence the practice of multiple-wife marriage and the maintenance of Muslim families. To explore these issues in concrete terms, I first differentiate Muslim polygyny from the household arrangements of some Americans who self-identify as Mormons. I examine questions raised about the practice of plural marriage among fundamentalist Mormons in the United States and about their possible relationships to the growing debate over the definition of marriage and same-sex partners. Furthermore, the Mormon-centrist approach taken by a number of observers of multiple-wife marriage as well as explorations of Muslim family life in Muslim-majority nations has made it possible to ignore African American marital discourse with impunity.

This social history not only sheds light on the richness and struggles within a type of family whose form and function is contrary to civil law in all fifty U.S. states,[1] but it illuminates a particular identity of "Muslimness" that meets at the intersections of religion, ethnicity, and culture.

Next, I consider Muslim womanism, the central thread that extends through the pages to follow. I characterize Muslim womanism as a critical reflection upon the beingness of African American women or the way female Muslims assert themselves in their homes and mosques as they strive to represent themselves as good Muslims and good citizens. As an interpretive tool, Muslim womanism challenges scholars and others to speak holistically about Islam and the diverse experiences of its female adherents by accomplishing for Muslim women what Katie G. Cannon and other Western womanists have endeavored to achieve for their Christian subjects: in this case, documentation of the agency and moral formulas African American Muslim women construct and pass on to succeeding generations from within the social conditions of membership in both a racial class and religious group that are marginalized in the United States.

Attendant to this discussion is the influence Christian womanist scholars have had on my own ideological and spiritual journey and the path I traversed to adopt a womanist identity. Both themes help to unpack my own positionality and to construct a framework to translate the social realities of my subjects into a legitimate lens for any study of African American Muslim life. They also provide a frame for ideas about living Islam through marriage and the foremost rationale African American Muslims use for living polygyny.

Mormon Polygamy versus Muslim Polygyny

The household arrangements of members of the Church of Jesus Christ of Latter-Day Saints and its splinter groups continue to dominate explorations of multiple-wife marriage in the United States.[2] As early as the battle over Utah statehood in the 1890s, when federal government officials forced the Mormon-majority region to choose between statehood and plural marriage, deep-seated American stereotypes linking primitive and perverted sexuality to the practice of men having multiple wives have abounded in U.S. society. Even the 2002 Winter Olympics, held in Salt Lake City, drew headlines that linked Mormons to multiple-wife marriage when the Wasatch Beer Company unveiled its advertising campaign for a beer called Polygamy Porter. The findings of a 2006 Gallup poll that Americans think most Mormons endorse polygyny accompanied the premiere of the HBO series *Big Love*, which aired for five seasons. No doubt, the 2008 public raid of the West Texas community and the subsequent criminal prosecution and imprisonment of its Fundamentalist Church of Jesus Christ of Latter-Day Saints (FLDS) leader, along with the reality show *Sister Wives* that debuted two years later, helped to reinforce perceptions that the practice of multiple-wife marriage is limited to remote desert enclaves or to current or former Mormons.[3]

Not until 2008, the year African American Muslim subjects of this book celebrated the thirty-three-year ministry and mourned the death of their leader, Imam W. D. Mohammed, did mainstream media outlets like National Public Radio begin to seem curious about the practice of polygyny among African American Muslims. Since 2001, Americans appear to be more accepting of multiple-wife marriage, according to Gallup's annual Values and Beliefs survey released in May 2013. The percentage of Americans who say polygamy is morally acceptable has increased to 14 percent, up 7 percentage points since 2001. In contrast, the survey results indicate a majority of Americans (83 percent of respondents) continue to consider the practice morally wrong.[4]

Throughout their religious histories, Mormons and Muslims have sought remedies for the care and support of widows and orphans in their communities. The racialized history of African Americans has prompted many who promote polygyny to expand the definition of the word "orphan" to include "a people" who have been rendered "fatherless" rather than its more narrow definition denoting individual and underage children. Crucial differences do exist, however, between Muslim and Mormon polygyny, whether as practiced by Mormons prior to the church's ecclesiastical prohibition in the nineteenth century or as practiced by FLDS congregations today. In addition to the difference in the number of wives a husband is permitted to marry—up to four for Muslims, no more than 999 for Mormons—Muslim polygyny does not lead to eternal unions. That is, unlike Mormons, Muslim couples do not participate in ceremonies with the intent that their marriages last beyond death and through eternity. Muslim males have fewer options as to whom they are allowed to marry. Forbidden are sisters of their fathers, mothers, and brothers, as well as marriage to biological sisters, for example. A Muslim husband rarely brings all of his wives together to live under the same roof. Muslims do not enter into "nominal" marriages, in which neither spouse has sexual access to the other, or into "convenient" marriages, whereby fathers have no parental rights.[5] Whether they are married monogamously or polygynously, the rights and responsibilities of Muslim spouses remain the same. Next I turn to the ways in which *Polygyny* expands consideration of multiple-wife households.

Polygyny's Contribution and Methods

This project breaks new ground on two significant levels. First, it fills a void in the scholarship on the study of polygyny among African American Muslims. To date, no comparable book-length work that focuses on African American Muslims exists, though Dixon's 2002 examination of polygyny through the testimonies of twelve African American women comes the closest.[6] Instead, scholars have included brief discussions about polygyny (though usually in the language of polygamy) and African American Muslims in chapters of larger studies or as independent essays. Most notable are two works whose authors sprinkle limited explorations of polygyny throughout their texts: Dawn-Marie Gibson and Jamillah Karim's *Women of the Nation: Between Black Protest and Sunni Islam* (2014) and Carolyn Moxley Rouse's *Engaged Surrender: African American Muslim Women* (2004). In addition, Robert Dannin's *Black Pilgrimage to Islam* emerged in 2002, offering an exploration of polygyny with the larger subject of patriarchy. Finally, D. Hadayai S. Majeed, an African American Muslim, draws upon firsthand experience and personal interviews for *Emerging Victorious,* a pamphlet-size study introduced in 1997 in which she recounts the Old Testament practice of polygyny both within her family and among early Mormon groups.[7]

Explorations of polygyny among Muslims around the world are more prevalent. These works usually are dualistic in tone, choosing to strongly affirm or advocate "Islamic plural marriage" as "one of the most beneficial components of Islam," one that is a right of Muslim men, or to complicate the notion of female choice and agency as they address the abuses of the practice.[8] Works that support polygyny include *Polygynous Blessings*, a touching 2007 memoir under the pen name MizAzeez. The seventy-eight-page, self-published work was adapted from the author's blog of the same name and features a forward by her husband. Some works, such as *Islam and Polygamy*, are context-specific, but feature global applications. The Malaysian nongovernmental organization (NGO) Sisters in Islam produced this pamphlet in the form of nineteen questions and answers that amplify its "Memorandum on Reform of the Islamic Family Law on Polygamy." More recent publications like the anthology *Love, InshAllah: The Secret Love Lives of American Muslim Women* include polygyny among the brief and personal reflections American Muslimahs (female Muslims) offer of life in the United States.[9]

Second, my portrayal of polygyny and African Americans introduces a new framework for engaging the voices of African American Muslim women and the authority of their experiences. Comparable to womanist theology, Muslim womanism is an emergent voice of African American Muslim women and an interdisciplinary approach to the study of African American Muslim life from their points of view.[10] Drawing on the theoretical activism of Muslim scholars such as Amina Wadud and the African-centered ethos of womanist thought, Muslim womanism asserts that the daily realities of African American Muslim women are a legitimate subject of scholarly inquiry. It grasps the connection between the racist and patriarchal culture of the United States, the nuances of black struggles for survival, and quests for Islamic legitimacy as they affect the social construction of womanhood for African American Muslim women. Let me now explain the impact of womanism on my positionality, in terms of research and personal identity.

Muslim Womanism as Ideological Window to Experience

I came to Islam in 1998 as a former Christian pastor who considered herself to be in service to a genderless Benefactor who brought women into existence as fearfully and wonderfully made creatures. For me, this G'd does not harbor gender biases, including those I have mentioned about Muslim women. Thus, my embrace of the spiritual equality of males and females in Islam was auto-matic. I was surprised, however, by the depth of communal (and particularly, female) acquiescence to maxims that begin with "the Qur'an says" and result in actions or expectations that challenge the mental, spiritual, and/or physical health and well-being of Muslim women. To err in this way is to deny the spirit of justice that permeates divine revelation.

The more time I spent among African American Muslims, the more aware I became of the emotional attachment many women feel to an idealized notion of community and authority, one in which women adhere to past practices rather than appear to disagree with divinely instituted codes by embracing their personal choices. For example, while the findings from this social his-tory concur with Dixon's assessment of the abuse of polygyny and assertion that the practice should be viewed as a responsibility, they also reflect parallel revelations about "back-door" marriages. By "back door" I mean marriages to second, third, or fourth wives without the awareness or consent of the existing wife or wives.[11] (Imam Mohammed taught his community that justice, fairness, and advance notice are required for the proper practice of polygyny, but a wife's consent is not.)

An apt example is the decision of the husband of one of my interviewees,

Karimah, whom we meet later in more depth. Here, she explains the manner in which she was introduced to multiple-wife marriage:

> This was definitely not my idea. My husband came home one day and told me that ours was to become a polygynous household. We had been married for fifteen years. Our children are adults. We work together. Nothing was missing in our relationship, yet he goes and gets a woman who was not a Muslim but who lived in a polygynous environment. She had no children so this wasn't an example of him helping out a single mother. He didn't ask my opinion. He said the Qur'an says he can take another wife and he wants to whether I like it or not. I'm trying to decide what to do. Sometimes I have to use an electric heater because he hasn't paid the utility bills, but I'm not in position to move just yet.[12]

Clearly, Karimah was taught to accept an inferior status. Such subjugation is characteristic of women whose marriages are regions of oppression. Karimah's story also indicates the absence of a key form of agency—being willing to interrogate one's environment.

Simmons explains:

> Surprisingly, there is much less questioning by American Muslim women converts of the supposedly Islamic patriarchal perspectives on gender than there is among Muslim women in Egypt, Jordan, Morocco, Palestine, Senegal, and Syria.[13]

The spiritual, emotional, and cultural dynamics of African American Muslim women like Karimah led me to seek a "mechanism for unlocking a way of thinking which ascribes authority," in Wadud's words. I sought an approach that might be able to rekindle in women with experiences like Karimah had a sense of their divinely inscribed agency and purpose.[14]

I want to uplift their spirits with the reminder that the freedom they possess as Muslim women sanctions female (and male) power that is incompatible with coercion, oppression, and abuse. Such approaches challenge women to avoid the role of victim and instead recognize their role in their own liberation. Ronald Shaheed, a resident imam in Milwaukee, raises inquiries about women's agency this way:

> So, since we are to believe in the whole of the book, what is the Muslim woman's responsibility regarding polygamy? Is she just the object of polygamy as established by our Prophet, just as she is seen as a sex object in today's world? I have never been able to discuss the Qur'an's revelation

about polygamy with most Muslim women that I know because they want to cite instances where it does not work without first discussing the issue as outlined by Allah in His holy book.[15]

Imam Shaheed is a prominent and respected leader who worked closely with Imam Mohammed. I translate his concerns into a strong reminder that the Qur'an extends conditional permission for the practice of polygyny but does not sanction injustice—a perspective Imam Mohammed conveyed on numerous occasions.

I am also reminded of the encouraging examples of living polygyny, even as this study indicates they are in the minority. Throughout my research I sought to unearth the life stories of African American Muslim women who live emboldened lives that call into question generalizations of Muslim women, African Americans, and African American Muslims. Moving far beyond a one-dimensional track that situates all wives as victims and all husbands as oppressors has been my ultimate goal.

With Muslim womanism, I bring to a section of the womanist house a lens that challenges totalitarian discourses of marriage, partnering, and household organization.[16] In the process, readers are invited—and perhaps at points compelled—to foster knowledge about Muslim women who share their husbands based on the views and voices of these women.[17] Even as I construct this framework, I recognize that few African American Muslim women have yet to embrace it.[18] I take solace, however, in the realization that I am among a minority of African American academicians who embrace Islam while traversing the academy. Because I was already at home with this woman-centered framework, it seemed natural for me to explore ways in which a praxis that gives primacy to the experiences of African American Christian women could be fashioned to address Muslim women.

Thus, Muslim womanism draws upon the multiple and interlocking experiences of African American and other Muslim women of color. I identify it as a philosophical perspective with a bent toward praxis because it advocates for change for women and their families and challenges those who study them to represent with integrity the lives of their subjects/actors. With a set of research practices, including those used in this study—surveys, interviews, oral history, and ethnography—Muslim womanism reflects the contours of a method of inquiry with a praxis component that is a recurring thread in this book.

Muslim womanism is an epistemology, or way of knowing, that positions the experiences and wisdom of women at the forefront of any consideration of Muslim family life. Accordingly, womanist ways of knowing unapologetically interrogate Muslim marriages for the particularities of women's presence and female agency in Muslim family life, specifically in a form of marriage in which the agency women exert is routinely overlooked, misunderstood, or diminished.

My subjects relate stories that provide lessons for them and for us. Their stories "speak back to normative liberal assumptions about freedom and agency" in reference to Islam and multiple-wife marriage.[19] In some ways African American Muslim women define and redefine agency as they make decisions about whether and the extent to which they will be subject to the collective good. Both reading and hearing my subjects is a prerequisite to a deeper understanding of their judgments and nuanced experiences. In reference to other marginalized groups, Villalon has observed,

> The manner in which these voices are brought into the analysis is central: the mere inclusion of the voices is not enough and does not automatically provoke a change in the understanding of otherness. It is not only about including, but *how* to include; it is not only about voicing, but also listening.[20]

Muslim womanism is born out of the realization that African American Muslim women are concerned with personal liberty and with collective self-determination, strong markers for the perimeters of agency. As the experiences of my subjects make clear, the task of realizing the goal of marriage, family, and beingness can place women in conflictual relationships with a variety of structures of authority. Some of the structures are grounded in cultural responsibility and patriarchy, some in norms of communal interpretation, and still others in a personal sense of what it means to be women of status and respect in their communities.[21]

While it overlaps with American womanism and black feminism, Muslim womanism contains elements distinct from both, particularly in regard to its attention to the varied conditions of black womanhood and diverse perceptions of justice as experienced by African American Muslims and the values of Islam they articulate.[22] Admittedly, my personal encounters with American womanism are significant strands that undergird my theorizing on the framework for this womanist project. I have discovered that Muslim womanism is more than a perspective, a way of seeing, and more than an epistemology, a way of knowing, that answers questions such as "What can we know about the experience of African American Muslim women living polygyny?" Its activist element makes

Muslim womanism a way of being in the world, and its development denotes a reconstruction of knowledge by and about African Americans.[23]

One Scholar's Road to Womanism

I did not arrive at the term "womanism" independently of Alice Walker's musings in her novel *In Search of Our Mothers' Gardens: Womanist Prose*. As a doctoral student who regularly attended panel sessions at annual meetings of the American Academy of Religion arranged by its Womanist Approaches Group, I enjoyed the company and mentorship of Katie Cannon, Jacquelyn Grant, Renita Weems, Emilie Townes, Cheryl Kirk-Duggan, Dolores Williams, Rosetta Ross, Linda Thomas, Marsha Snulligan-Haney, and other African American Christian scholars whose intellectual curiosity with female participation in and contribution to the roots and ideals of black life mirrored my own. My initial engagement with these scholar-mentors and their research commenced when I was a Christian and served a local Methodist congregation in Evanston, Illinois. As my dissertation research on African American Muslims progressed, so did my awareness that I had embarked on a religious odyssey that would lead me to Islam.

Once Muslim, I began to recognize that womanism's concern with black sexual power, with class, gender, and race analysis, and with spirituality and unity as skillfully articulated by first-generation womanists could resonate with African American Muslim women but was being developed outside of their lived realities. When I carried my unease to Cannon, she lovingly and firmly encouraged me to bring to the womanist table the life world of African American Muslims. The process has led me to pursue a more relevant term for the religious world of my subjects (and me): "Muslim womanism."

In an intentional manner, Muslim womanism promotes internal critiques on at least two fronts: first as a challenge to followers of Islam to question limitations imposed on the roles and agency of Muslim women in the private or public sphere, including the exclusion of women from the family decision-making process, and second as an analysis of the burden on Muslim women who contend with a "position of domestic inferiority" in exchange for communal survival.[24] Thus, the discourse of Muslim womanism moves beyond the historical race analyses of black male intellectuals, the traditional gender analyses of many feminist (predominantly white female) intellectuals, and the socioreligious analyses of many Christian womanists and Muslim (largely non-Western and nonblack) feminists in its interest in questions of knowledge production, history, and human existence that form African American Muslim family life and the life stories of African American Muslim women.[25]

Finally, Muslim womanism removes the veil from the realities of African American Muslim life and uses scholarly and popular discourses to give public voice to and advocate justice for women and children. In doing so, Muslim womanism highlights what has long existed privately, though it has been misunderstood due to two "parallel" and internal structures.[26] The first structure is cultural patriarchy as expressed by some male Muslims and others who presume to dictate what are the realities of African American Muslim women in both the private and public spheres. The second structure, cultural exegesis, draws attention to the ways in which some African American Muslims approach the Qur'an for theological insight, gender liberation, and communal survival, especially in their adoption of polygyny as a necessary form of Muslim marriage. As my research has confirmed, African American Muslims are divided on various levels about the legality and fairness of polygyny.

Finally, Muslim womanism acknowledges womanist concerns for all members of black families. Granted, a major contribution of this book is the primacy it gives to the perspectives of women. Still, the positioning of Muslim womanism as a theoretical lens for the exploration of Muslim family life is to particularize the experiences of the single largest group of American Muslims and to promote the excavation of black reality that affects the women, men, and children who live it. In the end, this partnership of experience as authority and woman-centered method with praxis fosters an acknowledgement of and respect for the authoritative potential African American Muslims possess to influence the practice of multiple-wife marriage. In the pages that follow I continue to demonstrate a pro-woman, pro-family advocacy for the survival and empowerment of African American Muslims as I address as well the utility of Muslim womanism. These pages and the stories recounted to me serve as a reminder that issues of agency, vulnerability, authority, and communal responsibility are inextricably linked where the practice and discourse of polygyny are concerned.

Marriage, Responsibility, and "Living Islam"

Questions regarding gender roles, family responsibilities, and spousal rights of women continue to be pervasive lines of inquiry in contemporary studies of Islam and/or Muslims in the United States and globally. Ideas about Islam and

Muslims are routinely inscribed on the bodies of Muslim women; how women think and interact with themselves and others on a daily basis is conflated into the realities of the men in their lives. I contend that to understand "living Islam," in reference to polygyny, is to grasp the social realities of Muslim women and in this case, African American Muslim women.

Among African American Muslims, the expression of patriarchy is evident but less visible than in so-called immigrant Muslim communities. A significant number of African American female Muslims come to Islam from Christian congregations in which they were visible and active. As Muslims, they continue to contribute to the life of their religious communities, serving in nearly every leadership capacity. Moreover, in contrast to the experiences of most Muslim women born outside of the United States whose home environments were not subject to centuries of American racism, African American Muslim women are often more educated and financially stable than and outnumber their ideal mates: the marriageable male members of their communities.[27]

Thus African American Muslim women may choose polygyny because they believe it to be the only way they can retain their cultural heritage, authentically practice a significant aspect of their faith, and enjoy the status afforded married women. Yes, for some women living polygyny *is* living Islam. That is, polygyny affords single women a pathway to marriage and one that extends an opportunity for them to tick off an expectation of their faith. Imam Mohammed told an audience, "Islam encourages you to get married. Male and female are dress for the other. The legal wife dresses the male and the husband dresses the woman. Let us be a dressed-up people like Allah wants us to be."

Notable for any discussion of polygyny is the weight that personal experience carries as a confirmation that marriage, like motherhood, bestows on a woman a certain status and level of respect. Indeed, "The role of woman in al-Islam is motherhood" was a familiar concept audiences heard from Imam Mohammed in reference to the status and rights of women. Moreover, he challenged women to employ their "mother guidance" to "tell the men when [they are] neglecting their duties." Imam Mohammed spoke, too, about the public leadership of Muslim women. On more than one occasion he predicted that the next leader after his death could be a woman.

Regardless of background, Muslim men and women routinely agree that married women are perceived to be freer to converse with men, appear less threatening to other married women, and are less likely to be viewed as "less modest" if they choose not to cover their hair. Married and single women rarely socialize outside of the mosque in some African American Muslim communities, and they often choose to collaborate on community activities with women who share their marital status.

Indeed, from a research perspective, being married can serve as a means to gain access to information. I can recall the doors that opened for me—in the forms of resources and introductions—because prominent community leaders knew I was married and were acquainted with my then husband. Interesting, too, are the stories of single Muslim women who speak of "feeling the eyes" or sensing the discomfort of other sisters until their marital status changed. As a newly remarried Muslimah, I can empathize with the perceptions of these women as well.

By examining polygyny in light of recent legal attempts to preserve the traditional definition of marriage as a union between one man and one woman, I draw attention to contemporary cultural wars that confirm the singular importance of family life and marriage to most Americans. A growing number of people are concerned about challenges to what former president George W. Bush called "the most enduring human institution."[28] That thirty-three other states have joined Massachusetts in recognizing same-sex marriage and Texas has battled polygynist residents over alleged child and sexual abuse suggests that disputes for control of the definitions of "marriage" and "family" have been joined.[29] Yet to be answered are two other questions that prompted this study: How do we define family units in marriages that have no legal status? What level of responsibility should Muslim communities accept for the well-being of families, regardless of form?

What is certain is that the peculiarities of black life in America have historically distinguished the lived experiences of African American Muslims from other practitioners of Islam regardless of individual nationality or citizenship. African American Muslims trace their roots to the arrival of Muslim traders, slaves, and free people as early as the tenth century. Indeed, three-fifths of all Americans who convert to Islam are African Americans, and their increasing numbers are routinely cited as the force behind a resurgence of Islam on the North American continent.[30]

I agree with Moxley Rouse that to best understand polygyny, one must approach the phenomenon mindful of its multidimensional context. Many African American Muslims who practice polygyny do so because they believe they are following the teachings of Islam. Some contend that the conditions of twenty-first-century black America mirror the social fabric of seventh-century Arabia when the Prophet Muhammad first received the revelation of the Qur'an. Then, as now, according to my sources, the lack of marriageable (single, heterosexual, and available) men, and/or the high number of female-led households, and the continued economic disparity experienced by mothers and their children make the practice of polygyny both mandated and permissible.

Others may be as surprised as I was to discover that some African American Muslim women initiate communication with potential wives for their husbands. They are the proactive ones, seeking some level of control or influence in the marital selections of their husbands. While for some, maintaining autonomy and independence was of foremost importance, others have indicated that they believe polygyny to be the only way they authentically can practice their religion fully. Indeed, Aisha, a Muslimah and attorney living in London, has explained her choice this way:

> I wanted a partner and man-hunted for one using a marriage agency and this [polygyny] suits me. I didn't want to remain single and I wanted my relationship to be endorsed by my religion, so sleeping around or living with a non-Muslim wasn't an option.[31]

With Muslim womanism we engage women like Aisha as "living human documents" whose language is worthy of our attention.[32]

Returning to Nissa, her case offers a view into the paradoxical journey living polygyny can be. In our private conversations, she shared with me the pain she experienced when her husband informed her of the impending addition of Salimah to their family system. At the time, Nissa was nine months pregnant and in no financial position to leave the marriage or her home even if she desired to do so. Arguably, her level of agency was extremely restricted. That said, she says she stayed to retain a stable environment for her children, out of her love for her husband, and because she believed, as her husband did, that polygyny is the "straight path" Allah called them to travel. Even as she and Abdul Hameed struggled financially and personally and she and Salimah wrestled with the possibility that their husband would choose a third wife, Nissa remained convinced that they had made great strides individually and collectively in their journey to live polygyny. So the anniversary day that opened this chapter was a special milestone for her, her husband, and her co-wife. The choices the two women made to make polygyny work for them speak to the diverse forms of womanist action African American Muslim women who share husbands encounter every day. While few of my female informants have been as successful in creating the workable friendship and understanding between co-wives as Nissa and Salimah have, all of them have used their experiences to shape their practice of Islam and the social circumstances that influence their marital decisions. Their stories and those that appear in the rest of this book confirm for me the danger of essentializing living polygyny for African American Muslims.

2

Agency and Authority in Polygyny

Mistresses we keep for the sake of pleasure, concubines
for the daily care of our persons, but wives to bear us legitimate
children and to be faithful guardians of our households.

Demosthenes, Against Neaera

I knew the blessings in polygamy.

Sawdah, thirty-something, from Michigan

At fifty, Karimah stands tall, her walk fluid, graceful. Her eyes glisten as if they
possessed drilling power. She and her husband of fifteen years are models of
style and the Protestant work ethic. They own a comfortably furnished home in
the suburbs of a metropolis, drive his and her Mercedes, run a successful business. Although weight never found a place of refuge on her 5'8" frame, these
days Karimah seems much thinner than the runway models for whom she is
often mistaken. Publicly, this mother of two, grandmother of two, is resource-
ful, a highly sought organizer who is a pillar in her local mosque. Yet few of the
women and men with whom she prays, converses, and works are aware of her
private pain. Though no major local or national Islamic event in this African
American Muslim community is held without her visible leadership, privately
she is anxious and lives in fear.

Karimah, a divorcee and former Christian, and Abdul Aziz, a Muslim, met
in 1988. She describes the first encounter with her soon-to-be third husband
this way:

I was leaving work and walking through the corridor leaving the building, and he was walking through the building going in the opposite direction and he said, "Are you going to the south side?" And I looked like,
"You must be crazy. I'm headed west. I'm not going to the south side." So
he said could he walk with me. And I said, "No, you can't walk with me."
He walked with me anyway.[1]

Their fortuitous meeting compelled Karimah to reconsider Islam, a faith she had only known through the daily living of a former husband, likewise a Muslim.

> So, after that relationship was over, you know, I decided, I don't want to be bothered with Muslims, period. I didn't even want to look at the religion. Didn't want to consider it. Didn't have, you know, any desire whatsoever to even ask what it was about. And then . . . I met Abdul Aziz.[2]

Although friendship evolved and Karimah became more attracted to Abdul Aziz, her teenage daughter remained a skeptic. Still, the more Karimah was able to observe Abdul Aziz, the more something deep within her persuaded Karimah to disregard her daughter's concern:

> Originally, he was just a sweetheart. Anything he could do. . . . He would come over, mow my lawn for me. He would be the only guy out there with a towel mowing the lawn, you know. Anything he could do to accommodate me, you know, he was willing to do that. So I was very impressed with that when it's at a time when you have to beg a man to do something for you, you know, I needed. I had the locks changed, and he was Johnny on the spot and never, never one time approached me sexually. So, I was really impressed with that. I said, "Hmmm. Maybe we've got a gentleman here. Maybe we ought to check into this and see what's to this man." My daughter, on the other hand, she said, "Ma, we better wait and see if he takes his mask off."[3]

If he possessed or wore a mask, Abdul Aziz did not reveal it during the first decade of his fifteen-year marriage to Karimah. But when he informed Karimah that he was taking a second wife, any agency—capacity for action—she thought she had to influence his personal decisions departed with her marital security. In her view, her husband's approach was both heavy-handed and subtle. Though speaking more from the perspective of personal and immediate angst than quantitative research, she also claimed that material, economic, and emotional hardships are common aspects of the polygynous marriage system in African American and other communities that feature them.

In this chapter I consider the concept of womanist action as performance and authority in the lived reality of African American Muslim women married to polygynous men. I begin by describing my use of the terms "agency," "power," and "authority." I then move to explain the performance of polygyny in the form of dialogue. In setting up the created drama, I introduce three categories of multiple-wife marriage and my rationale for assigning the twelve participants to them. I conclude with a conceptualization of authority in terms of gendered experience by building upon the theoretical and activist vision of Amina Wadud.[4] My intent is to situate multiple-wife marriage in two interlocking contexts that demonstrate the potential of my subjects to become both actors and authors.

Agency, Power, and Authority

I deconstruct three significant themes, fully cognizant of the fluidity among them. With womanist action, I point to what African American Muslim women do and say to preserve their civil and religious rights as autonomous agents. Conversely, I raise questions about what they do not say and do not do. I show how the cultural experience and religious understandings of African American Muslim women frame their agency that is both structurally and situationally constrained. Otherwise put, agency does not always equate with resistance but may be compliant, unintended, and the result of conscious planning.[5] With regards to polygyny specifically, agency can encompass unanticipated and innovative action that may hinder, reinforce, or serve as a catalyst for social change.[6] It also reflects the multiple positionalities of women who share their husbands.

My use of "power" imagines the extent to which women living polygyny make decisions in their public and private spheres and govern the organization of their households.[7] Gendered power, as Norton explains it, refers to the unequal application of power to men and women in household arrangements. In relation to polygyny as traditionally understood, gendered power represents the way a husband is situated to determine when and how many women he takes as wives and for whom he assumes responsibility. As the subjects of this book confirm, gendered power is reflected as well in the proactive efforts and negotiations women married to polygynous men choose to engage. As it resides in the private sphere of Muslim homes, "power" means to act on the ability to help determine how one's household is arranged.

By "authority" I refer to the use of the female experience of living polygyny as a legitimate source of knowledge about the practice and as a lens to interpret and understand the Qur'an's teaching on the subject. While the men in their lives reside on the margins of this work, African American Muslim women are not rendered invisible. Their presence enables me to more fully understand the attitudes of women as the primary subjects of this work.[8]

To most outside observers of Islam and to many Muslims, women living polygyny occupy an uncomfortable, submissive place, especially within a Muslim-minority society. They pursue and/or engage a form of marriage embedded within their understandings of their religion that suggest that polygyny is antiwoman, antichildren: an institution of oppression and exploitation that should be condemned. Drawing from scholarly conversations about "the nature of harm," in chapter 6 I explore some of the harmful aspects of multiple-wife marriage.[9]

Here, I limit consideration to one core finding: that the assumptions enunciated above are true for many African American Muslim women who share their husbands but not for all. I focus on the ways in which discourses about Muslim women, African American family life, and gendered power in Islam complicate and have complicated understandings of Muslim female agency and gender justice, particularly since 2001. To fully recognize the complexity of marriage decisions for some Muslim women, it is essential to demystify constructions of polygyny that erase female agency. Specifically, we must grasp thoughtfully the multiple levels on which women who share their husbands can and sometimes do wield authority in their marriages. It is helpful to note that such women are subjects with agency, though they may be unaware of it or may have ignored or resisted their options. Their lived experiences as a central authority merits closer scrutiny in any discussion of multiple-wife marriage.

There is no singular identity for women who share their husbands, just as the experiences of women in traditional monogamous marriages take different forms. The experience of living polygyny does not shape the realities of all African American Muslim women in the same way. That is, for my informants, multiple-wife marriage cannot be summed up in a single portrait. Women living polygyny can be and should be represented as actors who epitomize a force that shapes perceptions about and practices of the family structures they inhabit. Understanding these variations requires further exploration.

Dialogical Performance as Ethnography

My approach here[10]—as distinguished from approaches elsewhere in the book—is the inclusion of a staged, performance text with which I create fuller portraits of my informants and multiple-wife marriage.[11] This dialogical performance brings together twelve people living polygyny in an attempt to illustrate an imagined interplay among them.[12] "Performance" means gathering together different voices so they may be in conversation—talk—with each other or, as Conquergood notes, "a way of deeply sensing the other."[13] The social drama I present is fictive and real at the same time. It is fictive in that my informants and I never encountered each other as a group and at the same time. This performance is real in that it is based on interview transcripts and secondary research data. In the end, dialogical performance draws expressions of self- and communal identity from my subjects themselves and illustrates one of the three positions of qualitative research articulated by Fine:

> The positionality of voices is where the subjects themselves are the focus, and their voices carry forward indigenous meanings and experiences that are in opposition to dominant discourses and practices.[14]

I was drawn to performance particularly because dialogue permits the creation of space through which the researcher and her subjects may question, debate, and challenge one another. I recognize the possibility that my subjects would not communicate the same words they told me to each other face to face. Even so, I situate the utility of dialogical performance as a tool in one of its aims. As Madison puts it, "The performance strives to communicate a sense of subjects' worlds in their own words; it hopes to amplify their meanings and intentions to a larger group of listeners and observers."[15]

Performance as a Womanist Act

Using dialogical performance connects with womanist approaches in its acknowledgement of my ethical responsibility to address injustice, in its reliance on the lived experiences of my subjects as its primary source, and in its recognition of the distinctive angle of vision possessed by women living polygyny.[16] It pays homage to the broad appeal of Walker's definition and the self-naming sensibility woven into the souls of all African American women.[17] I submit that I am asking readers to suspend real-time expectations of the social drama I lay out. Time spent with my informants—some on multiple occasions, by different means, and ranging from sixty minutes to more than four hours—enabled me to make note of their gestures and deportment and to imagine the dialogical process that they might have with each other in an everyday conversation. As with the rest of this book, I use pseudonyms and slightly alter other recognizable markers to shield their identity.[18]

Finally, dialogical performance offers two central benefits for this study. One, it affords my informants the opportunity to speak to each other rather than to me alone. Hall has argued that Muslim women are represented and constructed by others along contrasting binaries both within and outside of Muslim contexts.[19] Even so, women living polygyny are comparable to other ethnographic subjects in that they, too, possess a "constitutive voice."[20] Removing myself from the discussion—even as I help construct it—and aiming for conversation among my informants furthers this idea. In the ethos of womanism, the participants in this performance can establish the meaning and articulate the existence of their experiences for themselves, even if they do not appear to be fully conscious of the consequences. They can do this alone, and as evidenced in the conversation, they can speak for themselves with/in the presence of men. In the words of Hill Collins, they can "talk back," giving their experiences and perceptions a visibility rarely seen.[21] Like other aspects of womanist thought, the performance constitutes a self-disclosing discourse, reaffirming my insistence on the lived realities of women as the central source of any study of polygyny.

The dialogical stance promises a reward for readers as well. Though the terrains for our ethnographic works differ, I agree with Rosen that interview transcripts can lend themselves well to storytelling on multiple levels.[22] Staging the performance in this manner draws comparisons to the development of methods used to examine other marginalized groups in which research subjects are invited to pose questions and teach the audience.[23] Moreover, what Isasi-Diaz writes about Hispanic women can be contextualized to include African American Muslim women living polygyny:

> What they have shared in their narratives they understand as relating not just to themselves. They understand who they are and what they go through as something that goes beyond them, as something that has to do with the Hispanic [and in this context, African American] community at large and with the whole of society.[24]

I concede that the actors in my social drama were not aware that their oral scripts would contribute to a fictive performance.[25] Frankly, neither was I. But as I began to outline the book and review the ethnographic data collected, I became convinced that the shift from representation to performance could "unsettle taken-for-granted assumptions."[26] I believe I have stayed true to what was said to me and what I discovered about this form of marriage. In the end, dialogical performance is designed to extend its heuristic hand and draw us into the discursive world of African American Muslims living polygyny with more depth and, I hope, particularize our engagement with their motives, expectations, and experiences.

By incorporating dialogical performance, I offer "representational scenes that present the illusion of an ethnographic present."[27] I acknowledge the value of dramatization as a means of intensifying the representation of individuals who live in a world surrounded by spoken and unspoken prohibitions, whose stories are "otherwise out of reach," and whose voices have validity as well as authority.[28] I strive to make the realities of African American Muslims more understandable. In sum, the dialogical performance helps make it possible to present, interpret, challenge, and take in the daily living of the subjects. Together, we—informants/authors, readers, and author/interviewer—can think collaboratively about ways to make meaning of and better understand the creation of polygynous households in terms of female agency.

My research confirms the suspicions of Muslim leaders like Khalil Akbar, resident imam of Masjid Ash Shaheed in Charlotte, North Carolina. Put simply, Imam Khalil contends that most of the examples of polygyny among African American Muslims reflect "misuses" of multiple-wife marriage—a commonality shared with their coreligionists in the United States. His perspective was shared by our religious leader, Imam W. D. Mohammed, who routinely reminded men of the difficulty of taking care of one wife, not to mention multiple wives. As our dialogue will make clear, where female power and moral agency are acknowledged and embraced, misuses of polygyny are less frequent and less toxic. In fact, the decisions women make to either enter into or remain in marriages with polygynous men often inadvertently reproduce the injustices they seek to avoid, such as a lack of maintenance, absence of public recognition as married women and the accompanying rights such recognition affords, unpaid *mahr*, and unequal treatment from their husbands. The experiences of Karimah draw attention to some of the jeopardies encountered by women living polygyny.

Some might charge me with blaming the victim, and those who do simply do not understand the essence of this complex, pro-woman, pro-family study. I counter such assertions with a few claims of my own: that interrogating the ways in which African American Muslim women acquire knowledge about their marriage options, what their experiences mean to Allah, and how to embody agency and authority rightly theirs can transform oppressed women into empowered ones, regardless of the form of marriage. I assert, perhaps more surprisingly, that female power serves as evidence that polygyny can be a form of marriage that some African American Muslim women intentionally seek and zealously protect.

Collaborative Voices, Forging Alliances

I encourage an alliance between women who share their husbands and the rest of the African American Muslim community in helping to establish a new social order, one that visibly reflects what this study suggests is absent in many households—Islamic marriage as justice.[29] That is, Islamic marriage is viewed as the command of G'd and thereby "bears witness for God's sake in justice."[30] I see at least two tendencies in polygynous households where women feel coerced to stay (or enter) because they feel they have no other options or out of misplaced cultural loyalty or in response to an Islamic mandate that does not exist. First, these women are unaware of or have neglected their rights and moral agency to choose for themselves the forms of marriage in which they engage. Second, we as a Muslim *ummah* have neglected our collective social responsibilities for the development and maintenance of healthy families.

The collaborative voices of my subjects coupled with Wadud's contributions to gender justice help to sustain my contention that three forms of multiple-wife marriage exist in Islam. These forms of polygyny—coercion, choice, and liberation—usually look alike when considered through the experiences of polygynous husbands rather than the realities of their monogamous wives.

I choose not to build justification for or opposition to polygyny based exclusively on individual or communal readings of Sura al-Nisa, "The Women," chapter 4 of the Qur'an. This is the chapter in which the two most cited passages on polygyny are found. Exegesis alone is a limited, human enterprise open to multiple perspectives, as is evident in the varied interpretations of the Qur'an and other Islamic sources that currently influence Muslims globally. Rachel Jones concludes that "there appears to be a disconnect between rights that women are guaranteed in the Qur'an and rights that they are given in reality."[31] Thus, I recommend an added focus—the experiences of women living polygyny. I further assume that the ethos of Islamic sources indicates a movement toward gender justice that sanctions a reconsideration of womanist action and authority from the perspectives of women living polygyny.[32] To choose this path is to empower African American and other Muslims to build marriages of monogamy or polygyny that authentically represent the teachings of their faith and thus affirm mutuality instead of male privilege. Striving for gender justice means to draw attention to the role of civil authorities in the private decisions Muslims make as it questions the civil responsibilities of Muslims in a Muslim-minority environment. Such an approach would demand an advocacy of the embodied realities of Muslim women, making visible an often "invisible community of the text."[33] I will address this community through consideration of the verbal and silent cues that signal to African American Muslims specific routes to polygyny. First, we prepare to eavesdrop on what is staged to be a real-life dialogue.[34]

"Can We Talk?"

I have long wondered in what manner a conversation would ensue if I invited some of my informants to chat with each other. I envisioned something akin to a polygyny-focused episode of The View TV program or a response to comedian Joan Rivers's well-known question "Can we talk?" which snowballed into TV and film projects for her and became the title of an R&B song as well as of a relationship conference session.[35] In addition to brief demographic information about all participants, I assign to them the form of polygyny they most embody from the three forms introduced above and described below. I use their ages and other personal data at the time of our interviews, though I have altered some details as a second level of security for their anonymity. As might be expected, some participants may not characterize themselves in the manner I have. In organizing this dialogical performance, I have assumed the presence of two elements of real time: that the doctrines and beliefs underlying their practices of polygyny have been in place for decades and that religious and cultural stipulations of multiple-wife marriage continue to conflict with legal mandates.

A few participants clearly are familiar with the Mormon practice of polygyny, which, though adopted by some contemporary fundamentalist Mormons, was prohibited by the Mormon Church in the nineteenth century. Evident as well is that some African American Muslim women unconsciously embody womanist action with the language they use to describe their marital status in polygynous households.[36] As they do, these women demonstrate the utilization of Muslim womanism in their dedication to self-definition and self-determination. For many of my female informants, naming their status in their marriage—wife, co-wife, polygynist—is a means of exerting agency in their interactions with their husbands' other wives and on their terms. But self-definition is only a first step on the road to justice, and it does not guarantee the communal liberation and accountability that womanist action demands, as the stories in this book demonstrate.

Mir-Hosseini argues that "justice and equality are intrinsic values in Islam," even as she and other feminists recognize the varied ways in which justice is contextualized.[37] Still, Soroush promotes justice and liberty as inseparable.[38] In discourses on women and polygyny, liberty operates as self-definition and self-determination. To exercise true autonomy is to critically interrogate laws, customs, and thoughts, including the basis upon which polygyny becomes an acceptable practice. Sometimes such interrogation challenges my subjects to be prepared to refute what others read to be a divine mandate. In other words, sometimes they must just say no.[39] Women living polygyny with experiences like Karimah's could benefit from such critical reflection.

On many levels African American women living polygyny are recognizably similar: they struggle with comparable emotions while also wrestling with competing desires for autonomy and private time with a man who also is another woman's husband. Such women confront stereotypes from both Muslims and non-Muslims about what it means to share one's husband, and they grapple with a form of household economics that requires a husband to consider the needs, desires, and demands of more than one household and one woman. They consider polygyny an Islamic form of marriage through which, I contend, women position themselves (or are positioned) along a continuum of coercion and liberation.

But women married to polygynous men differ from one another, too. Their lived reality helps to establish their identity. That is, their private experiences, sense of self prior to living polygyny, motivations for and expectations of this form of marriage, and sense of power coalesce to shape the category of polygyny each embodies and how comfortable she feels talking about her experiences and to whom. Regardless of the depth of their similarities or their differences, African American Muslim women living polygyny are often marked women—legally, socially, financially, emotionally, and spiritually.

Some willingly contract marriages that do not afford them the civil status of "wife," and they deny suffering any financial repercussions as a result. Other women living polygyny acknowledge that they have little civil recourse against financial setbacks, if not ruin, in the event their marriages end in divorce or the death of their husbands, compelling them to turn to relatives, friends, or social agencies for support. Their experiences contribute—and for most, confirm—perceptions of polygyny as harmful to women. In the United States, the primary manner in which the politics of markedness plays out is in the imposed social stigmatization these women experience in a society that privileges monogamy and in a religious culture that could benefit from the creation of resources to support and empower the family creations it permits.[40]

Three Forms of Living Polygyny

The experiences of Muslim women who share their husbands suggest three cat-egories that could aid in understanding their choices and living situations. Let me describe the categories I uncovered in this study, all with unstable and over-lapping boundaries. "Liberation" refers to the practice of polygyny in which husbands and wives are overwhelmingly content with their experiences and view multiple-wife marriage as a mutually beneficial family affair. Wives de-scribe polygyny as a blessing, may seek other wives for their husbands, and are eager to counsel women on how to create a dynamic polygynous life. Women who live polygyny of liberation do not have stress- or jealousy-free marriages, and they may at times consider divorce. But in the end, these women view multiple-wife marriage as a conscious choice that they freely accept. Some as-sert, as did a woman in Atlanta, that their husbands are not "right" unless they have multiple wives. Others voluntarily take the lead in securing potential wives for their husbands' consideration. Women living polygyny of liberation do not insist on contracting marriages that are registered with civil authorities.

For them, to be married is a blessing in itself, regardless of the amount of time or resources a husband is able (or chooses) to share with his wives. For the most part, they are not concerned about the conditional regulation of polyg-yny, though they realize that their position may not be shared with their hus-bands' other wives. They do not privilege polygyny over monogamy, though some prefer the former because of the communal status and freedom it affords. For women living polygyny the matter is simple: Islam permits polygyny even if all of a man's wives are not in full agreement. Clearly some women experi-ence polygyny as liberation. The question is, do all wives married to the same husband experience polygyny as liberation, and if not, should they?

The second category, "choice," encompasses marriages contracted by women who knowingly seek polygynous men and have few if any reservations about the practice. Those in this category who are already married decide to retain their husbands even if the men choose to take additional wives. Clearly, such women are a minority. Their motivations range from preference for independence rather than full-time responsibility for husbands to acceptance of polygyny so that other needs of their husbands may be met. Like those who live polygyny of liberation, women of choice unquestioningly accept the Qur'an's discourse on the permis-sibility of multiple-wife marriage but without the explicit conditions.

Although most would argue that polygyny is a voluntary course of action, it is important to acknowledge the nuances in these women's concept of choice. Even those who claim that they have few if any options beyond remaining married to polygynous men are inclined to let their understandings of Islam determine their course of action. They agree that husbands should notify any existing wives before they take additional spouses, but the women differ on what existing wives should expect from their husbands. An important question here is "In what ways can a woman exercise choices that do not ensure justice?"

"Coercion" rounds out the three forms of multiple-wife marriage I uncover in this study. The category of coercion reflects the experiences of women who believe their husbands are not financially, emotionally, or spiritually able to maintain multiple-wife households. These women say their standards of living decreased when their husbands became polygynists, they were not informed prior to their husbands' subsequent marriages, and/or they saw polygyny coming out of nowhere. Women who live a polygyny of coercion say they often feel they have few if any options to leave unhealthful situations.

Consulting religious leaders affords little comfort, they claim, given the numerous ways in which women say an imam can justify a husband's decisions regardless of the imam's personal viewpoint. Even some of the imams who refuse to officiate a marriage ceremony if the couple has not obtained a marriage license concede the permissibility of polygyny in a Muslim-minority context. In the end, most women living polygyny of coercion find themselves settling for being married "Islamically" or in a publicly witnessed ceremony officiated by a Muslim in which the bride and groom recite vows to each other and to Allah. This ceremony may or may not accompany a written marriage contract that stipulates the terms of the union and the dower the groom presents to the bride—an Islamic requirement to most Muslims. Here the question is the validity of a contract in the absence of justice.

Our Dialogical Performers

Table 1 illustrates the metaphorical spaces our twelve participants inhabit.

Table 1. Respondents, by category of polygyny

Polygyny of liberation	Polygyny of choice	Polygyny of coercion
Sawdah	Lamisha	Agnes
Walladah	Ahmed	Zuhara
Abdul Hameed	Lisa	Karimah
Salimah	Rashad	
Nissa	Amaya	

Polygyny of Liberation

In this classification are Sawdah, a thirty-something native of Michigan and mother of five; Walladah, a PhD-educated sister who advertised on the Internet for her co-wife; and Abdul Hameed along with his two wives, Salimah and Nissa. The depth of Sawdah's favorable experience is sufficient for her to carry this category alone. Of all my informants, male or female, Sawdah is the youngest and most exuberant about the benefits of polygyny. I cannot yet speculate about how common multiple-wife marriage is among previously never-married, under-thirty African American Muslim women, though the issue is an intriguing one.[41]

Walladah, a fifty-something mother of five, has lived polygyny twice and blames her eagerness to get married and having made a poor choice for the breakdown of her first marriage. One of the benefits polygyny has provided Walladah is having a sister, figuratively speaking, who becomes part of her family.

Salimah and Nissa are both in their fifties. They are not best friends, but they do work together with their husband and often headline workshops on polygyny. During the fifteen years they have shared Abdul Hameed, each woman has grown in self-awareness and in her appreciation for the talents of the other.

Polygyny of Choice

The performers in this category are Lamisha, a fifty-something Midwesterner in her second polygynous marriage, and two couples, Ahmed and Lisa, both in their sixties and married to each other for the second time, and Amaya and Rashad, a fifty-three-year-old divorcee with five children when she became his second wife. Lamisha and her second husband, Tariq, have known each other for decades. It was at the prompting of Lamisha that Tariq took Abeer (who chose not to participate in our study) as his second wife. Lisa remarried Ahmed, prompted in part by her love for him and desire for a father for their two children. At the time, he was in a marriage that was not working out. Lisa admitted that "it was in the air" that Ahmed and his wife Akifah might break up. She also conceded that as far as polygyny was concerned, she was only "okay, somewhat" with the arrangement. Akifah did leave the marriage, and eventually Ahmed married his other current wife, Grace, who was unable to join us in the interview. Though apparently in agreement with polygyny, Grace was unwilling to share her experiences, according to Ahmed. Finally, Rashad and Amaya had been married nineteen years at the time; his first wife divorced him soon after Amaya's arrival. Last year he suggested that Amaya tutor a young Muslim woman, his choice of a prospective second wife.

Polygyny of Coercion

Agnes, a forty-year-old graduate of Grambling University and mother of six children; Zuhara, a thirty-seven-year-old who married for the first time less than one year before our interviews; and Karimah. Agnes disregarded early warnings about polygyny. On numerous occasions, one of her sisters-in-law warned Agnes that her husband, Hussein, might take another wife. Even after Hussein's youngest brother became a polygynist, Agnes said she remained secure in her own marriage because her husband had not raised the issue of multiple-wife marriage. Zuhara initially agreed to polygyny because of where her co-wife lived—outside of the United States.

In this fictional mixed performance of females and males, some participants feel more comfortable speaking frankly and intimately than others do while also maintaining their modesty. And because this is a female-focused work, the males tend to stay in the background.

The Dialogue of Polygyny

"I guess I'll begin," announces Sawdah, as she scoots to the edge of her chair and corrects her posture. "I chose to jump in because after talking with some of the sisters, I realize that I may be a minority here."

"You mean because you're the only mother here with five children under twelve and you're only thirty?" asks Agnes with a smile, recalling the arrival of her own six children by the time she was forty.

"No ma'am," Sawdah says, "because I am a woman and I identify as a polygynist."

"You're brave," Karimah says softly.

"I'm curious about your language, Sawdah," says Lisa. "Most of us women don't refer to ourselves as polygynists, since only our husbands have more than one spouse. Each wife contracts a monogamous marriage. Personally, I think of myself as a wife and Grace, who is also your wife [glancing at their husband], as my co-wife since together with her I share you."

Lamisha raises her arm to claim the floor. "Sawdah, before you explain the way you use the term, I want to state up front that 'co-wife' doesn't work for me; sorry, Lisa. In college, we learned about Mormons in a world religions class.

They use the term 'co-wife' to describe a particular kind of relationship that features women who are related by blood, sisters who are married to the same husband, and wives who form strong bonds.[42] That's definitely not my experience. I mean, well, we get along, you know, we share a husband, but we're not best friends. Actually, I prefer the term 'wife' for both of us because that's what we are. That's all we are."

"Perhaps our experience defines the language we use," Sawdah suggests, now feeling more like an equal in the conversation. "I didn't go to college, but I do read, and I have learned that language informs identity formation. Language is endowed with special meaning in specific contexts, such as ours.[43] Now, to answer your questions is to explain the social meaning that I derive from the term 'polygynist': the choice to freely live a multiple-wife marriage and even with the crazy stuff polygyny can bring, be willing to chip in to ensure the survival of the family. It means to recognize that multiple-wife marriage is not an obligation on Muslim men or women but permissible, *halal*."

"Just permissible? But the Qur'an says men have a right to have more than one wife, doesn't it?" Zuhara interjects before realizing that her voice was louder than intended. "I came off a horrific life experience before coming to Islam, and I wanted to be chaste. So I needed to get married to live half my *deen*. I don't have a written contract because [my husband] said it was 'just a piece of paper.' My *wali* said, 'It's about the words of the contract,' and because we had witnesses we didn't need a written contract. My husband is bringing over a wife from Mali. He promised her family that he would marry her, so she will be his legal wife. I am off balance right now. I want to leave but I do love him, and besides, where would I go? Not only that, but another imam told me, 'If you divorce for the wrong reasons you won't even smell *jannah*.'"

Zuhara can't hold back the tears now.

Moments later, Salimah dares to break the silence. Speaking gently, she turns to face Zuhara. "We have a lot to learn about polygyny and marriage in general, frankly. I'm sorry that you are hurting right now and really disappointed that you didn't receive the best information or guidance. That's why we have to read the Qur'an for ourselves and not depend upon others to tell us what it says."

"Her problem is interpretation, surely," Nissa jumps in, "and the lack of Islamic knowledge. Too many women sit passively and receive interpretations about the Qur'an that are so off the mark it's not funny. And often we do not or cannot distinguish between the mandates of culture and the primary sources of Islam. So, yes, the Qur'an says that polygyny is permissible. But that permissibility actually means responsibility, and the responsibility of polygyny comes with conditions. Every man cannot and does not meet them. That's why the Qur'an also says one [wife] is better. Shoot, it's awfully hard for the men who try," she said, glancing over at Abdul Hameed.

"That said," Nissa continues, "Zuhara also has come up against the wall of indifference. That's what I call it. We say there are too many women without husbands, but we don't provide the resources, support, or education that focuses on the bigger picture—healthy married life. Some brothers marry young, single sisters and don't consider marrying anyone middle-age. Another issue is we are directed to marry from within the global *ummah*, but most of us want to maintain our culture, so we need to address this. We don't instruct women to ensure that they have a contract and *mahr*. What training do we give those in the position of *wali*, anyway? So, our silence or acquiescence as individuals and as local communities tells women it's un-Islamic not to accept polygyny, even from unqualified men. Please, don't get me started."

Nissa takes a moment to exhale. "I guess I'm just sick of hearing about women in vulnerable positions and we as a community, mandated to maintain widows and orphans, turn our backs because we say it is none of our business. I was nine months pregnant when Salimah joined our family, and I wasn't feeling that good about either issue, really. Plus, Abdul Hameed made mistakes, screwed up royally." "We believed G'd in doing what was new to all of us," he interrupts. "Sometimes our financial situation was dire," Nissa continues, "and I felt it wouldn't have been had he not taken on the additional responsibility. He was one of the first, and we were learning. But then as now, he is an honorable man. That is, he chose to step up and provide for a widow while also keeping his eyes on my house. I stuck it through because I wanted to. But that's me. I had a choice. You have a choice, too. I hope you leave here knowing that and start trying to figure out what you need to do to get to a healthier place. I'd like to help you with that if you'd let me, and I'm sure Salimah would too."

Zuhara looks up and smiles.

"Polygyny can bring out the best and worst of emotions, can't it?" Amaya asks as she stretches out her legs, and she notices the heads around her nodding in agreement. "We need to have more conversations in each mosque about the emotional toll of marriage, particularly polygyny—especially in regard to jealousy, honesty, and secrecy. Too many children have been abused, too many women are desperate to get married, too many men are plain ridiculous. Where is Islam in all this?"

"It's in family structures like mine, where decisions are made in the open," Sawdah says assuredly. "My husband, now deceased, may Allah give him rest and peace, had four wives and twenty-two children! At one point, all the wives and some of the children lived under one roof with him. We used to sit around the television watching *Big Love*, and the wives would compare us to the fictional female characters. I remember being asked by another sister, 'How do you feel about how the first wife feels about you coming in on the relationship?' I said, 'I can't help that, I'm not doing something *haram*, I am not doing something bad, I'm not fornicating.' But I could appreciate that the situation may have been difficult for her. She had only one child with him, and she was older. I tell women now that each relationship is separate. You have to focus on your relationship, your sex life, your marriage. The moment you wonder if she is better to him, if she looks prettier in her lingerie, that's the moment your relationship is going to suffer. If you can't get your mind off it, get a hobby, learn to sew, get a job. That's what women have to do to get past what he's doing with her."

"I'm glad you brought up the issue of sex," Amaya says, as her husband and the other men present feign embarrassment. "One of the misconceptions of polygyny is that sex plays a huge part in it. I admit, my husband has a higher sex drive than I do. Sometimes I think of looking for another wife to share the burden," she says, smiling. "But seriously, well, I was serious, sort of, the issue of jealousy goes beyond sex, to the allocation of time, resources. Some brothers can be the best providers but emotionally bankrupt, just simply unaware that they just can't go from house to house or room to room, share a meal, chat a bit, have sex, and think they've met their responsibilities. Like any form of marriage, we need to learn how to be emotionally present."

"But we also need to compel brothers to be honest, especially up front," Agnes chimes in. "I kept telling my sister-in-law, 'not us,' when she warned me that Hussein was going to take a second wife. I really wasn't worried because he knew [I did not desire polygyny], I thought. But when I was eight months pregnant, he contracted marriage with another sister in our *masjid*, one who was ten years younger and used to help me with our kids. And while I blame him, I was ticked off with the sister, too. You see, he asked me to meet with her, and I did. I thought I'd let her know up front that I was not interested. I asked her why she wanted to practice polygamy. She said she needed a husband and wanted to be married and wanted to be a second wife. Then she tried to make me feel guilty. She said, 'You should want for your sister what you want for yourself.' I said, 'I do, just not my husband, and you are not going to come between me and my family. And don't look at this house thinking we're living large.' I was getting emotional and pushed her, and I slapped her and I said, 'So you stay away from my family and never come back here or you're going to get hurt.' Later she said she didn't want to hit me because I was pregnant but figured since I called her bluff she'd fix me and do it [marry him] anyway."

"I understand you being upset with him particularly when you were carrying his baby," Lamisha says. "As a domestic violence worker, I also am not that surprised by your behavior. But we've got to get to the point where we position ourselves better and that our community steps in when private issues begin to impact the community in a negative way. I'm embarrassed to hear that others failed to see your situation as their business, including the imam. Even so, you and I both know that some folks in the *masjid* act differently around you if they know you're not married. Sometimes men look at you and you know they're looking through you. They don't look through another man's wife. There's some security, some status, some honor in being a married woman in Islam. That's why we need to rethink our *masjid* culture. We need to be accountable for our own actions and require the community to hold us to it. We have to stop treating our marriages as if they're some sideshow for other people's amusement."

"But part of what fueled your anger was secrecy, wasn't it, Agnes?" Amaya asks. "Marriage is a social contract in Islam. That means it's public. We need to inform sisters that they can write into their contracts a stipulation against polygyny and of course encourage them not to marry without a written and enforceable contract. A sister can't deny a brother what Allah has made permissible, but she can alert him to the likelihood of her response, as is her right. Neither has to sign the contract, which means the marriage shouldn't take place. If we had more honesty and less secrecy up front, more women would have a better handle on their options. But let's get back to Agnes's case."

"The *athan* is about to be called, and I really wanted to speak to that if I may, dear," interrupts Rashad. Amaya acquiesces, and he proceeds: "In addition to having a better understanding of the Qur'an and the life example of the Prophet—who was, by the way, never abusive to his wives—we need to train leadership to address these and other crucial issues in our community. Imam Mohammed taught us to think for ourselves, to study for ourselves. Polygyny, as outlined in G'd's revelation, is for me very clear. But I don't think we have the kind of leadership, and here I mean imams, nationally that can move us in a G'd-centered direction. It may take generations before this is the case. And until we have a viable national Muslim community in America that follows the leadership direction solidly established by Imam Mohammed as he guided us with solid Qur'anic principles, polygamy or no other Islamic concept or practice given to us by Allah in the Qur'an will find success among us here in America."

"I don't know that we settled a lot here," Amaya concludes, as a sense of quiet reflection descends. "Last year Rashad said he wanted to take another wife to have more kids. For a number of reasons I was against that and told him so. I recognized that he had the power of choice; he realized I did, too. In any type of marriage, including polygyny, there are times when we must negotiate what we believe is healthy and just for us. I'm glad to report that after several back-and-forths, he told the sister who was interested in joining our family that he could not proceed and said, 'I love my wife too much to lose her.' In the end, neither of us got all we wanted," she concedes, stroking the shoulder of her husband to whom she's been married nearly two decades, "but we did address the issue openly and honestly."

"That's what I mean," Walladah jumps in, smiling. "What's important is being in a *halal* relationship. We can leave here with that awareness and more. I do agree, for example, that marriage licenses have value for some people, and when that's the case they should not marry without one." Amaya nods. "But for me and many others" continues Walladah, who is seeking a second wife for her husband, "registering my marriage is not an essential component to feeling married or having a real relationship. While my former co-wife was married to my husband, Omar, and years before when I was in polygyny, my rights were never in question or lessened in a polygynous marriage. I have an excellent husband, *alhamdu-lillah*. I don't have any notion, thought, idea, or suspicion that because he takes on an additional wife or wives, which I fully support, that that will in some way change him into something other than what he is."

"I can't imagine a time in our history when there won't be a need for polygamy," Abdul Hameed interjects, noting the time for prayer is upon them. "But now, perhaps we should end with a *du'a*." They proceed to call upon Allah for those in or considering polygyny, for those for whom the weight of the desire for marriage leads them to make poor choices, and for their *ummah* to become surely focused on the commands of G'd, visibly attuned to gender justice.

As the dialogue above expresses, the ways women approach, experience, and react to living polygyny vary substantially. The responsibility for a healthy, *halal* marriage, regardless of form, does not rest with the husband alone. Indeed, women, too, are accountable for the extent to which their unions reflect justice and are pleasing to Allah. Equally apparent is that some families recognize the challenges that accompany living polygyny, but their experiences have convinced them that the benefits outweigh the struggles.

In a transition back to the real world, I next explore the concept of authority by laying out the theoretical guidance for valuing the experience of women living polygyny. As an expression of a living human document, female experience is an apt form of authority for evaluating the legitimacy of polygynous practices. Debates about and struggles for social justice are meaningless in Wadud's terms unless the cogency of experience as a form of authority is recognized.[44] Wadud has been successful and controversial in her efforts to promote a reinterpretation of the Qur'an that is pro-woman and pro-justice.

Experience as Authority

Just as Wadud has persuasively argued that "multiple, contested, and coexisting meanings of Islam are integral to struggles for justice in Islam,"[45] so too does the practice of polygyny among African American Muslims reflect the presence of diverse understandings of legitimacy, agency, and responsibility. Multiple-wife marriage, as the dialogical performance confirms, draws attention to how the authority women have in their life choices is often negotiated, limited, and nuanced. Approaches to these related threads, even if only on a subconscious level, speak to the ways in which African American Muslim women face the structural inequality of polygyny as well as its social utility and religious validity. At the core of the process is the nature of experience. Wadud theorizes about experience as authority in this manner:

> Too often the ordinary Muslim will think of authority only in terms of its political and social manifestation and might best be defined as legitimate leadership. And, while leadership itself can be the reason for complication, I wish to avoid that complication by positing several considerations on different types of authority including, most importantly, the authority of experience in order to move towards a more nuanced consideration of authority.[46]

If, as Wadud contends, "Islam is what is lived by the people, such that all people are equal contributors to what is Islam and each circumstance creates its own authorities," then female experience owns "an essential part of the claim for authority" for the practice of polygyny.[47] In other words, we rob women of all agency and volition by making religion responsible for their actions. Gross furthers this idea when she writes that "women's experience possesses a religious authority of utmost importance, never to be overlooked or denied, never to be sacrificed in order to conform to external or traditional sources of authority."[48]

Consideration of the link between agency and responsibility cuts both ways. For example, when Karimah relies on external commentaries she encounters about polygyny, she demonstrates her confidence and trust in her marital partner and religious leadership. Neither, she has come to realize, is all-knowing, even with the best of intentions. Naturally, they were not designed to be, but like many new to a faith, Karimah tended to become overly dependent upon others as she negotiated Islam. And given that many with whom she associated were unquestioning about what they were taught and experienced, it later was easier for Karimah to endure what she initially assumed was her fate.

Since her 2005 divorce, Karimah has come to demand more of herself and her community. She now realizes that, well, to put it bluntly, she wasn't crazy. She remains convinced that polygyny can be a workable solution for some. Even so, Karimah now is certain that her husband was not a good candidate for it and that by remaining in a toxic situation, she performed a disservice to herself, her husband, and his other wife. In other words, the terms dictated by the Qur'an for the practice of multiple-wife marriage were disregarded, ignored, or subsumed by other issues.

Furthermore, Karimah has concluded that her husband's behavior ran contrary to the Qur'an and the guidelines for the proper practice of polygyny as outlined by Imam Mohammed. Finally, over the years, Karimah has begun to wrestle with the Qur'an for herself. She no longer seeks legitimation through marriage but rather through her *taqwa*. Her more focused and consistent study, individually, with other women, and in mixed groups, resonates with the idea expressed by Anna Piela that "knowledge of religion is not a masculine thing, it's a Muslim thing."[49] Today, Karimah refuses to remain married "just because." The transformative process through which Karimah has traveled echoes Wadud's theorizing about women's experience as authority. Put simply, "Women's lived realities are one measure of the success or failure of Islam in all its dimensions."[50] In this case, the dimension is polygyny.

The daily living of women is critical to our understanding of polygyny in relation to social justice. To validate the role women share with men as *khalifah*, representatives of Allah on earth, is to draw attention to the right and responsibility of Muslim women to be among the authoritative voices that establish the canon, so to speak, for determining the presence of gender justice and the proper practice of polygyny. Indeed, female experience provides a mechanism for unlocking a way of thinking which ascribes authority and representation only to men, male needs or desires, and male understandings of directives on polygyny that Islamic sources provide.

These are issues with which Nissa has become more consciously familiar. As she indicates in the dialogue, her husband made mistakes. But she did, too. She permitted herself to become lost in the anxiety of the moment, assuming that to be a good Muslim was to accept polygyny as a mere *jihad*, a struggle sent from Allah. Theirs was a family attempting to learn about polygyny while they were in the process of living it. She had no role models, and she chose periods of silence over confrontation and decided to retreat to focus her energy on raising her children. Nissa admits today that she is more self-aware and secure—in herself and in her faith—and that she would do a lot differently now. She is a different woman today than she was. Nissa and Salimah have begun to speak publicly about the way they live polygyny, offering a useful examination of gender relations in their family.[51] Each time they do, the progress they are making in their journey toward caring for each other is obvious, as is their willingness to help others avoid their mistakes.

Salimah concedes that the way she and Abdul Hameed married could have been difficult for any woman to whom he was already married, but Nissa's pregnancy created additional stress for her and the family. Too little attention is given to the level of Abdul Hameed's recognition or understanding of the pain he has caused the women he loves and its impact on his children. Now there are times when Salimah regrets and acknowledges the pain her marriage to Abdul Hameed has caused Nissa. Even then, however, Salimah and Nissa push back against opposition to multiple-wife marriage and remain adamant that polygyny is the will of Allah for them.

Without a doubt, the realties of women like Sawdah and Zuhara place them at opposite ends of the polygyny spectrum. Just as Sawdah eagerly self-identifies as a polygynist, Zuhara's experience could easily personify what most people regard polygyny to represent: injustice and abuse. I agree with Wadud in her assertion that "agency is not subsumed under the status of marriage."[52] Several leaders in the association of Imam Mohammed would agree. In an August 5, 2006, marriage workshop held in Charlotte, North Carolina, presenter Imam Yahya Abdullah told women, "You let these brothers off too easily. If they want more than one wife, they should be able to handle them." By marrying or staying married to men who clearly lack the resources to care for multiple households, he said, "you are not helping them. You're crippling them."

Zuhara's sense of self, however, offers evidence of the wide gap that can exist between theory and practice. Her actions were often directed at and limited to the presence of her husband's other wife rather than to her husband and his readiness for the household organization he instituted. Surrounded by the ma-

jority chorus—that is, most members of her mosque—she never felt it necessary or possible to question the prevailing view of polygyny as a potential "sixth
pillar of Islam."[53] In doing so, she subjected herself to voices that pay little heed
to the positionality of men who take on additional wives, particularly in regard
to the men's physical, psychological, and financial stability.[54] Neither do they
provide counsel to women about the potential realities of husband-sharing.
Add to the mix those who hold onto social and religious power through the
inertia of their communities, and the environment is ripe for women like Zuhara and Agnes to experience less than ideal marriages. More often, theirs is a
world of male domination and female subjugation. These women were never
in positions to characterize their husbands' other wives in terms other than
rival, threat, or enemy. Still, these experiences do not adequately capture the
complexities of agency as a force for the restructuring of gender relations and
for creating change.

How is justice available to women who share their husbands? Does Islam
have a role in the public life of African American Muslim communities, particularly in terms of ensuring gender justice? In what ways does a disjuncture
exist between what African American Muslims promote as the ideal of Islam
and what African American Muslim women experience? These are inquiries
that an experience-as-authority model helps to bring to the forefront of polygyny discourse, especially when the goal is to draw women into a reflective
process that challenges directives about a practice they are living. There are
no easy answers, but my informants have begun to wrestle earnestly with the
questions.

Obviously, multiple perspectives of polygyny can be derived from women's
experiences and can influence the rethinking of family, as the dialogical performance illustrates. Madison notes, "We learn something from performance,
it has an impression upon us."[55] Women living polygyny should be the people
who determine the rules and representations of their own realities, as Walladah and Sawdah believe they do and as Salimah and Nissa say that are learning to do. Together with the men in their lives, women living polygyny can
use their experience as an authority to point to the larger structural features
of their society that can produce both liberation and oppression. After all, the
responsibility to implement justice in Islam falls to all of its adherents.

The three motifs I use to describe the ways in which African American
Muslims practice polygyny—liberation, choice, and coercion—serve as evidence that the Qur'anic mandate of justice and fairness is not experienced
by all multiple wives. They suggest that a link exists between the absence of

justice and the absence of women in decisions about their roles in family life. A woman-centered approach to considerations of polygyny enables us to better appreciate the circumstances that might compel some women to remain in it, solicit it, or choose to share their husbands. It is my hope that such an interpretive framework will help prompt a shift in the teaching and practice of Muslim marriage where needed in African American (and other) Muslim communities.

Using performance as an ethnographic device, I have introduced the threads that weave together this study of Muslim polygyny. This is not an exploration of multiple-wife marriage within the global community of Islam, within the United States, or among all African American Muslims. Rather, the purpose is to shed light on the practice of polygyny primarily among the community of Imam W. D. Mohammed.[56] Some informants were adamant that I use their actual names. Others encouraged me to photograph them and their residences. I did not follow either option. But I was encouraged by their confidence in me to share the stories as their stories, with their complexities, contradictions, and paradoxes. Thus, I approached the writing of this book as an entrée into their truths. I continue this approach with consideration of the role and construction of textual authority. I argue that the practice of polygyny in African American mosques should be read as an embodiment of textual interpretations particular to the black experience in America. While this communal exegesis produces husbands for single female Muslims who may otherwise remain unmarried, it also masks textual and patriarchal approaches that can further subjugate women and make healthy African American family life more elusive. In the end, an exploration of textual interpretation provides an opportunity for the association of Imam Mohammed to assess how it translates his teachings for the furtherance of gender justice. Imam Ronald Shaheed cautioned me at the outset of this research project:

> I don't think many Imams fully understand polygamy as outlined in the Qur'an and the life of Muhammad the Prophet, Peace be upon him, and Imam Mohammed sees an urgency in helping all of us to grow in our understanding. So, you know if the Imams don't understand, how much more the congregations do not understand.[57]

3

Religious and Experiential Prescriptions

Oh, you already know who it's going to be and you haven't talked to me?
Rashidah, spouse of soon-to-be polygynous husband

*So I said, I want to meet her. I want to talk to her. I want to meet her
because I don't want this to be done ugly. I don't want this to be done
behind my back. I don't want her to think that I don't know.*
Jamillah

As her husband makes the call for the predawn prayer in the adjoining room,
Jamillah rises from bed and readies herself for a ritual that is written into the
rules of the Islamic way to begin each day. A tall, slender woman whose high
cheekbones and complexion rival those of many magazine cover girls, Jamillah has come to especially enjoy this part of the day, this aspect of her marriage. She and her second husband, Rahim, both in their fifties and parents
of adult children, decided to follow the first prayer of the day with meditation and Qur'anic reading as a way to draw closer to Allah and to each other.
When Jamillah met Rahim, a year before their wedding, she was impressed
by his work among new, younger Muslims. Like her, Rahim was a teacher of
Islamic practices and beliefs, and Jamillah looked forward to the intimate time
they would share as husband and wife, together focused on the Qur'an, their
guidebook for living. Once married, and as their familiarity with each other
grew, Jamillah felt more comfortable expanding their predawn ritual to include
conversations about their marriage. To her, such an environment, already filled
with prayer, meditation, and recitation, is as healthy a place as any to relieve
anxiety and reclaim internal peace. On this morning in particular, Jamillah
is after answers, or better yet, a confirmation. And if a showdown is the only
means to her goal, she's fine with that, too.

For days now, Jamillah has observed the comings and goings of a different
man than the one she married five years earlier. She felt like she and Rahim
now existed in parallel spheres, separated by the thinnest of veils. After all,
Rahim's communication with her had not been as open and forthcoming, his

schedule had become more erratic, his manner more aloof. The more often Jamillah prayed and slept alongside Rahim and the more meals they shared, the more convinced she was that he had something to tell her but was having difficulty piecing together the words. Armed with "the weirdest feeling," Jamillah decided on this morning to toss her husband a declaration: "Look, you just need to talk to me about something!" That's when Jamillah learned that her husband would take another wife within the month.[1]

In this chapter I interrogate the use of the Qur'an and other teachings of Islam as a prescription for polygyny among African American Muslims. I explore the interpretive frameworks with which African American Muslim men and women promote multiple-wife unions and tolerate or dismiss a controversial form of Muslim marriage that conflicts with U.S. civil law. I propose an alternative Qur'anic hermeneutic, one that depicts Muslim women as autonomous agents whose surrender to their faith need not be viewed as synonymous with submission to spousal desire or communal survival. This chapter's examination of Muslim marriage affirms further the merits of experience, this time as textual exegesis, whether the text is the divine word as revelation or the divine word as embodied female reality. It situates experience as a another doorway to re-envisioning the position of the Qur'an on polygyny. I consider some of the faith commitments African American Muslim women embrace and the value they attribute to polygyny as a fulfillment of both spiritual and earthly goals.

Two of the basic assumptions many Americans appear to hold of women living polygyny are that they have no authority over their lives and have no agency in their homes.[2] Testing such assertions, however, requires a more nuanced look at polygyny based on the perspectives of women who live it and the theological and religious sources on which they form their decisions regarding marriage. Debates about polygyny have been too narrowly conceived as issues of male sexual lust and patriarchal power within the private sphere. Recognizing that some women experience one or both scenarios, my hope is to problematize what Muslims and others privilege as household arrangements within patriarchal structures that reach beyond the family into the public sphere, where the mosque and the larger African American Muslim community are sometimes situated. With regard to Muslim women, I position the local mosque and the larger African American Muslim community as sites that represent an extension of the private sphere.[3] Universalizing Qur'anic interpretations that support patriarchy and eliding multiple settings as a single space in which patriarchal relations occur, in my mind, are significant obstacles to healthy Muslim family life. More formal collaborations of Muslim women,

Muslim female scholars, and others that raise awareness of women's rights in Islam in regard to marriage and communicate these rights throughout local mosques are much needed. Such endeavors are crucial on a global scale but especially in secular regions like Europe and the United States, where religious law supersedes civil law for many Muslims and marriage rights intersect at the nexus of "state law and 'unofficial law.'"[4] Polygyny is contextual, often involving multiple and intersecting spheres of influence. For African American Muslims, the contextualization of polygyny involves a spectrum of sociocultural experience and religious norms, both nurtured by patriarchal power, that limits the options women believe are available to them.

Patriarchy and Polygyny

The term "patriarchy" has become the vernacular for the coupling of male privilege and power with female subordination that defines women primarily by their relation to men. Patriarchal power is derived from conscious authority more than physical force and is most visible in gender dynamics that occur within society and the home.[5] Home and society coalesce in Islam in the family, the basic building block of Muslim life. The authoritative sources of Islam instruct males and females alike to be modest in dress, action, and thought; patriarchy routinely places more responsibility for the expression of modesty on women. Syed has observed that the mingling of male supremacy and female modesty has led to the belief in many parts of the Muslim world that to be a good Muslim woman is to be obedient and modest and that a modest woman is duty-bound to submit to her father or husband.[6] Outside views tend to conflate modest dress in public with a persona of submission. For many married Muslimahs, the idea of submission extends to household formations and the unilateral decisions husbands make to live polygyny.

For Americans, patriarchy has become a way of viewing the world and envisaging Islam as a religion of male domination. Western Muslim feminists, believers, and others challenge patriarchy (and gendered portrayals of Islam) by proposing instead a methodology for rereading Islamic sources or unreading patriarchy to recover female-centered readings and gender justice.[7] In doing so, they offer evidence in support of the Qur'an as an antipatriarchal text and Islam as a religion with multiple and contested meanings and experiences. By "antipatriarchal," I defer to Barlas in her *Believing Women in Islam*. There she presents the Qur'an as a historically contextualized sacred text and Allah as the Creator who does not "violate women's rights by denying them agency and dignity."[8] I will return to these issues. For now, it is important to articulate the point of view of a few antipatriarchal-Islam scholars, which, in turn, questions the legitimacy of any method that is inconsistent with the spirit of the Qur'an.

Barlas, Wadud, and others who promote an antipatriarchal view of Islam dispute the use of the term "Islamic" for any practice that can lead to injustice. For these scholars, such a practice is contrary to the spirit of Islam and therefore un-Islamic. They contend that polygyny is similar to patriarchy in that the latter uses the weapon of domination to unleash a mechanics of power that determines how men may have control over women, not only so that women may do what men desire but also so that women may act as men wish them to act.[9] Patriarchal power exists within Muslim communities as this two-pronged enterprise, maintaining "both the idea and the practice of gross hegemony in the private and public spheres."[10] These spheres intersect in the family, where patriarchal power is most evident in decisions surrounding the structure of the family unit—and authority exercised over women by men. For antipatriarchy proponents, the Qur'an makes no distinctions between public and private spheres.

Given that monogamy is the only form of Muslim marriage available to women, polygyny is Islam's singular representation of domestic power that clearly—and some would assert, divinely—demonstrates a gendered imbalance in the human dynamics governing family relations.[11] More often than not, women living polygyny are balancing their self-accepted, other-imposed, or husband-directed existences with their desire to live lives pleasing to Allah. In so doing, Walby, among others, might argue that such women reside in multiple sites of oppression—and its in oppression that patriarchy feeds.[12] These interconnected, dynamic, and complex spaces span the private and public spheres and hold particular relevance for Americans of African ancestry, as this exploration of polygyny demonstrates.

Though few in number compared to the overwhelming presence of single-spouse unions, polygynous marriages are becoming more visible among African American Muslims.[13] So, too, are the varied ways in which multiple-wife marriages challenge the women involved and the sites of patriarchal authority and power they traverse. For example, wives who share their husbands may struggle with identity issues, particularly in regard to personal freedom for self-determination in the domain of family life. In some cultures, language clarifies the way women sharing a husband perceive each other. In Arabic, for instance, the word for co-wife is *darah*, or "one who makes trouble." The same term in the language of the Luo of Kenya is *nyieka*, "my partner in jealousy."[14] Similarly, Hausa women in Nigeria refer to their co-wives as *kishiya*, the word for "jealousy."[15] Unlike self-identified fundamentalist Mormons and most women involved in other forms of multiple-wife marriage, the majority of my female Muslim informants routinely reject the label of "polygynist" for themselves. Other than two who spoke in the dialogical performance, each of my informants says she is monogamously married to one man; thus, only their husbands have multiple spouses and are polygynists.

Their public insistence on self-definition may appear to give women living polygyny access to a greater sense of legal independence and sometimes more control over their material possibilities. But while the latter may be true for some women, few of their households in the United States come under law enforcement scrutiny unless other crimes are involved. Couples in unregistered marriages have few issues they can successfully bring before a U.S. court. Women boast about their ability to maintain control over spousal and familial relationships in their individual living quarters, though some complain about the lack of courtesy and/or respect shown by co-wives who find reason to contact husbands when they are scheduled to spend time with their other wives. Co-wives in each family usually collaborate on their husband's schedule with each wife and her children and the personal time the women share with their mutual husband in common spaces such as appearing as a couple in the mosque, among other Muslims, and within the larger society. Still, the women exert little power over where they live unless they are financially able to make such arrangements independently. That is, although women are involved in some decisions regarding their families, men continue to maintain "power and dominance over economic structures and hold a position of power" over their wives—and the number of wives they marry.[16] With few exceptions, Muslim polygynists establish separate households for each wife. Only rarely do African American Muslim women who share husbands view themselves and their co-wives as part a combined family unit, though they may acknowledge the plurality of households for which their husbands are responsible.

Polygyny in the Public Sphere

One way in which the borders of the public and private spheres appear more fluid involves attempts by women to uphold their own, their husbands,' and communal expectations of the roles of women in polygyny. Such endeavors include public displays of agreement with and/or encouragement of multiple-wife marriage for their husbands and acknowledgement of polygyny as an Islamic remedy to the social context of African Americans. By offering up an issue of the private sphere to public scrutiny (at least among fellow Muslims), women married to polygynous men confirm the fluidity of the domains and the extent to which they are willing to maintain an unpopular practice for what they perceive to be a greater good. Indeed, a common rationale for female support of polygyny concurs with the statement of a fifty-nine-year-old widow from North Carolina: "I would consider being in a polygynous marriage if the wife was unable to take care of herself and family due to illness."

While the primary loyalty of African American Muslim women in polygyny is reserved for their husbands and children, the somewhat insular nature of Muslim communities and the centrality of family life in Islam often compel women to maintain ties with and seek approval of and/or validation from other Muslims in their local mosques. In most instances a wife is expected to show her support for and agreement with her husband's decision by proclaiming Qur'anic validation for polygyny or to acquiesce so that her husband might shoulder responsibility for an "imagined community" of "orphans."[17] Izak-El Mu'eed Pasha, a pioneer and resident imam of the Masjid Malcolm Shabazz in New York, among others, characterizes black people as orphans in a foreign land and polygyny as a response to the domestic war waged against his community. His "We're at war" perspectives further illustrate the complexities of the practice of polygyny. They also draw to mind the lack of viable support systems in our communities to empower and sustain healthy marriages regardless of form. While some Muslims and others question any correlation between such expectations and female agency, the lived realities of women married to polygynous men suggest the need for more nuanced considerations of such terms as "autonomy" and "agency."

African American Muslim women who share their husbands routinely serve as the standard bearers for the right of Muslim men to take up to four wives. In doing so, they mirror the practice of medieval Muslims who, according to Rahman, took the "permission clause" of the fourth chapter of the Qur'an to be "absolute."[18] While in due time I will introduce Qur'anic references to multiple-wife marriage and take up their central role in consideration of the legality of polygyny for African American Muslims, for now it is noteworthy that even co-wives who struggle with jealousy, lack of resources, and marriages to men who are incapable of treating all their wives with justice are often among the first to reinforce a divine basis for husband-sharing.[19] Some of these women remain committed to men who fail to live up to Islamic standards for marriage. By declaring faith in what they believe Allah has ordained for their husbands, they contextualize a form of "household patriarchy."[20] That is, they process a type of social organization that affects their communal status and through which they may speak for themselves to the world outside of their homes. Perhaps surprisingly, their speaking involves a range of communication from supporting communal interpretations of Islam's sacred sources and acknowledging the legitimacy of other children born to their husbands to identifying and interviewing prospective co-wives.

Polygyny Comes to the African American World

Few Muslims espouse the view that polygyny privileges women, as scholar and author Patricia Dixon does.[21] Among those who do, however, are women comfortable initiating contact with other women who might be potential co-wives for themselves and spouses for their husbands. Indeed, the behavior and sentiments of such proponents of the practice echo the pre-reform legislation of Muslim-majority nations. For example, as late as 1979, Egyptian women were believed to possess "the psychological make-up to accept polygyny." Those "eager for their husbands' happiness" were presumed to find happiness themselves if their husbands took other wives. Sometimes these purportedly eager women were potential second wives who were familiar with polygyny. In 2010, an amendment to the law guiding marriage and divorce in Egypt, the Law on Reorganization of Certain Terms and Procedures of Litigation in Personal Status Matters, was passed by Parliament. While the legislation expanded divorce rights for women, it did not restrict men's rights to polygyny and only motivated a few women to include conditions or stipulations in their marriage contracts about husband-sharing.[22]

Back in the United States, a case in Texas is particularly telling. This state is home to at least one "polygyny mosque," or Muslim community with a reputation for the practice and promotion of multiple wives for Muslim men. A pilot for a reality show about an African American Muslim household that features a multiple-wife family was filmed during the summer of 2009. According to one disgruntled source there, African Muslim women who migrate to the Houston area visit African American mosques in search of future husbands, hoping to attract men who desire polygyny. When one successful woman was asked by her African American co-wife why she didn't find her own husband, the new wife replied, "I did; he just happens to be your husband." Within African American polygynous households specifically, pro-polygyny women promote this form of plural marriage and freely challenge conventional depictions of their household arrangements within their communities. Theirs is a history that traces roots to indigenous practices in Africa—a continent more than eight thousand miles away where nuclear-family orientation was not the norm in domestic life.[23]

With the arrival of the first bound Africans in the Americas, through to the late eighteenth century when the transatlantic slave trade reached its peak, until Congress abolished slavery in 1864, the enslaved African American family as a formal structure had "no legal existence."[24] Some scholars argue that slavery is guilty of being the saboteur of African American marriages.[25] Additionally, through 1878, Muslim polygyny was perceived to be a foreign practice. One analysis of *Reynolds v. United States* (1878) explains that "the Muslim religious tradition allowing polygamous marriage had so little influence in the United States that the United States Supreme Court denounced it as 'almost exclusively a feature of the life of Asiatic and African peoples.'"[26] Nevertheless, Christian ministers discovered and prohibited the continuation of polygyny during slavery. Slaveholders—and later plantation owners and other white males of whatever age—continued to control the sexuality of African Americans, limiting their ability to form independent unions of their own design or to safeguard or provide for each other. Dixon asserts that

> because of the kinds of cruelties that African American women could be subjected to, many African American men vowed to never marry a woman from the same plantation. . . . This was so that they would not be forced to watch a woman for whom they had feelings be "beaten, insulted, raped, overworked, or starved without being able to protect her."[27]

Astoundingly, two years before Congress closed the legal door on the practice of human bondage in the nation, it passed "morals-based legislation" that criminalized polygyny within U.S. territories.[28] By then, popular novelists and others intertwined the practice of polygyny with the institution of slavery.

Similarly, once Utah chose statehood over plural marriage to enter the Union in 1896, polygyny as then practiced by the leaders and followers of the Fundamentalist Church of Jesus Christ of Latter-Day Saints (FLDS) ceased to be a legally recognized way for any U.S. citizen to marry or organize households.[29] By several accounts, plural marriage continued on Indian reservations during the nineteenth century—practiced by the Blackfeet and Kiowa tribes, for example. Considered "domestic dependent nations," Indian reservations were permitted to determine some of their own affairs; thus Native Americans upheld their marriage customs as "a natural and necessary expedient growing out of their tribal organization."[30] The first community of Muslims in seventh-century Arabia shared common systems for household arrangements with nineteenth-century Comanche Indians, though, like early Mormons and later FLDS members, requirements for eligibility to become a wife differed. Still, as with the experiences of some of their Muslim counterparts, polygyny among Native Americans was believed to be an egalitarian system, as John Moore explains:

> From an American Indian standpoint, the institution of polygyny was seen to benefit both husbands and wives. For men, a larger household meant [an] increase in wealth and status. For women, polygyny usually meant they could get daily help with childcare and other household chores, and have an increased probability of keeping their mother in the household.[31]

Albert Gilles Sr., a writer whose family store catered to his Fort Sill Comanche neighbors, reported that some Indians retained the "soul-destroying and reprehensible" practice of multiple wives in spite of U.S. decrees to the contrary.[32] When directed by the Department of Indian Affairs to reduce his number of wives to one from five, based upon such criteria as "the wife you love the best," Parker, a Comanche neighbor of Gilles, responded this way:

> I have had a number of wives. Sometimes a wife dies and I take another to replace her. Once I had seven wives but now I have only five. Each of my wives I have for a different length of time. . . . I love all my wives equally. I could not call my wives together and tell them that now that the white man is coming, his law says that I can keep but one wife. White man says I should keep the one that I love the best. The rest are surplus and must go and live somewhere else. . . . This I cannot do. You come to my house. You pick out a wife for me to keep. Then you tell 'em.[33]

Apparently Parker—or perhaps more importantly, his wives—convinced U.S. officials to reconsider their demands. Soon after this event, the revised ruling limited polygyny to Comanches already practicing it, though even they were prohibited from taking additional wives. After all, as Gibbs and Campbell assert, many Americans during the nineteenth century opposed polygyny because of its association with Native American cultures considered to be primitive and savage. Scholars also record encounters during this period between Native Americans and African American Muslims, suggesting the possible continuation of polygyny through the end of that century.[34]

In some cases, scholarship challenged Orientalist portrayals of polygyny as an uncivilized family formation. John Moore has noted, "The pervasive Anglo-American idea that polygyny is sexually motivated on the part of the husband probably tells us more about the sexual fantasies of Anglo-American males than about the culture and values of Arabs, Africans or Native Americans."[35] Yet this view continued through the twentieth century, when some male members of the original Nation of Islam (NOI) are believed to have taken multiple wives; the NOI's legendary architect, Elijah Muhammad, among them. Interestingly, the foremost rationale for African American Muslim multiple-wife marriage, according to Gibbs and Campbell, is that African Americans "think of themselves as a Nation."[36]

Whenever they enter into a marriage contract, African American Muslims confront the complexities of family life that all U.S. Muslims do. As minorities in a secular context, they are governed by both religious and civil rules. They must decide how far they are willing to sacrifice their religious identities on a secular altar.[37] That is, "Islamic law governs the family relations of those Muslims who want to validate before God their most intimate relations, while simultaneously, United States law binds them through simple territorial sovereignty."[38] Daily living at this intersection of private and public spheres draws attention to applications of marriage and divorce procedures to which African American Muslims turn when polygyny is the goal. Like their ethnically diverse counterparts, Muslims of African ancestry organize their marital lives around the certification of their unions along one of three tracks: marriages authorized solely by religious law, only by civil law, or in a combination of the two. I now will briefly introduce these paths.

Which Law, Religious or Civil?

To be Muslim in America is to wrestle with a type of legal pluralism that challenges African American women and men to choose between two legal systems when considering the higher authority for marriage formation: religious law, as the unofficial law whose power is limited to their community, or secular law, as the official law legislated by the state. In a secular context like the United States, the cultural values that African American Muslims bring to their Muslim and American selves often shape how they interpret these paths of law and authority. With the added consideration of cultural values—in this case, the retention and transferral of culture and the survival of family life—culture joins religion and secular obligations as a third form of social ordering, each influencing the other. Ultimately, these official and unofficial laws, as Estin explains, "are sometimes closely interwoven, as with the formalization of marriage, and sometimes stand directly in opposition, as with laws prohibiting the practice of polygamy."[39]

The importance of determining how and under what circumstances one should organize a household and of continuing conflicts between blacks and law enforcement officials leads many African American Muslims to focus on the interplay of culture and religion. Yet, the absence of a single earthly authority with the power of final decision means, in the words of Quraishi and Syeed-Miller, that "the field is open" for African American Muslims to turn for guidance to the leaders and specialists of their choice.[40] Routinely, most turn to their resident imams and other religious leaders. Some approach those whom they perceive to be learned individuals regardless of their official positions within the religious community or, sometimes, their gender. With no requirement for education or practical experience, the knowledge of these types of resources on marriage and divorce proceedings can vary, as can expectations of their guidance and service.

For example, Farid Esack, a South African-born scholar who teaches in the United States and his native country, demonstrates his personal opposition to polygyny by refusing to conduct marriage ceremonies for a husband and his second, third, or fourth wife. The marriage contracts presented by couples who come to him must stipulate that the proposed union will be a monogamous one for both parties. Ronald Shaheed, leader of Sultan Muhammad Masjid of Milwaukee, will officiate at monogamous and polygynous marriages, while Khalil Akbar, who shepherds Masjid Ash Shaheed in Charlotte, requires a license that is registered with the state before he will perform a marriage ceremony. Nevertheless, Shaheed and Akbar, followers of Imam Mohammed, are willing to issue an Islamic or religious divorce decree for any marriage not entered into with a state license as well as any for which a civil decree is necessary to end the marriage. The decree they issue, however, is often a verbal rather than written one. Usually, no permanent record is kept at the mosque of either form. The same holds true for the contract itself for some Muslims, which creates opportunities for disparities for women. By religious divorce the imams mean a formal declaration that the marriage contract (*nikah*) by which the parties agreed to live as husband and wife in accordance with the guidance of Allah in the Qur'an and *sunna* and the laws of Islam is terminated.[41] While either party may be expected to continue to fulfill certain stipulations of the contract such as alimony or child support, no religious leader, mosque, or other Islamic body in the United States has the power to enforce those stipulations.[42] This is one of the issues that can make living polygyny a peculiarly troubling proposition.

Not all divorcing Muslims—married under religious law, civil law, or both—pursue an Islamic divorce to end their marriages. The husband of Martha, whom we will meet later, refused to meet with an imam to religiously terminate their *nikah*. For her husband, as with many other Muslims in religious-only marriages, their divorce was a private matter. For complete assurance that they were divorced, however, a civil decree was necessary since Martha and her husband were wed under religious and civil laws.

A key distinction between the two forms of marriage authority is that the unofficial religious law fulfills the requirement for an Islamically sanctioned decree to organize or disband a family. Among the reasons African American and other American Muslims opt for the Islamic-only form of marriage or divorce is their skepticism of government or their preference not to involve its oversight into private matters. Interestingly, some Muslims choose to limit the involvement of civil officials in their marital affairs even if theirs are monogamous unions. Ultimately, civil-only marriages are limited to unions of one man and one woman, even though the husband may later decide to take another wife. Those who prefer that their marriages or divorces be authorized solely by religious law risk unplanned challenges in the event of divorce or death of a spouse. Men who enter into Islamic and civil marriages simultaneously often leave the choice of the type of validation to the first wives they marry. Regardless of the label associated with their particular unions, African American Muslim women recognize that their mosques or local religious communities represent "semi-autonomous fields" that often generate their own rules.[43]

The Path to What Islam Says about Polygyny

Let's return to Jamillah and Rahim, the couple on the verge of an early-morning confrontation. Jamillah has braced herself for the news that Rahim has decided to expand his marital "covering." In our interview, she indicated her awareness that in Islam, spouses are a covering for each other, an adornment that protects husbands and wives from the dangers of moral transgressions.[44] Still, she acknowledged the possibility of polygyny when she married Rahim but failed to prepare herself for the reality of sharing her husband. When Rahim confirmed Jamillah's suspicions, one could argue that she was about to do what nineteenth-century Mormon converts did: "step out of the profane world and into a new spiritual space."[45]

Like many other Muslims, Jamillah trusted the teachings she heard and read that situated polygyny in the Qur'an as a male right or at least a permissible practice for contemporary Muslims. She was aware that some Muslims disliked the practice or challenged communal interpretations of its legitimacy in the presence of civil laws that criminalize plural marriage.[46] She also was acquainted with the experiences of local leaders whose marriages were portrayed as "model Muslim," whose multiple wives were described as happy and pious believers, and whose journeys to polygyny were told and retold as responses to a divine directive.

Logically, Jamillah realized that she was free to leave her marriage at any time, thanks to the Muslim marriage directive to "live in peace or separate in peace." Furthermore, in the absence of a civil registration of her union, Jamillah understood that she was not bound by any state-imposed restrictions. Spiritually, however, she felt trapped by a series of paradoxes. That is, she was caught in competing social notions: the freedom to depart, the idea that "Allah hates divorce," and the appearance of being un-Islamic by using the imposition of polygyny to end her marriage. Like all women living polygyny, she read her options through consideration of two passages from the Sura al-Nisa (The Women), the fourth chapter of the Qur'an.

Islamic Authority and Polygyny

Though incidental to the Qur'an's more than six thousand *ayat*, the passages in the Sura al-Nisa routinely serve as the guiding principle on polygyny in Islam. Moreover, my informants have described numerous ways to interpret their meanings.[47] Ultimately, Jamillah decided to remain in the marriage given that polygyny was the sole motivation for divorce. She characterized that decision as choosing Islam—or what she still insists is the Islamic rule of law on plural marriage. As with other women who support or reject sharing a husband, the process by which Jamillah arrived at her decision was a three-tiered one. This process involves gaining knowledge and understanding of Islamic rulings of polygyny from the three primary sources of authority: the Qur'an, *sunna*, and *hadith*. I offer preliminary reflections on each before returning to the Qur'an in more depth.

Given its importance in rituals such as daily prayers, meditation, weddings, and funerals and its revelatory significance, the Qur'an is the single most consulted, read, memorized, and recited source. Each Muslim home features at least one copy, depending upon the size of the family; mosques retain several editions for the use of believers and visitors. Some Muslims believe that *sunna* represent a second form of revelation and are referenced in the Qur'an. These Muslims tend to limit authoritative consideration to the Qur'an and *sunna*. For them, the latter is granted equal authority with revelation because it reflects the traditions of the Prophet and the seventh-century community in Medina, where the Prophet lived for the last decade of his life. Even as informants reminded me of the supremacy of the Qur'an, the manner in which some of them lived the Qur'an, particularly in regard to the rights they believed they possessed, often contradicted the spirit of justice inherent in the Qur'an.

Generally, many Muslims engage *hadith* less frequently in their private lives and primarily during lectures at Friday congregational prayer services, in classes on Islamic belief and tradition, and at conferences. Books of *hadith* address specific issues such as divorce, temporary marriage, the importance of accepting wedding invitations, the obligatory *mahr*, the types of women available for marriage, and the experiences of the Prophet and his multiple wives. *Hadith* that convey information on polygyny provide guidelines on time spent with, responsibility for, and treatment of wives. I translate the lack of familiarity with *hadith* among many of my subjects as their dependence upon religious teaching that occurs outside of their homes.

Some *hadith* clearly indicate that jealousy is an expected emotion experienced by women who share their husbands. At least two of the foremost *hadith* collections confirm that the Prophet refused to marry his daughter to a polygynist against her wishes.[48] Others are more specific in terms of consequences and ambiguous with respect to context, as illustrated in the following report from a collection of *hadith* on marriage:

> The Prophet (peace be upon him) said: When a man has two wives and he is inclined to one of them, he will come on the Day of Resurrection with a side hanging down.[49]

This recollection of Abu Dawud declares the consequences of preferring some wives over others as partial paralysis of the husband on the Day of Judgment, without clarifying what forms preferential treatment might take.

The process of gaining legal knowledge about an issue in Islam and striving to understand it is called *fiqh*. The above-named sources along with directives from Islamic schools of law represent Islamic jurisprudence. Even so, few Muslims outside of academic environments use such legalese to describe how they go about deciding what is an Islamic action or practice and how they apply it to their daily lives. More often, their actual practice reflects adherence to three stages—Qur'anic exegesis, communal tradition and responsibility, and personal consideration of theological and practical options. While the weight devoted to each stage varies, the importance of *asbab al-nuzul*, the occasion of revelation, as part of Qur'anic interpretation is a common starting point. Mudzakir has argued, "The interpretation of the Qur'an cannot be separated from its context, in which political, social and economic factors play a role."[50] In other words, among African American Muslim women living polygyny, discerning how they think through the Qur'an and construct rationale for their decisions as black people in America is a significant signal for why they remain living polygyny or oppose it. In this regard, my interviews expand the evidentiary base.

Reading and Approaching the Qur'an

Regardless of social context, most Muslims regard the Qur'an to be the direct word of G'd to humanity through the Prophet Muhammad. Although portions of the Qur'an have been translated into at least 114 languages, Muslims tend to ascribe more authenticity to the Qur'an as written in Arabic, the language of revelation. Most Muslims first encounter the Qur'an as an oral experience whose *ayat* are recited, memorized, and prayed in Arabic, even though less than 20 percent of the estimated 1.3 billion Muslims converse in Arabic.[51] Thus, for some Muslims the multiple non-Arabic translations are at best "approaches" that never completely recapture the original meaning.[52] Nevertheless, translations can be beneficial because a translation "is a kind of explanation" that can "throw light on the original through offering possible interpretations."[53] Of the multiple English-language approaches, *The Quran: Text, Translation, and Commentary* by Abdullah Yusuf Ali has sustained popularity among African American and other Muslims in the United States since its first publication in 1934, due in part to backing from the Saudi government that enabled wide distribution.

Yusuf Ali's translation is routinely presented as a gift to new Muslims because it is accessible to non-Muslims, nonspeakers of Arabic, and individuals who are fluent in Arabic but whose native language is English. For many followers of Imam Mohammed, the Yusuf Ali Qur'an replaced the Maulana Muhammad Ali translation after W. D. Mohammed succeeded his father in 1975. At the time, Mohammed characterized the change as a move from the edition preferred by NOI founder W. D. Fard to the highly readable "best Arabic to English" translation available.[54]

While they are aware of the aforementioned language issues that surround the Qur'an as text, most African American Muslims refer to whatever version they use as the Qur'an, leaving others to make distinctions between Arabic and English editions. The sentiments of Barlas, a Muslim female scholar, resonate with the perspectives of African American Muslims: "There is no substitute for reading the Qur'an in Arabic, but, to me the word of God is equally real in *all* languages."[55] African American and many other Muslims tend to privilege the version of the Qur'an used by their imams and other teachers. Thus, African American Muslim women across the United States, like those who regularly gather for weekend sisters' classes at Masjid Ash Shaheed in Charlotte, Masjid Al-Taqwa in Chicago, and Sultan Muhammad Masjid in Milwaukee depend on Yusuf Ali's Qur'an as their primary English translation to discern the will of G'd for their daily lives and circumstances.

Although the Qur'an addresses general issues relevant to marriage, it appears almost silent on the question of multiple wives—a practice that is as controversial today in the United States as it was in seventh-century Arabia. Until the advent of Islam, tribal customs dictated that a man could marry as many wives as he chose. While evidence of polyandry, or women with multiple husbands, remains questionable, concerns about paternity would ultimately limit wives to only one husband. As with other revelations given to the Prophet, directives about polygyny were "deeply consonant with the sociocultural systems already in place throughout the Middle East," in Ahmed's assessment. Wadud explains, "It was impossible to mutually recognize and thus protect the father's paternal rights when a woman had more than one conjugal partner."[56] Though brief, the two verses on polygyny are part of a larger discussion of moral and social rules for the developing community that had migrated to Medina from Mecca. They are compiled as part of the third-longest chapter in the Qur'an, here translated by Yusuf Ali:

> If ye fear that ye shall not be able to deal justly with the orphans, Marry women of your choice, Two or three or four; but if ye fear that ye shall not be able to deal justly (with them), then only one, or (a captive) that your right hands possess, that will be more suitable, to prevent you from doing injustice. (4:3)

> Ye are never able to be fair and just as between women, even if it is your ardent desire: But turn not away (from a woman) altogether, so as to leave her (as it were) hanging (in the air). If ye come to a friendly understanding, and practise self-restraint, Allah is Oft-forgiving, Most Merciful. (4:129)

Unlike other *suras* in the Qur'an whose titles may not fully describe their contents, al-Nisa focuses particularly on the rights and status of women. When revealed, *ayat* 3 and 129 attempt to address an inequity concerning the rights and maintenance of women and children and the existing customary practice in pre-Islamic Arabia that both became the property of men when they married.[57] Understandably, they do not signal an awareness of contemporary situations in which women could be financial providers.[58] Neither these passages nor the Prophet Muhammad instituted multiple-wife marriage. Instead, the revelation restricted the practice. Even as men commonly use these verses to justify satisfying sexual desires, the historical context of the passages prevents any thoughtful use of them to sanction multiple-wife marriage for the purpose of sex. The transmission of the passages to the Prophet followed the deaths of dozens of men from the nascent Muslim community in 625 during the Battle of Uhud, the second of three major early conflicts.

Examinations of Islamic legal materials routinely promote these *ayat* together as a divinely inspired reform in Arab history that served to repudiate one expression of patriarchy and protect women and children from abuse and destitution. Indeed, some scholars argue that one valid interpretation of these passages is that the Qur'an advocates against "generalized polygyny" while also presenting a compelling case for "justice and accountability for unjust actions."[59] Yet no consensus exists about how, where, or when al-Nisa should be invoked in contemporary societies. Today, these passages are regularly treated as isolated prescriptions for the practice of polygyny that limit egalitarian constructions of relationships between husbands and wives and among co-wives. Qur'anic interpretation, then, can be complicated, especially when one seeks confirmation for an established or preferred position. It also can be challenging when particularities of the past do not appear to be present or when modern contextualization methods expand consideration of terms such as "orphan" to include an entire ethnic group.

To African American women, the process of discerning what the Qur'an says and means and applying that knowledge for twenty-first-century Muslims can be a deeply personal one that varies depending upon the individual and her religious, emotional, and practical resources. Throughout this work, I argue that the process of interpreting and understanding the Qur'an, along with the practical application of interpretation, is vital to gender justice for African American Muslim women and others who encounter polygyny. These stages—interpretation, communal tradition and responsibility, and personal consideration of theological and practical options—leave their mark on the practice of polygyny among African American Muslims. I begin with the interpretative stage because scholarly hermeneutics alone can empower or oppress African American women in ways that neither the communal nor the practical stages can.

Scholarly considerations of al-Nisa *ayat* 3 and 129 contextualize the Qur'an's position as one of three related but distinct discourses: those that interpret the Qur'an to endorse polygyny, those that stress Qur'anic ambiguity on the issue, and those that speculate that the Qur'an no longer permits multiple-wife marriage.

I call the first discourse "traditional literalism," to refer to the debate promoted by advocates of polygyny ("TL" scholars). I label the second discourse "ambiguous pragmatism" to refer to arguments (by "AP" scholars) that place the Qur'an on the fence, so to speak, regarding the validity of polygyny. "Reformers for justice" round out the trio of discourses to highlight efforts (by "RFJ" scholars) to halt the practice of polygyny on the grounds that it fails to meet the Qur'anic (or Islamic) goal of gender justice. The boundaries between these groups remain fluid in some areas, as I hope will become clear. Nevertheless, these discourses suggest that the answers to whether polygyny is legitimate today are, respectively, "yes," "maybe," and "no."

The Discourse of Traditional Literalism

Like their AP and RFJ counterparts, advocates of traditional literalist approaches to the Qur'an agree that Islam did not institute polygny but modified and regulated a practice already in place. For TL scholars, however, the answer to whether Islam sanctions polygyny was answered more than 1,400 years ago when Allah said yes. They communicate divine agreement by

- interpreting 4:3 as an absolute statement that embraces the possibility of up to four wives;[60]
- characterizing the marriage of up to four wives as the "way of the Prophet." In fact, they often lean on a popular *hadith*: "Whoever revives an aspect of my *sunna* that is forgotten after my death, he will have a reward equivalent to that of the people who follow him, without it detracting in the least from their reward";[61]
- defining polygyny as a valuable service and thus not only a right but also a duty of men to alleviate problems that would exist otherwise (surplus women, homosexuality, uncared-for widows and orphans, barren couples);[62]

- promoting polygyny as a form of marriage that elevates and protects the rights of women and children;
- portraying multiple-wife marriage as does author and co-wife Jameelah Jones as "a complicated aspect of marriage in Islam in which the welfare of the community supersedes the desires of the individual (woman)."[63] Does this conflate the desire of men with the desire of the community?

Whether what the Qur'an says about polygyny means it is an unbridled right for Muslim men or a practice permissible regardless of time or context, one issue is without doubt for TL advocates: polygyny is "not a decadent or indecent relationship but a valid part of the marriage system" of their religion.[64] As part of their examinations of the subject, TL scholars turn first to the Qur'an and *sunna*. They also consult *hadith* and rulings of the major schools of Islamic law and thought—Maliki, Hanafi'i, Hanbali, Shafi'i (and multiple Shi'a legal traditions). At some time in Islamic history, TL scholars have been able to draw from each school as they searched for legal codes that sustained their hermeneutical project on polygyny.[65] I will highlight some of the most prevalent academic and popular works on polygyny that have circulated throughout African American and other Muslim communities.

Some contemporary proponents of the traditional literalist discourse lean heavily on the traditional Islamic sources cited above as they generate resources that reflect their personal journeys with polygyny. The authors of *Polygamy in Islaam*, Abu Ameenah Bilal Philips and Jameelah Jones, and of "Pedagogy of Polygyny," Chanda Green, are two noteworthy examples. They are highly visible and respected individuals within African American Muslim communities and share their cultural concerns, particularly in regard to the sustainability of the black family. Their educational credentials and the depth of their interactions with traditional sources, along with the personal narratives they incorporate into their intellectual discourse, suggest to those around them that these authors know a lot about this subject and their knowledge can be trusted. The female authors are African American women who came to Islam prior to establishing polygynous households.

A husband and co-wife who discuss their own marital experiences wrote *Polygamy in Islaam*. Both of the authors possess master's degrees; Philips also holds a doctorate in Islamic studies. Both have studied and worked in Saudi Arabia, the cradle of Islam for many Muslims. According to the publisher's note, Philips and Jones are "reverts" whose "western background facilitated a deep understanding of the subject. They have dealt with multiple-wife marriage in the light of the Qur'an and *sunna* and have described the important characteristics of marriage in Islam. They have provided a straightforward reply to the question of why Islam allows four wives."[66] *Polygamy in Islaam* appeared in 1985 as one of Philips's first self-published works, after Jones joined his family as a second wife. Since then, it has been reprinted at least four times; the latest edition (2005) is available on the Internet.[67] Part of the rationale for its popularity is the authors' claim that *Polygamy in Islaam* is "one of the only books of its kind in English devoted solely to the highly controversial topic of polygamy in Islam."[68]

Philips explained the motivation for the book during a 2010 appearance on *The Deen Show*, a Chicago-based online radio and cable television program. As an introduction to the topic, the host legitimates his guest's treatment of polygyny by saying that "the Creator has legislated and approved that a man is able to [marry up to four wives]."[69] During the fifty-six-minute interview, Philips indicates that his research on plural marriage emerged from his personal entry into polygyny during the early 1980s and his decision to examine and translate one of the classical works of legal interpretation, *al-Mughni* by Ibn Qudamah. "I realized that it was important for me to have a thorough knowledge of the legal structure [aspects of Islamic law] governing plural marriage," he explains. "It is a requirement of every Muslim that whatever field they enter into they should be thoroughly grounded in the knowledge of that field so as to avoid doing what is displeasing to God and ensure that what they do is pleasing to God." Philips contended that polygyny provides protections for women and children that are absent in monogamy. For him, unions of one husband and one wife can serve as "an escape from legal polygyny":

> Monogamy protects males. The decision makers of society are males, and males do benefit from polygamous relationships. . . . By making it illegal to have more than one wife, they remove from themselves the responsibility for looking after more that one wife. That's the point. So they can have a wife, and they can have girlfriends, mistresses, prostitutes and all these other things without any responsibility. They can have these relationships but they are not held responsible. . . . By making it a crime for a man who decides to have one wife, and he decides to be just and honest and fair and take a second wife, he's labeled a bigamist. That's a crime for which he can spend time in jail. Whereas a man who has girlfriends, he's got a wife, but he's got girlfriends, mistresses, he's got children coming here, there, all across the country, he's labeled a hero.[70]

Like other TL promoters, Philips acknowledges that polygyny is not problem free:

> There is some smaller harm that comes to [a woman who shares her husband with his other wives]—it hurts. . . . But you are trying to avoid a greater hurt. So we just have to keep focused, that this permission in Islam is trying to avoid a greater hurt in society as a whole. And, the smaller harm that comes to the wife that she is patient with it and that it becomes purification for her as Allah promised. . . . The harm that [polygamy] prevents is obvious; the good that it brings is clear."[71]

"The Pedagogy of Polygyny" is Chanda Green's 2011 doctoral dissertation.[72] Like other TL scholars, this thrice-married mother of five recognizes polygyny as one of two ways to be lawfully fulfilled in marriage but a practice that women who share their husbands "reshape and reform" on a daily basis.[73] She agrees, too, in the promotion of the Qur'an, *sunna*, and *fiqh* as the primary if not sole sources to answer such queries as "Is polygyny permitted in Islam?" and "Must I stay with my husband if he takes another wife?" About the times she has lived polygyny, she writes, "I went through huge paradigm shifts from detesting polygyny no matter what, to objectively viewing polygyny and examining it for the positive and negative that can go with it."[74] Still, she adheres to the more conservative continuum of traditional-literalist discourse when she writes, as was the practice of the Prophet, that "the husband is not required to notify nor consult with his wife or wives prior to marrying additional wives."[75]

Philips and Jones would concur with Green, though all three do encourage men to inform their wives. So strong is the consensus of TL advocates in the rightness of polygyny that, like the Assembly of Muslim Jurists of America, they would also agree that husbands and their multiple wives may marry in the United States without registering their marriages with civil authorities—a position to which Imam Mohammed likewise subscribed. Another appropriate spokesperson for this perspective is Jamal Badawi, whose out-of-print pamphlet *Polygamy in Islamic Law* is available online. He considers polygamy to be a fitting remedy for men with barren wives. This is another rationale often used for the practice, but it is one scholars like Wadud and al-Hibri strenuously disagree can be supported with these conditional verses. The TL discourse contends that Muslim men strive to be fair to their multiple wives and that some Muslim women prefer polygyny. For these polygyny proponents, Islam is a religion with a proven standard for living for all Muslims—one that Muslims should affirm rather than revise to fit popular norms.

Most of the discourse of traditional literalism proclaims that wives cannot unilaterally opt out. They cannot say no to husband-sharing simply because of their personal preferences unless their marriage contracts stipulate monogamy. For TL thinkers, such women disobey G'd. These scholars claim that the Qur'an, *sunna,* and *fiqh* comprise sufficient support for polygyny in Islam and its practice today. Specifically, they interpret the Qur'an as saying polygyny is at least permissible and at best a right, and that settles the matter. In the end, theirs is a discourse that, like a popular *hadith,* warns against making unlawful what Allah has made lawful.[76] Perhaps how the proponents of this discourse describe polygyny holds the key to our better understanding of the rationale of women living polygyny who, like Jamillah, say they do so because they have no other choice.

The Discourse of Ambiguous Pragmatism

The second discourse links the permissibility of polygyny to the presence of justice. It is a middle-of-the-road discourse that offers a clear rationale for situating AP scholars between the discourse of traditional literalism and reformers for justice.[77] Indeed, they stand symbolically in the shadows of generations of *ulama* like nineteenth-century Egyptian Muhammad 'Abduh and his disciple Muhammad Rashid Rida. Both conditionally situated themselves within the camp of permissibility depending upon the unlikely presence of justice and/or equal treatment. According to Tucker, 'Abduh considered polygyny to be "an act permitted by the Qur'an" on the condition of equal treatment of co-wives. She contends that Rida based his position on interpretations of the Qur'an and *sunna* that suggested that the difficulty in extending justice to multiple wives might lead a "responsible Muslim" to monogamy unless "national priorities" suggested otherwise.[78]

In "Muhammad Rashid Rida on Muhammad Abdul on Polygamy," posted on the Internet long after Rida's death in 1935, the disciple appears to confirm his teacher's qualifications about polygyny. Rida writes of Abdul, "Polygamy is like one of those necessities which is permitted to the one to whom it is allowed (only) with the stipulation that he act fairly with trustworthiness and that he be immune from injustice." Yet, later in the essay, Rida claims that 'Abduh also laid the blame for the difficulties of polygny on women:

> The wife stirs up enmity and hatred among them [children, father, relatives]; she incites her husband to enmity against his brothers and sisters, and she incites her husband to suppress the rights of the children which

he has from other wives. The husband, on the other hand, follows in the folly of the wife whom he loves the most, and thus ruin creeps into the entire family.[79]

In other words, husbands are responsible for successes in living polygyny, wives for its downfall.

The translators, annotators, and linguistic consultants of *Quran: Reformist Translation* could be characterized as "The Qur'an said it, and that settles it" camp. They are AP scholars. The three collaborators of the 520-page manuscript are Edip Yuksel, an author, activist, and legal scholar who teaches philosophy at Pima Community College in Tucson, Arizona; Layth al-Shaiban, an author, founder of Progressive Muslims, and co-founder of Islamic Reform who works as a financial adviser in Saudi Arabia; and Martha Schulte-Nafeh, an assistant professor at the University of Arizona and an administrator in its Department of Near Eastern Studies. Published in 2007, *Quran: A Reformist Translation* offers "a non-sexist understanding of the divine text" that "explicitly rejects the right of the clergy to determine the likely meaning of disputed passages." Though billed as a "reformist translation of the Qur'an," its identification of the Qur'an as the "sole legitimate scriptural source of religious law and guidance in Islam" is unacceptable to some reformers like Wadud, even as she "supports the efforts of these translators."[80] Still, in the view of AP scholars, governments are free to establish regulations as they see fit, and individuals are free to follow their consciences as they navigate their marital options. The contributions of AP scholars can feel especially frustrating to women living polygyny who seek definitive answers to combat the certainties about polygyny they encounter.

The Discourse of Reformers for Justice

Finally, RFJ scholars adamantly oppose polygyny and contend that the Qur'an clearly articulates the required context and the impossibility of following both the law and spirit of the Qur'an on the matter. Furthermore, the Qur'an counsels husbands with the declaration "One is better." Advocates of the RFJ agenda realize that multiple interpretations exist in regard to what the Qur'an says and what the Qur'an means. But they insist that in the absence of justice—and thus the impossibility of the Qur'anic ideal—monogamy is the only available option for marriage. The RFJ discourse is not persuaded by the lack of potential marriageable Muslim mates for African American women.

With the New York edition of Wadud's dissertation published in 1999 as *Qur'an and Woman: Rereading the Sacred Text from a Woman's Perspective*, she produced the second edition of the first female-exclusive exegetical text. In this book, Wadud raises important questions about the acceptability of polygyny today. Other works have followed, including *Feminist Edges of the Qur'an* by Aysha Hidayatullah, *Women's Identity and the Qur'an: A New Reading* by Nimat Barazangi, *Believing Women in Islam: Unreading Patriarchal Interpretations of the Quran* by Asma Barlas, and *Women Shaping Islam: Reading the Qur'an in Indonesia* by Pieternella Van Doorn-Harder. In addition to their scholarly work, proponents of RFJ also advocate for the type of social activist work produced by Malaysia's Sisters in Islam. That is, they support activities within mosques and other venues that emphasize mutuality, dignity, justice, and freedom—themes they say are visibly present in the Qur'an.

Finally, the RFJ discourse is designed to push back against patriarchal assumptions about marriage and women's roles within the family. In the place of injurious representations, this discourse strives to normalize the idea of questioning any exegetical process that leads to the oppression of women or denies women human dignity and fair treatment. Having weighed these three approaches, I translate RFJ's campaign for gender justice to mean that women have the right to choose whom they marry and the context in which they do so. I am sure that most if not all RFJ advocates may disagree with any acceptance of polygyny even when all parties are in full agreement and their rights are protected. I do hope, however, that they may perceive this book as a contribution toward mechanisms that shift the discourse about the rights of men in family formations to justice for all.

This research project has irrefutably demonstrated to me that many men and women involved in polygyny in the United States are victims of erroneous communal teachings and explanations of the Qur'an based on faulty and/or culturally specific interpretations. Theirs is a romantic attachment to polygyny, one that affords an opportunity to demonstrate their autonomy from America's racist and dominant culture at the expense of the well-being of women, children, and community life.

Equally apparent is that for some women, polygyny enables entry into marriage as the only legitimate arena for sexual intercourse and procreation. They are willing to use their marriages as their personal *jihad* because polygyny provides a "tool for cultural survival in which the otherwise marginalized are able to seize power" from those who have dominated them.[81] A few women who prefer to share a husband choose polygyny because they believe it to be the only way they authentically can practice, in words attributed to the Prophet, "half of their religion." They perceive polygyny as a way to live a morally good life, assume the higher status enjoyed by married female Muslims, and maintain their independence. Some pro-polygyny women even celebrate their periods of autonomy. As one wrote, "How I love my late nights and early mornings without a man. I hope you can enjoy yours too."[82] What is more, other women and men perceive this form of Muslim marriage to be a suitable response to continued black suffering and as "a method of survival that links African American Muslims to their first generational Muslim ancestors."[83]

The experiences of most African American Muslims who live in polygynous households across the nation compel me to question, as Wadud has, "How can there be justice if women do not experience it?"[84] Granted, some women do experience what they would consider to be justice. And while their journey of polygyny has not been without its own challenges, they advertise for wives for their husbands and conduct initial interviews. A subject in an NPR report explains why she did so: "I had to make sure that she'd be the right fit—not just for my husband, but for our whole family."[85] When African American Muslim women recruit potential co-wives through print advertising, Twitter accounts, Facebook notices, and listserv announcements, they mirror the endeavors of Muslim women in the United Kingdom, counterparts who "seek to become the second wife of a married man."[86] By retaining control over the selection of additional wives, these women also ensure their compatibility with them.

Some women, like Qaedah, a thirty-eight-year-old in Texas, have entered polygynous households multiple times. Qaedah declares, "I absolutely love polygyny. For the sisters involved it is, in my opinion, they who have all the benefits minus any of the stress and pressure. I don't lose anything through polygyny. I gain in every way."[87] Qaedah had begun to network among friends and others—electronically and by word of mouth—to secure another wife for her husband because "Inshallah [if G'd so wills] she will be a part of the family." Qaedah and other proponents contend that through polygyny all Muslim American women have access to marriage.

I am not surprised at the disagreements that surround the religious legitimacy of polygyny in the form practiced by most African American and other Muslims who organize households in the twenty-first century, especially given the diversity of perspectives women living polygyny encounter. Apparently, the constitutionality of multiple-wife marriage is not always clear, either. Even the congressional committee that confirms presidential nominees to the judiciary has been indecisive. That is, Senator Orrin Hatch (R-Utah), then chairperson of the Senate Judiciary Committee and the great-grandson of a polygynist, responded to a constitutional inquiry this way:

I don't think the Constitution is clear. I think the constitutional law is clear. . . . The Constitution is ambiguous with regard to this. It provides for religious freedom.[88]

Attempts to validate the experience of women as a strategy to ensure justice are common among scholars and other activists who seek for Muslim women the full application of their rights. Those who believe that Islam permits or gives the right to men to adopt polygyny may differ regarding whether a potential wife must be a widow or orphan and whether a husband should inform or gain approval of his first wife before taking a second, third, or fourth. There is also the question of whether Islamic law permits a wife to obtain a divorce and maintain her financial rights if polygyny is the issue of discord and her husband does not want to end the marriage. Yet all lift up al-Nisa as a timeless and culture-free authority, in effect the will of Allah for twenty-first-century Muslim families. In doing so, they raise family law issues that retain the visibility of maleness in African American family life,[89] but this can render justice elusive to too many Muslim women.

I approached this chapter with the goal to problematize the practice of polygyny. I also set out to urge Muslim women at the grassroots level to unite with Muslim women in the academy to challenge essentialist depictions of polygyny. My students have learned about the possibilities inherent in the Muslim female. One writes, "Muslim women are responsible for their own empowerment as members of not only a widely-practiced religious tradition and as contributing members of American society, but also as scholars, mothers, wives, writers, gamers, poets, dancers, musicians, activists, and any other roles which they fill as people, not solely as Muslimahs or Americans."[90] Perhaps together, grassroots and academic women can empower all Muslim women to view their personal experiences as legitimate authority that helps clarify their own marital options. If, as Kecia Ali suggests, there are times in which the Qur'an requires Muslims to "depart from its literal provisions in order to establish justice,"[91] the opportunity to help show American Muslim women what they can do about polygyny is one of those times.

4

Legalities and Emotional Well-Being

Without a legal marriage, wives can go to court for child support
for their children, but they can expect nothing for themselves.

Latifah, a Texas lawyer

We got married in 2006, and approximately one month after marriage during
a conversation he said his "wife." I asked him what was he talking about.

Lanita, new to polygyny

Martha exhales as she nears the end of her riverfront walk. Feeling accomplished, she smiles as sweat dampens her shirt. Though comfortably single for
the past three years, this health-care professional admits to periods of loneli-
ness and longing for companionship. Walking helps her feel connected to her
community and environment, but watching the scores of couples sipping wine
at outdoor cafes and tapping their feet to sidewalk musicians or just strolling
past her hand in hand on this summer evening suggest a deficiency that Martha would rather not admit. A mother of two and grandmother of three, Martha hopes to remarry and feels she's ready, but she wonders whether her entry
into the sisterhood of sixty-year-olds will limit her prospects. The outdoor
scenes before her elicit longing. Martha's ex-husband, fifteen years her junior,
has married again, taking another wife to join Martha's former co-wife—whose
presence led Martha to file for divorce.[1] Learning about his most recent marriage (to a mother of two) sends Martha into a free fall of remembering. When
she lands, she's back in her attorney's office late in the divorce process. Her
husband preferred to resolve the divorce privately. She and her attorney are
about to consider a strategy Martha hopes will compel her husband to end his
two-year-long obstruction of her petition. For Martha, as with most African
American Muslim women living polygyny, a public resolution is the only insurance against further injustice when a husband takes another wife.

The introduction of polygyny into their already stressed household made
this marriage unbearable for Martha. While her co-wife Rashidah frequented

local shops in a nearby town to furnish her new apartment, Martha lost weight, suffered through sleepless nights, and questioned her own worth. Although she did not intentionally ram the car of her co-wife with the latter behind the wheel, as one distraught subject did, Martha could relate to feeling that only she could end her own madness. So she struggled daily to maintain self-control. Yet even though she agreed to retract her demand that he repay thousands of dollars in bills charged in her name, even though she decided not to request that he pay the *mahr* he promised on the eve of their seven-year marriage, and even though she chose to keep private his verbal harassment rather than alert their mosque to imperfections in his shining image, Martha realizes that her fight is not yet over.[2]

Soon, the sight of her favorite ice cream shop jerks Martha back to the present reality. She exhales again—this time in gratitude that her engagement with family law courts in the United States is in the past and thankful, too, that the legal protection unavailable to Rashidah and Medinah, her ex-husband's current wives, was easily accessible to her. Should either decide to end her marriage, she can rely on neither civil courts nor her Islamic community to confirm that a legally sanctioned marriage ever took place; as far as the American legal system is concerned, Rashidah and Medinah are invisible, they are on their own. They embody the conclusions of the Texas attorney offered above and reflect the ways in which women living polygyny often have little control in the marital decisions of their husbands and sometimes of their own destinies.[3] In contrast, because Martha entered a union regulated through laws of marriage and divorce in the United States, she has more options.[4]

In other words, most women married to polygynous men are like Rashidah and Medinah: aside from any financial agreements they may have notarized, they have no legal standing as married women.[5] Moreover, Martha's district court decree defined the legal duties of both parties and represented a binding judgment—a level of reinforcement that neither her mosque nor the larger American Muslim community can exert.[6] If American Muslim women are unable to rely on their communities to help preserve their rights, what is the efficacy of Islamic family law to these women? For that matter, is Islamic law compatible with American civil law at all? Or are civil courts alone best suited to resolve marital issues that involve religious beliefs? And is polygyny defensible as a First Amendment issue, or is it just another feature of the latest culture war?

To begin to make sense of Islamic family law and its implications for African American Muslim women living polygyny in the Muslim-minority United

States, I start with a brief sketch of Islamic jurisprudence on family matters and the communal authority on polygyny for African American Muslims, drawing attention to the "space" of polygyny in the physical and mental landscapes of my subjects.[7] I focus specifically on the United States during the 1950s and 1960s, a period in which global reform of polygyny coincided with an era of social movements, black nationalism, and unrest—perhaps the best and worst of times for the original Nation of Islam and its architect, Elijah Muhammad.[8] Global examples of the challenges of polygyny among Muslim populations add salient contrasts for this study because of the possibility that their family law policies influenced the marital codes that Elijah Muhammad instituted after his visit to Turkey and the Middle East in November 1959.

I then turn to the concept of family law for the followers of Elijah Muhammad and W. D. Mohammed. The son dismantled many of the spiritual, physical, and psychological barriers that maintained the insularity of his father's movement when he assumed the helm of the NOI in 1975. Even before he did, Mohammed began to comprehend just how formidable was his father's hold on his followers and the depth of their willingness to believe that their leader possessed the quality of moral infallibility. What is more, Mohammed would join other NOI leaders in characterizing his father's relationships with several secretaries and other NOI female members as contemporary expressions of polygyny. I argue that women who initiate or welcome offers of marriage from polygynous men may view their legal rights and communal responsibilities differently than women who, despite reservations, feel religiously obligated to enter into or sustain polygynous households.

While some African American Muslim men and women strive to uphold their Islamic legal rights in American family courts, only African American polygynous men assert their rights in American mosques and Muslim homes by contracting both monogamous and multiple-wife marriages. I privilege husbands as initiators of *nikahs* because only they can choose to marry multiple spouses and assume responsibility for either monogamous or polygynous households. Such examples of male control of females fuel associations of Islam with patriarchy and perceptions that some of the laws of Islam—if not the religion itself—are incompatible with universal human rights and gender equality.

An informed exploration of multiple-wife marriages must take into consideration the effects of these unions on the mental health of women and children. In some ways, all members of polygynous households live the practice. It is to the ways that living polygyny figures into the emotional health of women that I turn now. Central to this discussion is Clara Muhammad, the only legal wife of Elijah Muhammad.[9] Clara chose to remain with her husband despite mounting evidence of extramarital activities because she believed his battle for the well-being of black people outweighed any personal failures. It comes as no surprise that the former Clara Evans never acknowledged that she or her husband lived polygyny. More than three decades after the death of Elijah Muhammad, the mothers of the children he bore would gather to publicly defend his honor and claim their status as widows of the Messenger.

I conclude by drawing attention to the work of Khaled Abou el Fadl, Asifa Quraishi, and Najeeba Syeed-Miller, who challenge local mosques and other designated community structures to assume the role of legal guardians for Muslim women and men as they seek to ensure gender justice.[10] Although I join Mormon scholar Janet Bennion in supporting the decriminalization of multiple-wife marriage, I am concerned by overt and tacit tolerance for polygyny in situations where abuse and misuse are supported by arguments that marriage is a private matter and polygyny a religiously sanctioned practice.[11] The social, religious, and legal relationships in familial structures of polygyny and monogamy are varied and multilayered; they demand and deserve regulation and support from local mosques and the larger Muslim society. A principled approach to the recognition of Muslim marriage is needed, and such consideration should begin with Muslims. I suggest that reinforcement of female agency coupled with communal education and regulation that undergird Muslim family life are key to gender justice for African American Muslim women. They also are useful in understanding an issue as complex as multiple-wife marriage.

Polygyny and Islamic Family Law

The legality of a polygynous marriage is heavily influenced by the legal system that governs the context in which the marriage takes place, the process that unites the parties, and their understanding of the meaning of legal or religious permissibility. To better appreciate the road to marriage legitimacy, let us begin with a clarification of religious law in Islam. Generally speaking, Islamic law is the binding code of ethical and social norms upon which Muslims structure their lives. It is, as John Esposito has noted, "central to Muslim identity, for it constitutes the ideal social blueprint for the good society."[12] The primary source of Islamic law is the Qur'an, though due to its minimal legal content—limited perhaps to as few as eighty of the more than six thousand *ayat*—other sources of law include the *sunna, ijma, qiyas,* and *ijtihad.* African American Muslims

who come to Islam through the doorway of Elijah Muhammad or W. D. Mohammed may lean on the lifestyle of Elijah as articulated through his son's
commentary on the Qur'an regarding polygyny and the latter's prescriptions
for multiple-wife marriage, as I will explain.[13]

After the death of the Prophet, the historical development of the juristic
discourses on multiple-wife marriage in Islam and other aspects of Islamic
law emerged as scholastic debates in the schools of law of Sunni and Shi'a
Islam, the two largest branches of Islam. Muslim scholars and others continue
to sift through the Qur'an and *sunna* for legal directives today, applying the
rulings of legal schools depending upon their context and association with a
particular school of thought. The overwhelming majority of global Muslims,
including my African American informants, are Sunni Muslims. Thus, I will
limit my overview of polygyny in Islam to consideration of the four schools
primarily aligned with the way of the Prophet.[14] Nevertheless, an encounter
with Sunni jurisprudence on polygyny underscores the relationship between
context and practice, as well as the importance of Muslims developing legal
reasoning for the environment in which they live. In Muslim-majority societies and in Muslim-minority societies like the United States, variance in the
principles of Islamic family law on polygyny confirms the plurality of perspectives Muslims hold on the matter and adds to the confusion of Muslims and
non-Muslims about what Islam teaches regarding multiple-wife unions and
the marital rights of women.

Context as a Legitimation for Polygyny

The significance of context cannot be overstated, particularly within a religious
framework whose jurisprudence "made no provisions for permanent as opposed to transient diasporic communities."[15] The concerns that my informants
bring to multiple-wife marriage highlight a particular sense of community
among Muslims with a shared religious and cultural legacy. It recognizes that
the social context of the United States can, according to those living polygyny
in this study, impose constraints that prompt some African American Muslims
to seek solutions to problems that are not shared by other Muslims.

The authority of legal opinions on polygyny to which many African American Muslims subscribe reflects the commentary of W. D. Mohammed. It is
one that mirrors the reform activities of Muslims around the world and, in
the words of Kathleen Moore, the development of "Islamic law from below."
In stressing that "environments change juridical concepts," Moore recalls the

significance of indigenous constructions of power and influence and reform campaigns to restrict or abolish polygyny that emerged in the early twentieth century. These grassroots efforts were organized by Muslims intent on pushing back against patriarchy and embracing gender justice.[16] One relevant site of comparison is Tunisia, the first nation-state with a legal system based at least in part on Islamic law. There, multiple-wife marriage was abolished in 1956, and grassroots activists continue to raise questions about the presence of justice in such arrangements today. That is, they frame polygyny jurisprudence, in the words of Abdullahi An-Na'im, as a "product of human attempts" to place authoritative sources in conversation with specific historical contexts.[17]

As with Mohammed's African American Muslim followers, these geographical examples reflect a particular application of polygyny for a specific time and cultural space. By conceiving the legal reasoning and cultural contexualization of Islamic discourses on polygyny as a plausible endeavor, I do not intend to establish support for or opposition to multiple-wife marriage. I do, however, wish to suggest that the juristic process of African American Muslims and their self-assumed authority of judicial construction of legal norms is an example of situated knowledge that is no less viable than other attempts to locate an Islamic position on polygyny in a different context across time and geographic space.[18]

Although the disapproval of one of the Prophet's daughters raised questions about the legitimacy and justice of multiple-wife marriage in the seventh century, the bulk of public and legal debate about Islamic polygyny has taken shape since modernization campaigns began during the eighteenth century and with the decline of the Ottoman Empire. Such contestations over family law matters draw attention to internal dissent among global Muslims and the significance of context, place, and space to culturally supported forms of marriage that occur in the United States. They also demonstrate the myriad ways in which tensions between Islamic practices and women's rights are challenged, defended, negotiated, and renegotiated, as Kathleen Moore's research confirms.[19] When the dust settles, concerns about the vulnerability of women, communal autonomy, and whether multiple-wife marriage leads to economic and social inequalities or is even Qur'anically approved keep polygyny in the forefront of debate and controversy.

Juristic Schools on Polygyny

Traditionally, Islamic family law functions through schools of Islamic jurisprudence. Muslim-majority countries take their cues on rules of polygyny from juristic institutions that began to emerge in the eighth and ninth centuries. For Sunni Muslims, the four principal schools of law—Hanafi'i, Shafi'i, Hanbali, and Maliki—are eponymously named for Muslim thinkers whose legal writings led to a degree of doctrinal consensus and distinct approaches on civil and criminal issues, especially family law matters like multiple-wife marriage. Indeed, classical and medieval scholars devoted such attention to household relations and personal status, usually code for men's authority over women, that anthropologist and activist Mir-Hosseini portrays family law as the "most developed field of classical Islamic jurisprudence."[20]

Even with the respect jurists of one school held for proponents of another (Malik ibn Anas taught Muhammad ibn Idris al-Shafi'i, for example), juristic differences became more apparent over time as these intellectual traditions have taken shape and become associated with particular characteristics. More than sixty countries whose legal systems have been established at least in part on Islamic law have adopted provisions of a single school or multiple schools based upon the self-interests of the government. Pakistan, for example, is committed to the more rigidly formalistic Hanafi'i school, but Pakistani law permits women to include stipulations in their marriage contracts against polygyny—a Hanbali characteristic. Syria is another nation where the Hanafi'i school, the oldest survivor of the Sunni institutions, is the dominant jurisprudence. In its Personal Status Act of 1953, Syria made polygyny contingent on proof that a husband is financially capable of maintaining more than one wife—a provision also adopted by Libya, another former French colony. It was in Libya that Muammar Gaddafi's first mentor, Gamal Abdel Nasser, received Elijah Muhammad in 1959.[21]

Islamic law requires couples to produce a marriage contract that is witnessed by representatives of both parties and registered with local religious authorities for reasons of inheritance and as proof that a valid marriage exists. (Interestingly, in Morocco and some other countries, Muslim women routinely carry their licenses with them when they leave their homes.) By drawing attention to this requirement, I make no assumption that all Muslims who say they adhere to Islamic law follow all of its directives. The same can be said for adherents of other legal systems. That said, such regulations transform otherwise private acts into public events. Personal status cases such as the registration of marriage contracts routinely occur in family court in the jurisdiction where the marriage takes place. But, for African American and other Muslims who reside in regions in which they are a minority and are governed by secular legal systems—like the United States—what connotes compliance with Islamic law or is contrary to it can be context-specific. That is, whether the jurisdiction is where the practice is authorized or illegal and whether authorization is required from both religious and civil officials significantly affects the level of privacy possible and how Muslims name it. Let me provide a brief explanation.

Although polygyny is prohibited in most regions of the world, adherence to its legality varies, regardless of the size or influence of the Muslim population. For instance, religious and civil authorities routinely converge in family court in Muslim-majority societies like Afghanistan and Morocco. Yet, Afghani men may take up to four wives with little if any regulations, while contracts for multiple-wife marriage in Morocco are valid only under "compelling circumstances and stringent restrictions" that involve proof of the husband's ability to guarantee equality among the wives and their children "in all areas of life."[22] In fact, polygyny is forbidden in Morocco—the first country to formally recognize the former colonies that became the United States as a single nation—if the wife stipulates in her marriage contract that her husband must refrain from taking additional wives or when there is a risk of inequity between the current and potential subsequent wives.

Examples of Western Polygyny

Muslim-minority societies, especially those in the West, continue to grapple with their uneven regulation of polygyny but not with its legality, which makes the lack of prosecutions of African American Muslims and other Americans living polygyny less surprising. Norway, for example, has seen an increase in men with multiple wives even though polygyny is against the law. In contrast to men in the United States, husbands in Norway are permitted to bring second wives into the country from regions in which the practice is permitted and the marriages legitimated.[23] Muslim women living polygyny in Britain became eligible for increased benefits in 2014 in an effort to "treat extra wives as single" so the state could not be construed as officially recognizing polygyny, according to the nonpartisan Gatestone Institute.[24]

Finally, when the British Columbia Supreme Court upheld Canada's polygamy laws in 2011, Western countries maintained their united front against the legalization of multiple-wife marriage. While declaring that the ban does infringe on religious freedom, the court ruled that criminalization is justified because of the harm to "women, to children, to society, and to the institution of monogamous marriage."[25] Obviously, tangible discrepancies exist in the official handling of polygyny regardless of adherence to law in Islam.[26]

Polygyny and Elijah Muhammad

Born in Sanderville, Georgia, the former Elijah Poole assumed leadership of the original Nation of Islam in 1934, shortly after the departure of its founder, W. D. Fard. Shortly thereafter, he moved the movement's headquarters from Detroit to Chicago. Under the leadership of the "emperor," as one grandson referred to Muhammad, the original NOI drew tens of thousands of African Americans to a movement that supported the self-sufficiency and self-determination of black people.[27] Prior to his death in 1975, Elijah Muhammad was legally married to only one woman, the former Clara Evans. Together they produced eight children, including his successor, W. D. Mohammed, who would steer the black separatist movement onto the path of mainstream Islam. At least thirteen other children were born to Elijah during the 1960s.

The framing of these children's status and the social position of their mothers continue to raise questions about models of multiple-wife marriage within African American communities.[28] Like many charismatic leaders, Elijah Muhammad led throngs of believers whose devotion was as legendary as their certainty that his actions reflected the will of G'd. By the early 1960s, the NOI began to slowly introduce the membership to the Qur'an. No consensus exists among current leaders about the depth of their engagement with the highest authority in Islam on multiple-wife marriage. Besides, NOI teachings would never question or contradict the actions of Muhammad. In the NOI, there were "big I's and little you's," explained granddaughter Laila Muhammad. "My grandfather and his leadership could do things other members could not. Everyone knew their place."[29] Even so, too little attention has been paid to links between Muhammad's public statements and private actions and what he learned and perhaps adopted from his overseas travels to Muslim societies where polygyny was permitted if not tolerated. Questionable, too, is how his biological and spiritual descendants struggle to distance themselves from or tie their philosophies to his views on Muslim marriage, especially in reference to polygyny.

A Chicago imam told me in the summer of 2013 that the NOI was a dictatorship, not a democracy. Even some leaders in the association of W. D. Mohammed held so firmly to the autocratic thinking of Elijah years after the leadership change that Mohammed chose to dismantle his leadership structure five years before his own death. I will briefly consider one of the NOI's worst-kept secrets, one that symbolized the expansion of Elijah Muhammad's family and led to maneuvers among his top disciples as they grappled with how to explain what appeared to some to be a personal and moral crisis for their leader. Given the high level of moral purity members of the Nation of Islam were expected to embody, the significance of transforming Muhammad's public denial about the status of the mothers of minor children into the language of doctrinal consistency cannot be overstated. Perhaps this discussion also uncovers the roots of his successor's teachings on polygyny.

The likelihood is great that for the tens of thousands of African Americans who embraced the philosophy of Elijah Muhammad during the 1950s and 1960s, the NOI leader symbolized political, economic, and religious independence. Concentrated in urban areas across the country, Elijah's Nation was distrustful of whites and skeptical of their involvement in any meaningful social justice campaigns or other endeavors to uplift the reality of black Americans. Thus, his followers waged their own campaigns to promote black pride and self-reliance. They cemented the NOI as an American Muslim institution, Islam as the religion of black people, and Muhammad as the Messenger of G'd and the "crowing glory of the black man and woman in America."[30]

Followers gave Elijah Muhammad unquestioned authority. When he told his followers not to vote, by and large they did not. When he told them not to eat pork, they turned their backs on what was then a cultural staple. When he promoted a socially conservative morality, they worked diligently not to disappoint. And when Elijah Muhammad's personal affairs appeared to show hints of a less than stellar portrait, they consulted and interpreted the holy book he gave them in accord with his thought. As they reconciled the biblical stories of Christianity and Islam to fit the needed profile, leaders of the Nation cast the Messenger's intimate relations in terms of what they concluded were their scriptural significance and contemporary relevancy and banished any other thoughts to the subconscious.

Explaining the Paradoxes of Polygyny

Today, more than five decades after the birth of the first of Elijah's children whose mother was not his legal wife under American civil law, controversy continues within and without the Nation regarding other relationships in which he fathered children during the 1960s. Central to the debate is the extent to which his movement and its leaders offered a rationale that permitted Muhammad a family structure that few knew existed and fewer still questioned. That is, the NOI came to legitimize the private affairs of its leader. To members, Allah afforded their leader special dispensations, and to question Elijah was to question G'd.

Relatives, followers, and observers contest how and to whom Elijah actually described these relationships. Less uncertain are the feelings of Clara, Muhammad's legally recognized wife of fifty-three years. The NOI's first lady threatened to leave her husband at least once. Extended time spent away from Elijah suggests that Clara did not accept passively the other relationships her husband created—unions that his successor and others would characterize as marriages and, thus, religiously acceptable. Clara Muhammad never followed through on her threats. To me, she, like other women living polygyny, reluctantly lived with a paradox—one in which a wife might be compelled to ignore any other women who claimed to be married to her husband while also defending his character. The paradox of polygyny also challenges notions of equality, as wives are required to share the resources of a family unit typically determined at the discretion of the husband. Maintaining her marriage and keeping her family together was non-negotiable for Clara Muhammad, even if it meant the ultimate exposure of other heirs of her husband. Even so, in private spaces, she mirrored the emotional conflicts of most of my female informants who stand by their husbands.

"I can tell you that Sister Clara was upset," A. K. Hasan said during a late-night telephone conversation in the summer of 2012. Resident imam of the Bilal Islamic Center in Los Angeles, Hasan became a follower of Elijah in 1956. He knew Malcolm X, served with and under the leadership of W. D. Mohammed, and shared private meals with Sister Clara, whom he described as "firm in a sort of quiet way." Imam Hasan's characterization speaks to his awareness of Clara as a woman who adopted the norms of womanhood of her generation—which often meant protesting quietly about personal matters, if at all—and accepted the selflessness required of her as the wife of the Messenger. What's more, in recalling her feelings about Elijah's other wives, Minister Louis Farrakhan cautioned people to resist focusing on Clara's emotional pain. Instead, he directed attention to what he believed to be the role of Elijah Muhammad in the plan of Allah:

> If only we were mature enough to put our emotions in check, our focus would not have been on our pain and the pain of Sister Clara Muhammad and the Muhammad family; our focus would have been on asking Allah (God) why He ordered His Servant to have what others did not have (wives); then we would have grown into the Wise Thinking of God and been more prepared for this reality in our own lives when or if it became necessary . . .

> Most of all, I want you to step into the shoes of the Honorable Eli-

jah Muhammad, whom we are attempting to follow, who loved his wife, Sister Clara Muhammad, who was with him when he was considered nothing and aided him in his growth from nothing; yet he had to carry the tremendous weight of his Mission even while he was in anguish over the knowledge of his Domestic Life which was tearing his family apart. . . . We must be careful, lest we become one whose emotions cause us to judge this situation as a grievous one and end up sentenced to death by virtue of our own judgment. The Honorable Elijah Muhammad was not the cause, he was the agent of that which Allah (God) ordered and which he obeyed. The Best Knower set this in motion and it would benefit us greatly to grow into seeing through His eyes.[31]

Nevertheless, Imam Hasan has no doubt about the secrecy that shrouded the personal life of his leader or about the devastation felt by the Nation's first lady, especially given the movement's moral code and her husband's protestations about her critiques of his behavior. Neither do at least two of Elijah's grandchildren.

In *The Evolution of the Nation: The Story of the Honorable Elijah Muhammad*, Muhammad-Ali, son of Elijah's fifth child, Herbert, claims that W. D. Mohammed was unable to "accept the hurt dealt to his mother when he learned of his father having chosen to lead a polygamous life (in contradiction to his espoused doctrine to his followers)."[32] According to Laila Muhammad, the eldest daughter of W. D. Mohammed and family spokesperson after his death, her grandmother was "very upset" about these relationships and "thought of them as affairs." Laila recalls written correspondence between her father and grandfather, with the former asking Elijah to call the mothers of his subsequent children his wives—a request Elijah refused. Instead, the NOI leader told his soon-to-be successor "the believers wouldn't accept that."[33]

Perhaps in his plea Imam Mohammed anticipated his future teachings about marriage in Islam—dialogues intended to benefit the diverse and international movement he would lead as he guided NOI members onto the path of mainstream Islam—and that a few would travel the path to polygyny. For instance, Mohammed, according to several of his leaders, would later declare that "once a man enters a woman they are married." To Laila, her father would have meant engaging in sexual intimacy makes the man "responsible" for the woman and that he "better make her his wife."[34] Elijah's refusal set in motion a profound question for his son and other disciples: Can their followers take multiple wives as Elijah Muhammad did? The choices of the NOI leader also reflect the presence of diverse understandings of the practice of polygyny and, obviously, varied interpretations of the most accurate way to characterize his behavior.[35] What, if any, responsibility the son felt for his young siblings and their mothers and his possible communication with them about his father's decision not to legitimate their familial connections is knowledge that likely will never be uncovered for public consumption.

The NOI's Family Law

From its beginnings in 1930s Detroit, the NOI promoted an internal family law that was consistent with that of many Muslim nations in regard to the value of marriage, distaste for sexual impropriety, and belief that marriage provides a sense of protection and security to women. The heterosexual, two-parent family was the pervasive ideal in the Nation. Men were viewed as the guardians and maintainers of women; wives were expected to obey their husbands and celebrate the care of their families as their primary if not only role. Through gender-segregated educational settings, NOI members were instructed to demonstrate self-respect and self-restraint by keeping personal matters private, even if doing so created moral and spiritual uneasiness. (When Martha's husband tried to maneuver out of obtaining a civil divorce, he was motivated by an allegiance to this perception of privacy.)

NOI members were warned against supporting or permitting governmental interference in their personal or communal affairs. Instead, they were encouraged to embody a motto prevalent among followers of Marcus Garvey and the United Negro Improvement Association: "Do for self." Those who failed to live up to these standards faced public discipline, humiliation, and isolation. In the end, the NOI's control over its members began on the individual level, seeped into the private sphere of the home, and continued to the public space of the temple. For many members, to be marginalized or lose face in the NOI was akin to social and spiritual death. By the 1960s, this ethic of insularity lay side by side with traditional family values in the larger society, even as Muhammad sought more visible separation from it. At the time, he declared, "We must have some of this earth that we can call our own and soon!"[36] To the NOI leader, part of being self-directed and autonomous meant being free to construct guidelines for the formation of family life that reflected the social realities of his disciples and the needs of black people as he understood them. In other words, the practice of polygyny symbolized a direct connection between "Do for self" and maintenance of community life because with it practitioners become the solution to the problem of the lack of marriageable men. Apparently, this was a notion his successor embraced.

As late as the 1990s, the principles of "Do for self" and black respectability were embodied in attempts by contemporary followers of Imam Mohammed and Minister Louis Farrakhan (who split from Mohammed in 1978) to situate Elijah's private life within Islam's particular construction of marriage. This construction featured both monogamy and polygyny. Such attempts have protested academic and popular investigations that refer to the mothers of Elijah's other children as "concubines" and their relationships as "extramarital affairs." They do not, however, address any emotional harm the women and their children may have experienced as a result of their relationships with the NOI leader.[37]

Inside the NOI of the 1960s, these women were ostracized for being unwed mothers, NOI officials refuted their claims about Elijah, and their children grew up "under the shadow of illegitimacy."[38] In 1993, however, four of these women, all of whom assumed the surname of Muhammad after the death of Clara, gathered together for the first time in an effort to reclaim an authoritative voice for their "husband" and for their personal stories of life with him. June, who gave birth to two of Elijah's children in 1960–1962, greeted the gathering, an assembly of the followers of Minster Farrakhan, this way:

> Brothers and Sisters, I know it is a pretty hard pill to swallow that the Honorable Elijah Muhammad took on wives. We are so mundane in our understanding of life. We have to think on a spiritual plane.[39]

The remarks of Evelyn Williams, who along with Lucille Rosary filed paternity suits against Elijah in a Los Angeles court, seemed to suggest that she revised her own recollections of Elijah's concern for the welfare of his wives and children:

> When he came to me and asked me to be his wife, he sat down, as beloved brother Minister Farrakhan has said, and opened the Holy Qur'an to the place where it dealt with the wives. He loved his wife, Sister Clara Muhammad, and his children, but he said Allah was forcing him to do this for future generations. I want you to know that he was an honorable man and he is an honorable man, and he stood for respect of all black women around the world.[40]

Differences of opinion as to how to best portray the intimate aspects of Muhammad's life can be attributed to any number of explanations, including the lack of readiness of the NOI to accept any moral failings of its leader, as his granddaughter has suggested, and the fealty afforded its officials, especially members of the first family.

In the late 1990s, two notable biographies of the NOI leader were published. In *The Messenger: The Rise and Fall of Elijah Muhammad* (1999), Karl Evanzz endeavors to distinguish Elijah Muhammad the individual from the message he delivered as the Messenger of Allah. In the other work, *An Original Man: The Life and Times of Elijah Muhammad* (1997), Claude Clegg supports his research with the "words and ideas" of NOI members, insisting that "the talk of multiple 'marriages' and 'wives' of E. Muhammad is a post 1975-phenomenon."[41] In an e-mail exchange, I asked Clegg what he thought might be his subject's reaction to this discussion. In his response, Clegg refuses to play revisionist:

> I think that Muhammad would have been bewildered by and opposed to efforts to have these women presented publicly (or privately) as his "wives." Even after these relationships and the resulting offspring became public news in the 1960s, he declined to embrace these women as spouses prior to his death in 1975—and neither Farrakhan nor anyone else dared to announce them as such during that time.[42]

The sentiments of Imam Hasan, Martha, and others, in my view, echo Clegg's assertion. In the United States of the 1960s, polygyny was not legally accepted or socially sanctioned except among some fundamentalist Mormons, a handful of Christians, and Black Hebrews, a group whose members migrated to Liberia in 1967 and two years later to Israel, where they renounced their U.S. citizenship.[43]

Nevertheless, during our telephone interviews and private conversations in the summer of 2012, imams who had embraced Islam since the 1970s through the teachings of Elijah and served as leaders in the ministry of his son never wavered in the consistency with which they characterized Elijah Muhammad's relationships as marriages. One could contend that they merely employed the language of marriage to dignify their leader's behavior and thus, in the words of Mattias Gardell, "closed ranks."[44] On the other hand, differences of historical time and space may have necessitated that Elijah and his son choose contradictory language to describe the same events. It is equally plausible that when followers of Elijah recalled the relationships that developed during his marriage to Clara Muhammad, mother of his first eight children, they strove to do so in reference to the specific responsibilities and dispensations afforded the Prophet Muhammad and other prophetic figures and the classical interpretation of the Qur'an on multiple-wife marriage.

In Defense of the Messenger

Two of Elijah's earliest disciples to articulate a rationale for their leader's be-havior were Malcolm X, the spiritual offspring who eventually left the move-ment in disgrace, and Elijah's biological son and successor, W. D. Mohammed. Malcolm and Imam Mohammed collaborated on a number of activities at the direction of Elijah, one being traveling to NOI communities around the coun-try in 1959 to explain the ritual of prayer.[45] Ronald Shaheed, the Wisconsin resident imam, said Imam Mohammed "confirmed" for Malcolm some of the rumors about their leader's private life, but he did not bring the discussion to Malcolm, as is alleged in the latter's *Autobiography*. Instead, Malcolm sought out Mohammed to confirm what he knew. Apparently, on the decision to use scriptural precedence to redefine Elijah's relationships, however, Imam Mo-hammed and Malcolm were in agreement. In his autobiography Malcolm re-called a conversation with Elijah in 1963 at the NOI leader's home in Phoenix:

> "I'm David," [Elijah Muhammad] said. "When you read about how David took another man's wife, I'm that David. You read about Noah, who got drunk—that's me. You read about Lot, who went and laid up with his own daughters. I have to fulfill all of those things."[46]

In fulfilling "all of those things" described in the biblical passages to which Malcolm says Elijah refers, he seems to imply incest and adultery in addition to polygyny; by all accounts, though, Elijah Muhammad never engaged in either.

Obviously, aspects of such biblical narratives contributed to Elijah's ideol-ogy. Imam Mohammed often declared that his father obtained his views about polygyny "biblically," as did at least two of his contemporaries, Father Divine and Sweet Daddy Grace. Evidence does not exist that either Father Divine or Daddy Grace practiced multiple-wife marriage. Still, their movements, like those of the NOI, zeroed in on the economic self-sufficiency of black people. Though Father Divine died in 1965, his Peace Mission's message of racial har-mony and his monogamous marriage to a white woman are the subject of a YouTube video uploaded in 2007. Sweet Daddy Grace, a railroad cook turned preacher, emigrated to the United States from the Cape Verde Islands. He built the first United House of Prayer for All People in 1919 in Massachusetts "from discarded rock and wood." By the late twentieth century, the United House of Prayer had amassed more than one hundred congregations throughout the United States and was a major real estate power.[47] As the son of a Baptist

preacher, Elijah shared Christian roots with these charismatic religious leaders, who ascribed to themselves the personae of biblical figures. In short, was
Elijah Muhammad a polygynist? "Absolutely," declares Imam Faheem Shuaibe
of Masjidul Waritheen in Oakland, California.[48]

Laila Muhammad assumes an alternative position from the teachings of her
father and some of his disciples. While Elijah led the NOI, W. D. Mohammed
was an unlikely successor, but when he assumed that role, it was as a leader
who taught his disciples to think for themselves. Speaking of him, Laila ob-
serves:

> [My father] may have said those were his [Elijah's] wives later on because
> you love your father and you want to think those are his wives. When I
> look at the situation, yes [Elijah] entered them, he had children [with
> them], he should have been responsible and he was responsible. But he
> didn't acknowledge [those women] in the way that probably would have
> been best for them and for the children so he lacked in that responsibility.
> So I don't call them his wives.[49]

The granddaughter of Elijah makes an interesting link between acknowl-
edgment and marital legitimacy. It is a link that women living polygyny can
achieve in their communities, at best, but not in the larger world as long as
their marriages remain unregistered.

Understanding the social and political climate that gave rise to the Nation
of Islam in 1930s Detroit permits some disciples to label Elijah Muhammad
a polygynist. This characterization along with attempts of other followers to
focus on the harm they say befell the women and children involved provides
some perspective on how many African American Muslims form their legal
consciousness on polygyny. Their perspectives ready us next to consider Imam
Mohammed's prescriptions for the practice of polygyny in the United States.

As described earlier, Islamic law and global reforms to its family law component in the 1950s and 1960s coincided with the expansion of the first family
of the original Nation of Islam in the United States. Published reports and
recollections of family members and observers who personally interacted
with Elijah and Clara Muhammad highlight the gendered reactions that polygyny can and often does elicit, as well as the cloud of revisionist history
that continues to hover over Elijah's personal life. Nearly forty years after his
death, his family members and supporters do not agree on whether using the
characterization "wives" for the mothers of at least thirteen of his children
reflected a marketing plan to right what appeared to be a flawed product,

privileges afforded a prophetic figure, an attempt to embody mainstream Islamic practices, an early example of polygyny within the leadership of the NOI, or something in between.

Regardless, the women involved self-identify as wives, and at least one of them, Tynetta Muhammad, is revered in Louis Farrakhan's contemporary NOI as the widow of Elijah even though the NOI leader never publicly acknowledged any wife after Clara. Apparently, the women's experiences were sufficient reason for Minister Farrakhan to discourage the practice of polygyny among his followers. During the 1993 Saviors' Day introduction of the women and their children, Farrakhan stated:

> I wouldn't advise nobody to do this. You better first take care of the one you have. These sisters have been the victims of slander and evil talk and abuse and they did nothing wrong but mother children that would be righteous guides and examples for us.[50]

When Farrakhan alludes to a victimizer, he does not mean Elijah Muhammad.

The reaction of Clara to the sexual activities of her husband mirrors the attitudes of many women when they discover their husbands are living secret lives, especially if the husbands are major religious or political figures. When asked years later why she threatened to leave her husband but never did leave, Clara replied, "I realized that his mission was greater than he was."[51]

African American Muslim women living polygyny routinely encounter and/or accept ideas that can be needlessly blindsiding, encouraging them to stand by husbands who do not meet the conditions for the practice of polygyny as outlined in the Qur'an. Such ideas also lead men, even some with the noblest of intentions, to move beyond their emotional or financial means. The experiences of these women provide evidence of the existence of different combinations of private and public patriarchy through which women negotiate and face exploitation in both spheres. Elizabeth, a fifty-four-year-old divorcee from Wisconsin, explains:

> I would consider being in a polygynous marriage where the sister chose me as a co-wife along with her husband. If I were already married, I would choose someone [as a co-wife] who complemented me (had characteristics I lacked) and who was a good "friend" and believer.[52]

In Elizabeth's view, everyone benefits, at least theoretically, when Muslim women share their husbands in polygyny. Her preference for a good friend and believer signals the value some female survey respondents placed on amicable relationships with co-wives and the importance of a shared understanding of Islamic guidelines for plural marriage. Her predisposition speaks as well to the emotional strain that some women experience and the ways they attempt to "get back" at their husbands to resurrect for themselves a degree of personal dignity. Karimah characterized her own actions this way:

> I began to renege on my charity. You know, I wasn't paying the light bill. When we had bills, whatever money was in the house went towards whatever the bills were. But I started using my money to do whatever I wanted to do. Me and my daughter would go shopping; I would take her to the show. I was doing things that I normally would not have been doing. And I guess it was me trying to deal with all of this traumatic situation that I had going on. I was like, okay, well, if you're still telling people I'm your wife, then you have to take the full responsibility. And my charity is not going to be part of it. So things were in disarray. Utilities shut off. And I would say, hey, well, it's gonna have to go off so I would show him that this is not acceptable. This does not meet the criteria that I think Allah gave the guidelines for.[53]

Evidence of marital distress did not alter the behavior of Karimah's husband; eventually she filed for and was granted a divorce.

As we have already seen, some women married to polygynous men fight their battles in secret, and some take out their frustrations against their husbands' other wives in public. How rank-and-file members deal with the complexities of polygyny in their contemporary context and what, if any, connections they make to the lifestyle of Elijah reflect the role of culture and socialization. Irfan Al-Alawi and others note that where the laws of Muslim-minority countries prohibit multiple-wife marriage, Muslims generally choose not to contest them—either overtly or covertly.[54] Clearly, most American Muslims, including African Americans, are most comfortable conforming to Western understandings of traditional marriage as a heterosexual union exclusively between two consenting individuals.

As I write, my mind returns to a telephone conversation just now concluded with Zuhara. I called her to offer a word of encouragement and a conversation partner willing to discuss her options as she decides whether she can continue to share her husband. I could tell that she was grateful for the call, but the tone of her voice also belied fear for the future and frustration with the present. It's the same fear that was evident during our interview. Then on the phone she said, "If I had to make this decision all over again, I wouldn't have moved so fast." At her wedding ceremony, she did not share with her friends that her husband would soon take another wife, "out of embarrassment that people would look at me like I settled or that I could do better."[55] For this sister and others in her position, the question to Imam Mohammed might be "How do we enforce any standards for living polygyny?"

5

Imam Mohammed's Commentary on Polygyny

I would definitely say that the second should have a *wali*. Since the first is already the one married, I wouldn't term it as her needing a *wali*, but I would say that the husband should tell her family of his intentions, demonstrate his capacity, and be open to feedback.

Lamisha

Lamisha possesses a commanding presence and not merely because of her stature. It's partly the gleam in her eyes that is captivating, and from them you are drawn to her freckles and then to her wide smile. But her activism is an even more dominant force and a source of community pride, as the plaques and citations in her private office confirm. The writer, entrepreneur, mother, and grandmother is well known among American Muslims on the local and national levels, especially when the topic involves domestic violence or interfaith dialogue.

Although we gather in the lobby of her nonprofit organization, Lamisha does not desire to impress with her entrepreneurial acumen. Nor does she wish to solicit applause with the latest challenge she has helped to resolve in her densely populated metropolis. Instead on this sunny Friday in 2012, hours after departing *jum'ah* at one of three area mosques frequented by African Americans, Lamisha is eager to share the story of her road to polygyny. She is keen to explain why she believes regulated and open multiple-wife marriage is a protection for women in the physical sense and a safeguard for their rights, hearts, and spirits. Why is Lamisha so confident? Because, as she tells it, she knows the right way to live polygyny due to her experience doing it the wrong way.[1]

In this chapter I draw attention to one of the central communal authorities for the practice of polygyny for members of the association of Imam W. D. Mohammed. The teachings on marriage and living polygyny that Imam Mohammed espoused from 1975 to his death in 2008 reflect the social context of black America in much the same way that the revelation on polygyny given to the

Prophet Muhammad spoke to the needs of seventh-century Arabia. Both men recognized the higher purpose that polygyny was designed to address, that is, the care and protection of widows, orphans, and "neglected women." By acknowledging the weight of culture and socialization in one's lived reality, Mohammed recognized experience as authority, a dominant theme of this book with regard to the situatedness of polygyny as well as to the Qur'an as a source of wisdom and guidance that establishes an ethical framework for multiple-wife marriage. I demonstrate that Imam Mohammed did not shy away from extrareligious forces—like the lack of marriageable African American Muslim men—as he shaped his philosophy on polygyny. Instead, he recognized that justice can be elusive in multiple-wife marriages and that few men, even among his followers, are qualified to assume the responsibility.

In addition, the teachings of Mohammed echo the contention of classical Islamic jurists, modern thinkers, and contemporary individuals who have lived polygyny that the Qur'an must be read in its time and context. Mohammed was fully aware that doing so may warrant a different application in twenty-first-century North America than it would in another time and place. Among the thinkers in Mohammed's ideological camp in reference to reading the Qur'an is feminist scholar Kecia Ali. For her, the practice of polygyny raises "broader debates over whether Qur'anic rules must always be literally applied or whether their specific provisions are context-specific, and thus liable to change with changes in social conditions."[2]

As noted earlier, Elijah Muhammad chose not to characterize as marriages the relationships he had that led to the births of some of his children. In contrast, his son taught that when a man has sex with a woman in Islam, he has either married her "or is an offender who should be punished."[3] The father explained that his NOI followers were not yet ready to accept their leader as a polygynist. Nevertheless, the women whom Elijah Muhammad refused to declare as his wives prior to his death in 1975 chose to identify themselves as his widows twenty-eight years later.

Precisely how much influence the decisions of the father had on the son's teachings about living polygyny is unknown. What can be stated unequivocally is that Imam Mohammed began developing his commentary on polygyny in the 1970s. By 2002 he instructed his leaders to talk more about polygyny and marriage in general, out of his concern for how the community engaged multiple-wife marriage and the number of women who desired marriage but did not encounter eligible, interested men.

W. D. Mohammed Talks Polygyny

Imam Mohammed began formally to clear a path for such dialogue by spear-heading gender-segregated discussions in 2003 in major U.S. cities. To packed houses, he articulated his "best practices" for living polygyny in this Muslim-minority country and invited questions from his audiences. While Moham-med disagreed with decisions of many of those who were associated with his leadership and were living polygyny, he did perform at least one *nikah* that involved an already married man exchanging vows with a second wife.[4] Clearly, sanctioning this union was an exception for Mohammed, a rare ex-ample of this religious leader publicly approving of a man assuming respon-sibility for an unmarried sister who may not otherwise have experienced the benefits of marriage. Conversations with wedding participants, those close to Mohammed, and leaders of the mosque at which the religious ceremony was held suggest the following. To Mohammed, the groom was knowledgeable about his religion and had prepared himself and his family for the challenges of bringing another woman into their family structure. The bride was fully cognizant of the groom's family dynamics and how her presence could alter their lives as well as her own. So supportive of the marriage was the groom's current wife that she assisted with preparations for the marriage ceremony and attended the celebration of her husband's marriage to the other woman. To many multiple-wife advocates, this is a healthy way to begin living po-lygyny.[5]

During his life, Mohammed could point to a few other African American Muslim families as strong examples of living polygyny, but he was convinced that most African American Muslim men were incapable of maintaining mul-tiple wives "Islamically." By this he meant even men with the noblest of inten-tions could not meet the Qur'anic ideal of justice. Mohammed recognized that a number of concerns underscore the difficulty of adhering to a core qualifica-tion for Qur'anic justice. Grave challenges can arise from the economic status of many black men, lack of Qur'anic knowledge about the practice, the psycho-logical trauma African Americans have endured because of institutionalized oppression, and the obstacles a man can encounter in trying to meet the physi-cal, financial, emotional, and spiritual needs of multiple wives. "Religion is all about man being a servant of G'd in his own environment," he told a group of male Muslims during a lecture in Detroit in March 2003. "You are not to marry out of lust, not to get another woman because you want more meat. It is very difficult to take care of one wife now days."

There is another reason of prime importance that adds to the burden of living polygyny in the West, and Mohammed knew that this problem is a reality for all men in America: the United States is a social environment that legitimates only one spouse at a time per husband. Indeed, for most Muslims the latter hurdle makes polygyny unacceptable.[6]

The teachings of Imam Mohammed point to the efficacy of the Qur'an and the life example of the Prophet Muhammad as the surest foundation for consideration of polygyny among twenty-first-century Muslims, particularly for Imam Mohammed's followers. His teachings question the practice and ideology of some members of his association. Perhaps Mohammed compared the way they lived polygyny to the priesthood ban of black Mormons. One Mormon scholar describes the church's rearticulation of the latter "as a matter of error or cultural and historical conditioning rather than as the will of God."[7]

Mohammed touched on the issue of polygyny in public lectures and private conversations throughout his thirty-three-year ministry, and some of his commentary on polygyny in his own words is available today in the form of articles published in the *Muslim Journal* and the videotaped messages he delivered a few years prior to his 2008 death and two to three years before his marriage to the former Khadijah Siddeeq.[8] The practice of multiple-wife marriage in the United States draws attention to the extent to which public accommodation and recognition should be made for religious identity and practice.[9] It also prompts the question of whether justice is available to African American Muslims whose marriages are conducted in "the shadow of the law."[10]

Divorce and Polygyny

In many regions of the United States, individuals who petition for divorce are required to appear before a judge, even if both parties agree to legally terminate the marriage, as was finally the case for Martha.[11] She was married in both religious and civil law, as are an overwhelming number of African American Muslims. She negotiated a marriage contract, her marriage was solemnized through a *nikah*, and it was registered with the state in which she resides.[12] With her civil marriage, Martha could bring her marriage and her divorce wishes into public view without fear of attracting attention to her husband from law enforcement that could lead to charges of polygamy.[13]

A religious divorce was possible, too. Obviously, not all Muslims seek both civil and religious marriages, as is true with civil and religious divorces.[14]

Martha chose both. So, when her husband informed her that he was taking a second wife, Martha considered his personal affairs, her preferences, and the circumstances involved and decided that she wanted their union to end. Had she married religiously only, obtaining a divorce would have been a less arduous road for Martha. She could have avoided the expense, the waiting period, and the legal requirements for a civil decree in her state.[15] But then, a marriage license provides legal proof of marriage and affords the bride and groom legal status as a couple and certain legal protections in regard to inheritance, division of property, support, and maintenance issues.

Access to the American judicial system for the civil dissolution of marriage is available only to women and men who first obtain marriage licenses and register their marriages with the state. Although this process is common among many first wives, it is not available to women who are their husbands' second, third, or fourth spouses and choose to end their marriages in the United States.[16] For these women, only religious resolution of divorce is available, though some marital disputes such as those that involve contracts, child support, or witnessed agreements may be adjudicated in American courts. Most women living polygyny steer clear of the American judicial system for fear of further scrutiny of their husbands. Those who attempt to pursue legal divorces may be surprised by their actual status.

For example, Sahar, a Texas mother of three, hired a divorce attorney believing that hers was a common-law marriage and therefore eligible for civil dissolution. While she and her husband lived as husband and wife in a common-law state (as he did with his other wife), the attorney explained that Texas could not recognize their union due to polygyny. Sahar further discovered that even if hers had been a traditional one-wife, one-husband marriage, theirs would not have been viewed as a common-law union because neither she nor her husband had completed a declaration of marriage within two years of the start of their cohabitation.

Sahar did manage to sue her husband for child support, and since he was not guilty of other crimes, her attorney assured her that Texas was unlikely to pursue prosecution for polygyny. Without access to the secular legal system, however, Muslim women living polygyny whose marriages are unregistered are often further marginalized when they seek to end marriages under Islamic law. The absence of Islamic frameworks in the United States to enforce divorce, child support, dower, or other agreements leaves Muslim women with even less recourse to justice for themselves and significantly less than those available to women of other faiths such as Orthodox Judaism.[17]

Mohammed's Backdrop for Polygyny Rules

When Imam Mohammed began to teach about polygyny in the 1970s, the mothers of his youngest siblings were in probate court to pursue claims against the estate of his father. At that point, Mohammed warned his followers that few people qualified for multiple-wife marriage:

> You can't put one in the Econo Lodge and the other one, the Marriott. You can't do that. So you know you're not ready. You can hardly put two in a station wagon. So that's a privilege for a very, very small minority in society.[18]

But by 1987 Mohammed's messages seem to link polygyny with communal responsibility. To an audience in Milwaukee he said:

> Polygamy is a provision to block and help us to overcome other threats and social problems in society. It is an answer, a remedial measure. It's not a principal of life for men in Islam that they should aspire to have four wives.
>
> War is not the only thing that causes women to be at the mercy of society . . . we need a whole lot of rich men in the black community to take care of our neglected women. Don't we? Now I know [some members] say, "Hey, that doesn't sound like our Imam. Is that him talking?" Yes, it is. Your Imam grows up. Things that I couldn't say yesterday, didn't have the strength to say, didn't want to look at, thank G-d I have the strength to look at today and I can say it.[19]

Mohammed's remarks also raise the likelihood that some women living in the United States do not and would not oppose polygyny, a conclusion that is consistent with the results of this study. They suggest as well that to this son of Clara and Elijah Muhammad, having a father figure in the home is one of the beneficial by-products of multiple-wife marriage:

> And don't say, "Oh, the American woman will never do that." I know better. I can tell you some American women have already done that and they say they're happy with their situation. One lady told me, she said, "This man that has taken me as his second wife accepts his responsibility. He lives with us. He comes to see us. He shares his time with us. He spends nights with us, as well as with his first wife. My children know their father." She said, "Brother Imam, I wish I could tell the women that I appreciate the provision of polygamy in Al-Islam."[20]

In 1998, Imam Mohammed congratulated a resident imam in the Midwest who took as a second wife a divorcee with five children. As he did, Mohammed proclaimed that such commitment by "qualified" men is necessary for the cultural survival of African Americans and black family life. At the time, Imam Rashad had been married to his first wife for nineteen years and had five children of his own with her. When he Islamically married the divorcee, he said he was financially able to support both families and accepted the additional responsibility with the knowledge of his wife—one of Mohammed's qualifications. Ultimately, Rashad's first wife left the marriage. Although he has seriously considered taking another wife in recent years, his second wife, Amaya, has made clear her opposition. Today, she remains his only wife.

Islamic teachings have never reflected ambivalence about marriage. Rather, they highlight its societal importance, Mohammed writes:

> The Holy Quran draws our attention to the burden that is placed upon the married couple and the good or bad consequences that result from such unions that affect the conditions of the world.
>
> If every couple from the early stages had been seriously interested in preserving the best of human life for generations to come and if they had conducted their lives in a way to safeguard the future world today, we would still have an "Eden" or a "garden of paradise," so to speak. It is not mysterious or supernatural things that make life or that destroy the "garden of Eden"—heaven is in the hands of the men and the women who form the union (marriage).[21]

Not only does Mohammed link marital decisions to the well-being of creation, but he also appears to situate males and females on a level field in terms of their responsibility for and to creation.

Understandably, then, Muslim men and women are strongly encouraged to pursue marriage. Prohibitions against sex outside of marriage are enforced in varying degrees, from capital punishment in Muslim regions to social rejection in non-Muslim areas. Whenever punishments are enforced, however, they are disproportionately directed at women. For the global Muslim community, a life of celibacy or choosing to live as part of monastic communities where voluntary virginity is the norm is considered contrary to the will of Allah. Like his father before him, Imam Mohammed understood through personal experience that some limits to freedom of religion imposed by the government must be opposed. He expected men living polygyny to uphold their financial responsibilities to their wives and offspring in cases of divorce.

His writings on marriage indicate that he would have agreed with the suggestions made by Lamisha in the epigraph. He wrote in *The Man and WoMan in Islam*:

> We should consult [Allah] before taking big or drastic steps that will bring about consequences that affect our children and our families, as well as us as individuals. Since we do not live our lives alone as a married couple, Muslims are taught to recognize Allah as the saving force in our lives and our marriage.
>
> The second saving power that is extended to us is the Muslim society. The couple can turn for health and strength to relatives of the two families, to God, and to the society of Muslims.[22]

Lamisha and her husband chose to involve "the second saving power" when he expanded their family.

To be clear, Imam Mohammed did not advocate multiple-wife marriage; rather, he was "resigned to the fact that Allah, in the Qur'an, authorized, encouraged, legitimized limited polygyny and outlined the rules and regulations for it." While some might not recognize this interpretation from the Qur'an, Mohammed chose language that resonated with his community. That is, to him the Qur'an explained that the purpose of polygyny was "to secure the future for orphans in the Islamic community."[23] Obviously, the household formations of various followers fail to demonstrate allegiance to some or any part of the rationale as Mohammed interpreted and taught it.

Given the deep admiration and love he held for his mother, Clara, and the pain he watched her endure, it is difficult to believe that Mohammed was immune to the hurt women can feel upon discovering that they are sharing their husbands or that their husbands desire additional wives. My conversations with him about his mother during the fall of 1997 suggest that Clara's experience was likely at the core of his position on polygyny, one of attempting to call to the forefront Islamic gender justice to mitigate the unhappy realities of some African American Muslim women, though it falls short of linking justice with enforcement.[24]

Over the succeeding years, Imam Mohammed drafted more detailed guidelines regarding polygyny that employed Islamic religious sources and his analysis of the state of black America, where marriageable men are in short supply. Undergirding his effort was the insistence that women have a choice—actually, the power—to accept or reject marriage with a polygynist man.[25] By 2002 he stipulated nine qualifications needed for the proper practice of multiple-wife marriage in the United States. One could argue this his prescriptions could be viewed as a starting rather than an ending point.

Mohammad perceived religion and law to be so ineluctable that he framed the two as elements of a single whole—a common practice for those affiliated with a faith of orthopraxy like Islam. In it, religion becomes the individual and communal values that Muslims hold based on their interpretations of Islamic traditional sources coupled with Mohammed's contextualization of their meaning for African Americans in a Muslim-minority context. As in other cultures, the way in which African American Muslims practice Islam reflects their particular social and cultural circumstances. Perhaps this helps to explain why Islam is embodied differently in different contexts.

As for law, Imam Mohammed conceived it to be the general order of existence by which African American Muslims govern themselves—again, as established by the Qur'an and *sunna*—and the sphere within which they face the consequences of behavior that is contrary to civil jurisprudence. In this way, law also was for Mohammed a "cultural system." By this I mean "a set of symbols and meanings, combined with a set of practices and rituals" that helps African American Muslims make sense of and orient themselves within their religious movement and the larger context of the United States.[26] Looking at his nine guidelines through the lens of a cultural system brings into focus his reasoning on polygyny for African American Muslims and the paradoxes that surround it. Granted, even attention to the benefits of polygyny through the window of culture is unlikely to persuade many other Muslims that multiple-wife marriage is just and a remedy for twenty-first-century African American Muslims. Though his guidelines for polygyny do not indicate a preference for multiple-wife marriage over monogamy, they are unlikely to convince his female supporters who have shared their husbands and still carry emotional, spiritual, financial, and sometimes physical scars from these experiences. They will not encourage me or most other African American Muslim women to consider polygyny. Still, closer examination of Imam Mohammed's position does increase understanding of what he might have hoped for his female relatives, children, and followers who are or have been affected by multiple-wife marriage.[27]

W. D. Mohammed's Nine Rules for Living Polygyny

I turn now to the nine guidelines that Imam Mohammed articulated in reference to the proper way to live polygyny in the United States. Given his mother's experience, it is not surprising that he focuses on male responsibilities. Thus, a husband must

- possess *taqwa*,
- avoid discrimination,
- provide individual living quarters for each wife,
- inform his current wife or wives before taking another,
- enter into marriages that do not contradict any previous contract or accepted circumstance,
- consider obtaining a marriage license,
- make the marriage ceremony public,
- not use the marriage as a means of preventing divorce or adultery, and
- enter polygyny for an important reason.

Let's now look at each rule more closely.

In stating that a husband must have *taqwa*, Imam Mohammed draws attention to the mental and spiritual state of men who choose polygyny. Mohammed counsels women to examine the level of G'd consciousness of potential mates even if they intend to be their husbands' only wives. If a man claims the responsibility of polygyny he must, in Mohammed's view, ground his justification in a reasonably observable level of *taqwa* that gives a prospective mate a sense of what her life would be like once married to him. With such advice, Mohammed encourages the woman to go beyond the public life of a prospective husband and seek understanding of how he lives his private life and who or what governs it by conferring with those who observe him outside of the mosque. Being a husband who strives to live in a conscious state of awareness of the presence of Allah was a constant goal of Mohammed throughout each of his six marriages, even though at times his desire may not have matched the reality experienced by his wives.

Here I refer specifically to the experience of his youngest widow, Khadijah Siddeeq-Mohammed.[28] Apparently, his wife of four years was surprised to discover that she was not his only spouse at the time of his death, though Mohammed lived solely with her during their marriage. Indeed, Mohammed regularly informed his followers that he lived as a married man with only one woman at a time as a way of stressing his personal monogamous home life.[29] He said that once a marriage ended, he financially supported each wife until she remarried, a practice that served as a model for at least one of my informants, who financially supported one of his wives throughout their four-year divorce ordeal. Such behavior is consistent with al-Baqarah 2:241, which states that providing financial maintenance for divorced women is the duty of righteous men; the verse implies a specific time frame.

By stating that a husband must avoid discrimination and provide each wife with individual living quarters, Mohammed points to the importance of a husband refraining from displaying preferences while also enabling his wives to live with dignity and respect. There might be significant differences in the needs of the wives, especially depending upon the number of children each brings into the marriage or has with her new husband. Nevertheless, equitable access to her husband's time, attention, and resources should be a reality for all wives.

Equally worthy of consideration is the notion of "regard for the feelings of others," a commonly used definition of "respect." While husbands may satisfy this reference in regard to housing, it is questionable whether the same can be said about those who tell pregnant wives they are about to marry, expect current wives to train their co-wives, and demonstrate clearly and early their inability to maintain multiple households. The issue of justice is situational, too. Omar, a fifty-nine-year-old New England entrepreneur and husband to as many as three wives simultaneously, is quick to admit that fair treatment is difficult if not impossible. Still, he remains committed to multiple-wife marriage:

> It's very difficult to have more than one wife and treat them all equally. I really realize this more now. It says in the Qur'an, you marry one, two, three, or four, but you can never treat them equally. You know why? And the reason is: if I was to have my two wives sitting in front of me today and give the first one a $100 bill and I give the second one a $100 bill. And I say in my mind, "I have completed what I wanted to give them for today," and I might smile, my first one would say to me, "You smiled at her; you didn't treat me right." I understand that is her perception, what she saw. I wasn't smiling at the last one. I was smiling that I made my commitment of what I already established. She'll never be able to see that. So it's no way possible that any one of them would ever see that you would treat them equally.[30]

For antipolygynists, the comments of this African American Muslim coincide with the Qur'anic verse that stipulates that one wife is better if justice is unobtainable.

Still, Omar was preparing to relocate to the South at the time of our interview, taking with him at least one of his two wives and leaving the door open to adding a third once he got settled. Regardless of the number of wives, however, this father of three adult children and two under the age of six was strongly considering purchasing an additional residence—for himself. Since 2010 his primary residence has been in a southern city that has become cosmopolitan. Neither wife has relocated with him as of yet; both hope to do so soon. As for a third wife, Omar believes he's set, at least for now. "The more I think about it, the more I think I won't do it again," he says. "It's a lot of work, time, and effort to try to do justice for them and to myself."[31]

The fourth and fifth are the most contentious of Mohammed's rules for polygyny. While he taught that "the family is too close, too private, too serious for secrecy," Mohammed left open to interpretation in the fourth item that a husband must first inform his present wife or wives.[32] It is not specified when such a notice should occur or whether by informing the woman or women Mohammed intended discussion of the ramifications for the current family. It was clear to him that a wife's permission or consent was not needed, even as his guidelines and the practices of some of his followers underscore one of the ethical shortfalls of multiple-wife marriage.

For instance, one of his female followers received notice when she was nine months pregnant that her husband was about to take an additional wife. For another, news came during chemotherapy treatments for breast cancer. A third woman, who did not realize that her groom was already a husband when she married him, finally agreed to polygyny as long as it did not include interactions with her husband's other wife. Rather than accuse him of fraud, she explained her change of mind in terms of how she views the Qur'an. According to her husband, the bride said, "I'm not crazy about it, but I can't find in the Qur'an that you can't take more than one wife."

To women like Aadila, a twice-married, now divorced East Coast Muslimah, their leader's recommendation that husbands inform their wives is a place to start but stops short of the goal line of justice. This forty-year-old, self-aware woman, from whom self-confidence oozes easily, could serve on both sides of a polygyny campaign. She is open to sharing her husband, whether in the position of his current wife or as one he invites into his life. Aadila is comfortable talking about multiple-wife marriage but only when characterized as an "act of charity" for one of the women involved. While Aadila concedes that she doesn't know one man who can responsibly handle being married to multiple wives—"not everyone is supposed to do it"—she proposes a surer way to meet the Qur'anic mandate:

If something's going to be taken from her, [a current wife] should be a part of the decision-making process. It would be easier for [her husband] to get along with her in that kind of situation if he does [take another wife]. If she has polygyny dumped on her without including her in the decision, [the family] is not going to be successful.

On the other hand, if the brother has the correct thing in mind as far as really helping someone—considered more as an act charity—than out of desire to just have someone else, I would question whether [a current wife] has the right to force him not to do an act of charity.[33]

For Aadila, a woman's "charity" means marrying a man whose wife is sick and unable to function or acquiescing so that her husband may take on a woman who needs help. Either way, Aadila is adamant that husbands talk to their current wives before approaching potential mates or making definitive plans, to ensure that the husbands "don't tear down one thing to add something to it."[34]

At the MARIAM conference in Chicago in 2012, Imam Faheem Shuaibe informed participants that women may incorporate language into their marriage contracts that rules out polygyny as long as it does not conflict with the Qur'anic stance on multiple-wife marriage. His workshop drew attention to his leader's fifth guideline, that any polygynous *marriage* should not contradict any contract or accepted circumstance previously entered into by the husband and his current wife or wives. This consideration specifically addresses verbal agreements or expectations with which spouses enter into marriage and that should be articulated in the marriage contract. None of my female subjects says she formally stipulated monogamy before or at the start of her life together with her husband.

With men's lack of sufficient resources, Mohammed could conclude that many of them living polygyny are not qualified for multiple-wife marriage. And he may have ruled out changes in spousal expectations: "If a man marries a woman whom he knows cannot have children and makes an issue about that," he has no legal grounds.[35] What is more, given that the marriage contract is designed to be a voluntary agreement, it should reflect the present and future expectations of the bride and groom. An option rarely discussed for those whose marriages are legally recognized is that the wives may be able to seek annulment if their husbands take additional wives, thanks to *Reynolds v. United States*, the 1878 U.S. Supreme Court decision that rendered polygyny illegal.

Muslim-minority countries such as Britain stipulate spousal consent, according to a member of the Muslim Council of Britain.[36] Imam Mohammed does not insist that current wives must agree to polygynous marriage, and neither does the Qur'an. But the ethical core of the Qur'an and the practice of the Prophet makes it doubtful that justice is achievable without wives' agreement. In the end, the presence of communal resources or stop-gap measures could reduce the number of unqualified men who become polygynists and the number of women who remain married to them primarily because they believe they are complying with the permissibility outlined in the Qur'an. It is noteworthy, too, that African American Muslims are not alone in thinking that polygyny is sanctioned. Indeed, as multiple-wife marriage has become ingrained in Islamic law and practice, Muslims around the globe have become accustomed to accepting that a husband has a right to four wives that is firmly established in Islam's authoritative sources.[37] Many of my subjects say another pedagogical approach is in order, especially if the goal is a more authentic representation of Islam's teaching on polygyny and the establishment of fairness and justice for all family members. Scholar Ali states my point quite elegantly:

> Individuals must be willing to take responsibility for acts of interpretation, rather than insisting that they are simply doing what "Islam" requires. . . . The values that are taught and especially lived in intimate contexts should be guided by deep ethical reflection on the overarching divine purpose for human life on earth: to command what is right, to forbid what is wrong, to do good deeds, and to be ever-conscious of God.[38]

The controversy surrounding the sixth guideline reflects what could be considered a recommendation to intentionally circumvent civil law. As in Britain, where a Muslim marriage ceremony must accompany a civil ceremony for legal recognition, in the United States *nikah*-only marriages do not provide women with spousal rights. Religious marriages that do not accompany marriage licenses are not registered with any U.S. state. When Mohammed said that "a husband should seriously consider obtaining a marriage license," he intended to challenge Muslim men to ensure that all their marriages carry legal recognition. He was pointing, too, to the need for recognition of each spouse as a legitimate wife.[39] Thus he instructs men to act courageously to protect what they believe Allah has permitted, even in the face of possible civil penalties—perhaps his most ardent invitation to civil disobedience. He told a group of men who gathered in Atlanta in 2003:

> You might say, "Well the state won't let me marry or have two wives." Well I would rather go down, get a license and take a chance on getting caught and marry, register with the state or at least have the Muslim marriage contract registered with the state. . . . At least it shows you weren't hiding

anything, you weren't trying to deceive the law. And know that you can handle two.[40]

Granted, most Muslims interpret Islamic law to steer Muslims in the opposite direction, one that encourages compliance with the laws of the land in which they reside. But by legal recognition, Imam Mohammed also could have meant that each marriage is acknowledged in the community and that legally enforceable documents exist to show how a husband plans to maintain his wives and children in the event he precedes them in death. For Judge David Shaheed of Indianapolis, leaving behind a notarized, signed, and witnessed will that outlines a husband's intent meets this condition; his understanding would have benefited the survivors of Mohammed upon his sudden death in 2008.

The final three guidelines—that the marriage ceremony be public, that it not be used as a means to prevent divorce or adultery, and that it be formed for an important reason—speak most specifically to the communal aspects of marriage by addressing the role of marriage within the family, broader Islamic community, and larger society. While all of Mohammed's rules on polygyny can represent the social harms and benefits implicit in polygyny, these three especially underscore questions about the dignity and equality of women as expressed in private religious and cultural practices. Marriage in Islam serves as a foundation for the structure of the mosque and the larger society, a reality Imam Mohammed understood. During his thirty-three-year ministry, he devoted significant time to family values in his public lectures and private, gender-segregated talks. He recognized that at stake in debates about polygyny—and Muslim marriage in general—is its effect on family life, female identity, and perhaps the future of African Americans in general as well as those associated with his leadership or the original NOI. Here he raised concern for marriage ceremonies held in secret, especially those entered into on less than honorable grounds, without the awareness of current wives or their mosque communities.

Perhaps Mohammed would be less enchanted with the route taken by Omar, among other polygynists. Although Omar was able to financially maintain multiple families and did, this African American Muslim husband and father married women who possessed little awareness of their Islamic rights and without the knowledge of his current wife or wives. In fact, he introduced his bride, Najilah, nineteen years his junior, to members of another mosque he attended before he informed his wife Nuri. Within six years, Nuri left the marriage. Such situations offer further proof of the need for measures in mosques to address them as well as for education and counseling on marriage and family life.

Implicit in Mohammed's directives is a caution to individuals who conduct polygynous marriages. Herein is the context in which the role of the Muslim community is most visible. More often than not, *nikahs* of single-wife marriages among his followers are public events that occur in mosques, public facilities, or private homes. Announcements of coming marriages are given after Friday congregational prayer services and before or following the Sunday lecture and are posted on building sites, on social media outlets, or both. The officiant, usually the local imam, conducts premarital counseling, though its depth and length vary greatly. The lack of legal recognition for polygynous marriages is one issue that contributes to the secrecy of such *nikahs*, as does the level of information that has been shared with the husband's current wife or wives.

My findings in this study indicate that a significant number of imams will not officiate at a polygynous ceremony unless they have discussed the pending marriage with the husband's current wives and have witnessed the marriage contract for the bride-to-be. Those who do are known to support the practice and often are in Texas or Georgia or Pennsylvania or other states where polygyny is much more visibly practiced. Some imams in these areas maintain strict adherence to a core of ethics and transparency that requires the notification and involvement of all current wives in any premarital counseling sessions arranged for a husband and his bride-to-be. Other imams refuse to perform multiple-wife marriages due to legal repercussions or on the principle that the American law should supersede religious permissibility on this issue. Still others distribute their self-designed marriage contracts that stipulate monogamy only or refuse to perform monogamous or polygynous marriages that are not registered with the state. Ultimately, such varied positions open the door to *nikahs* being performed in secret. News of the resulting marriages is often communicated by word of mouth. If a husband's current wife or wives belong to the mosque in which a polygynous marriage takes place and it is known that she or they did not support it, the union rarely is announced or celebrated publicly.

An Invitation to Polygyny

The liberty that Imam Mohammed suggests men possess to enter polygyny to increase their progeny, for example, has encouraged some Muslim men to approach as additional wives younger women able to bear children. Rashad's interest in expanding his family was fueled by his desire to "bring more Muslims into the world." Omar approached Kareema, never married and twenty years younger, after Nuri left the family and Najilah became his only wife. Omar's decision was motivated in part by the prodding of her father, who considered Omar to be an honorable man. By this the father meant someone he believed was trustworthy and would take care of his daughter. As plans for their marriage progressed, so did conversations about the groom's gift to the bride. "All she wanted was diamond earrings," Omar said, "but her father wanted a loan for his business." Prior to the marriage, Omar returned with earrings plus $5,000 for his soon-to-be father-in-law. Although Najilah recognized that her husband was not pleased with their marriage, she still hoped to be Omar's only wife. After Najilah spoke on the telephone with her co-wife, she later told him, "I'll deal with this [polygyny] as long as you deal with me." Omar said in return, "I'm just a bad brother. I'm learning to be better. I'm not the best of brothers, not the worst of brothers. I am not beating you, well, maybe I am beating you because I've taken another wife."[41]

When Omar married Hafeezah, his third wife at the time and with whom he exchanged vows without witnesses, he conceded that she was not familiar with *mahr*, the mandatory gift Muslim grooms are to give their brides. He said Hafeezah later assured him that he had met his Islamic obligation, telling him, "The dower you gave me is 'I do.'" When he informed Najilah of his marriage about two months later, she expressed her anger by "calling me a gigo-ho"—a derogatory term for a male whore. Omar claimed Najilah was jealous because she and he were unable to have children together. Soon, he said, they initiated conversation about adoption.

Family situations as intense and dramatic as the one of Najilah, Kareema, Omar, Hafeezah, and Nuri are as representative of African American Muslim polygyny as are the realities of women who await becoming co-wives. That is, neither situation is everyone's story. Rather, both and many others have the potential to turn our assumptions of polygyny, those who live it, and the foundations that guide them into questions about justice, agency, and the practice of faith in the United States.

Poor Health and Sisterly Fondness

When Mohammed declares that the proper practice of polygyny responds to an important rationale and Aadila equates the choice to share one's husband with charity, the experience of a warm-hearted widow who entered her third marriage on her fifty-eighth birthday could be seen as exemplary. Naeema's second marriage ended when her husband of nineteen years, an accomplished writer, lost his battle with sickle cell anemia. For the next fifty-two months, she prayed the *istikara* prayer of supplication and hoped for a marriage proposal from an upstanding Muslim man who could be "a form of protection" against unwelcome advances from other men. While unwanted pursuers elbowed each other for position, an acceptable proposal was received from a surprising source in a nearby city: Ronald, also fifty-eight, who was in a twenty-year marriage to a victim of multiple sclerosis who was bound to a wheelchair. "I was impressed by the way he carried himself," Naeema began, recalling Ronald's assistance and advice on home repairs. "He showed concern for me. Plus he knew my late husband and asked for one of his books. When I told him it was out of print, he gave me the money to have it republished. If that was a strategy, it certainly worked."[42]

Ronald's behavior matched Naeema's image of him. He consulted his wife, Shujana, five years his junior, before the *nikah* and even renewed his vows to her at their mosque about a week after his wedding to Naeema. He initiated provisions to ensure that both would be cared for in the event of his death. The three of them attend public events together; the co-wives, Naeema's term for them, share a sisterlike fondness for each other. "I admire her a lot," Naeema said. "Considering her condition, I think she has a great spirit." From Naeema's perspective, polygyny has enhanced Ronald's relationship with Shujana. "They are closer, and there is more appreciation between the two of them," Naeema said. Even with the comfort she now enjoys, two years into their marriage, Naeema knows what she would do differently. "I would require that we have a place of our own instead of him moving in with me," she explained. "My former husband's presence is here in too many ways. We built this house together. This doesn't seem to be a problem for Ronald, but it is for me." As for the future, Naeema and Shujana appear to be on the same page: "One of the first things [Shujana] said to me was, 'There will not be a number three.' We laughed about that."[43]

Ultimately, Imam Mohammed's rules on polygyny serve as stipulations for men regarding the proper practice of multiple-wife marriage and as reminders for women that they need not become victims. In other words, under Mohammed's policy, polygyny is not about male sexual pleasure in exchange for female subordination. To help ensure that the rights of Muslim men are not privileged over their responsibilities, his guidelines could—and in my view should—take the form of "law," or the general order of existence for African American Muslims who claim Imam Mohammed as their spiritual leader. His provisions could prove useful to other American Muslims engaged or interested in multiple-wife marriage as well. But his method of living polygyny deserves and requires further attention, clarification, and expansion for progress to occur on the road of ensuring justice.

In this examination of Imam Mohammed's nine rules for the proper practice of polygyny in the United States, I interspersed examples from the bittersweet experiences of some of his followers that highlight both the limited institutional resources within African American (and other) Muslim communities that focus on Islamic family life and the legal safety net that most women surrender when they marry polygynous men. Like Clara Muhammad, however, women have a choice in whether they remain in, enter, or seek multiple-wife marriage. In my view, the guidelines that Imam Mohammed articulated during gender-segregated meetings around the country may be understood to legitimize polygyny for religious purposes for African Americans Muslims, particularly those who view his teachings on polygyny as a confirmation of the Qur'an's position on multiple-wife marriage. They need not do so, however. What is abundantly clear is that his discourse widens the door of polygyny as a potential form of marriage to women who prefer the flexibility of a contract that affords autonomy and companionship as well as the identity of marriage. But they are not without their limitations.

Just as their ancestors who endured slavery married without legal sanction, African American Muslims construct lives together based on what they believe to be their cultural needs and religious rights. Those who affiliate with the ministry of Imam Mohammed strive to build healthy families based on the authoritative sources of Islam and commentary of their leader. In so doing, for me the central issue they raised is whether their protests bring justice to women and children in religious communities void of support systems and within societies hostile to polygyny. That African American and other Muslims in the United States adhere to components of Islamic law such as those regarding inheritance and interest rates suggests that Islamic jurisprudence is not incompatible with American civil codes.

6

Mental Health and Living Polygyny

Why don't they have two mommies?

Naim, as a child

Fatimah, as she has been called since the days she began to act like a younger version of her namesake in the mosque, is pacing the floor of her bedroom. She's a high school senior undecided about a career path, and the window of educational opportunities is closing rapidly for a student with her lower-than-expected grade point average. She'd like to travel and is considering the military, but she's concerned about leaving her mother alone. Her mother, newly single for the third time, seems to be the happiest Fatimah can recall in years. Just the thought makes her smile and want to run to the adjacent room and hug her mother. She stops short of grabbing the door knob, however, because she knows, upon arrival, her mother will turn away from the television and ask, "So, what do you want to do after graduation?" It's close to midnight now, so Fatimah prepares for bed. Before she surrenders to fatigue, she has an awakening. "There is one thing I know I don't want to do," she says to the figure staring back from her bathroom mirror, "follow my mother in polygyny!"[1]

Children raised in polygynous households are privy to a particular view of multiple-wife marriage, one whose vantage point determines whether they choose to replicate their parents' marital choices. Some, like Naim, whose inquisitiveness marks the epigraph above, have fond memories of their childhoods. A twenty-four-year-old graduate student pursing a doctorate in psychology, Naim says he and his two siblings celebrated a specialness he believes added benefits to his family that were denied their classmates: they had "two mommies." Others, like Fatimah, recall polygyny as having a less than desirable effect on their families and on their mothers.

For Farah, mother of Fatimah, sharing a husband meant she could expect to spend less time with her two youngest boys, not more; her new husband did not permit her young boys to live with them. She didn't realize that living polygyny would mean choosing between building a home environment for herself and her two eldest children and yielding primary custodial care of her two sons under the age of ten to their father, her ex-husband. Though Farah regularly speaks to her sons by telephone, she misses them and desires to be closer to them. She battles guilt, too; sometimes when they visit, she tends to be too lenient. She has noticed that the youngest is acting out more. Once he became so uncontrollable during their visit that she was forced to return them to their father earlier than planned. Circumstances such as this one created stress in the marriage of her ex-husband and her relationship with his wife. Farah is not that surprised that Fatimah refuses to consider polygyny. She wonders, at times with regret, whether her choices have skewed her daughter's attitude toward her faith and toward marriage. Farah is fearful, as well, that perhaps she has not been the best role model and that the manner in which she has lived polygyny has adversely affected her children's mental health.

We journey now into the subject of the psychological and emotional well-being of the women and children who experience multiple-wife marriage. First, I take a look at polygyny from the recollections of its youngest household members and parents who observed their behavior. My research findings concur with literature on the mental health of children raised in polygynous households in various faith traditions, that family dynamics directly affect the mental and emotional adjustment of children whose mothers shared their husbands. Second, I look into marital harmony and parental emotions, especially from the perspectives of women. I describe the common structures of polygynous families by sharing the demographics of the women in them. I conclude with a consideration of "commuter" polygyny.

The findings of this study of women living polygyny indicate that multiple-wife marriage is a "subculturally bound phenomenon."[2] Researchers interested in nontraditional American families like those in which Naim and Fatimah were raised have built a growing body of work in the past three decades. And as the public's awareness of polygyny has increased, so has scholarly attention to its effects on the behavioral, emotional, and academic adjustment of children.[3] I am not surprised that polygynous households can emotionally affect children, given their impact on the marital harmony and emotional well-being of parents. Of course, the same can be said for two- and single-parent households.

Respecting Parental Wishes

The potential for harmful effects on children of women living polygyny is the hardest issue to address, quite frankly. It has been one thing to solicit examples of the concrete effects of living polygyny, whether they reflect physical space, cultural identity, or financial considerations. I also have been more comfortable delving into matters of the heart, gently striving to listen to women, individually and in groups, as they articulate their painful and joyous experiences of sharing their husbands. It has been somewhat straightforward to observe husbands taking mental note of the vivid anguish expressed by their wives as the husbands sit between them. Even for subjects willing to tell me the most intimate aspects of their household arrangements—that only the bathroom separates the private spaces co-wives inhabit, for example—the journeys of their children were off limits.

Naturally, I chose not to request permission to speak to the offspring of my subjects who had not reached adulthood—meaning almost all of our interviews. But even when the road to polygyny for the parents was an overwhelmingly favorable experience and their offspring were adults themselves, one or more informants verbally chastised me for attempting to contact their children. Most of my subjects preferred to limit my queries to the choices they themselves made. In fact, with few exceptions, they would halt the interviews any time I attempted to go beneath the surface for their own anecdotes of their children's experiences or for their sense of their children's mental health. Even subsequent and independent contact with some adult children displeased their parents, who demanded that I respect their wishes not to include their children. I attribute their resistance to a number of factors, most importantly to concern about the children's walk of faith, protecting the privacy of their children, and limiting the potential harm to their children and others if their identities were revealed.

I recognize, too, that most of my subjects whose children were forced to live polygyny because of their parents' choices were not proud of some of the experiences their children have had or witnessed, and the parents feel responsible for some of the challenges their offspring have endured. Some have never gathered their children for a family chat about the impact of mom's or dad's marital decisions. Though I collected few firsthand accounts of their emotional health from children living polygyny, I nonetheless gleaned—from secondary research and direct revelations from co-wives about their own well-being—

information that led me to draw two conclusions: this arrangement can be detrimental to children, and its experiences can compel women to share their household arrangements with social work and health care professionals.

Unveiling Polygyny

My sampling does not indicate a higher risk of behavioral problems among children raised in polygynous households than in single- or dual-parent families. This is especially true where the household economy was sufficient to meet financial need, separate dwellings were provided for each mother and her children, and wives who did not have biological children aided and supported those who did.[4] Nor did I discover sexual abuse of children. Nevertheless, conversations with Muslim counselors and child care advocates paint a more disturbing picture and one that is consistent with the literature on risk factors associated with polygyny. Dialogue with two professionals in particular, one in New York, the other in North Carolina, indicate that state and regional social service agencies are becoming more aware of the practice of polygyny among African American and other Muslims as an increasing number of women seek help for or choose to identify their family structures.[5] The locations of these Muslim advocates—the East Coast and the South—suggest that abuse and other adverse effects of polygyny are not limited to a single city or geographical area but may indeed be a more pervasive problem.

For example, a consultant with the New York state court system revealed that some African American Muslim clients are women in multiple-wife marriages whose children have been abused by the siblings or relatives of their husband's other wives. "New York state doesn't accept common law marriage and is not going to accept polygamy," said the sixty-eight-year-old administrator, whom I call Marsha. "Right now, polygamy puts children at risk," she continued. "Typically, women who come to me haven't wanted to say they're in a polygamous situation since it is illegal in New York. Now, they will come in as 'mothers' of their children."[6]

Oliver Muhammad,[7] resident imam of As-Salaam Islamic Center of Raleigh and a North Carolina state chaplain, has witnessed a change in the number of women willing to name their family formations, especially when they adversely affect the mental health of their children. Muhammad is unclear whether polygyny increases the likelihood of family violence and disruption, as the literature sources suggests, but he is adamant in his belief that polygyny can cause harm to children:

I have counseled families experiencing problems with their young males. The father is not able to spend as much time with his kids, especially if theirs is not the "licensed marriage." You see a drop in young male attendance at the *masjid* and some getting into trouble with the law and experiencing a drop in performance at school. Some brothers [men] actually rescue sisters [women] who come out of abusive marriages by marrying them as second wives. Unfortunately, while a brother may be rescuing one family, his first family may become a victim in the process.[8]

Imam Oliver's evaluations reflect the effects a father's absence can have on children, particularly on his male offspring, regardless of the form of marriage he chooses. I found it particularly disappointing how few parents recognized that the choice of polygyny was theirs but also imposed upon their children. African American Muslims living polygyny often have claimed that maintenance of women and children is a primary motivation for structuring families in this way. Yet, few have reported consciously considering the emotional health of children when they contracted their marriages. (I realize that couples in monogamous unions are no more likely to consider the potential effects of their decisions on their offspring.) The experiences of children growing up happily, as Naim recalls, seem especially rare. Still, what children of those living polygyny see, hear, feel, and do helps to bring full circle the idea of experience as authority in its multifaceted streams.

Most of my informants bring children into multiple-wife marriages before the children reach the age of ten, and the mothers say the presence of co-wives actively involved in the physical, emotional, and spiritual care of the children is especially important. How fathers relate to the children of other men can also be an issue.[9] Some of the children were either born into polygynous households, as Naim was, or were too young to recall any other family structure. They say having at least one disciplinarian among the wives helps to limit acting out and other disturbances. Several young adults indicated that their developmental years were behind them when their fathers became polygynists; now living on their own, they refer to the homes of their fathers and their fathers' later wives as their parents' homes.

Modeling Living Polygyny before Children

What children observe of the relationships between wives, how husbands interact with their wives' children from other men, and the ages of wives in comparison to adult children in the family can help shape their self-perceptions and security, both personally and in relation to polygyny. The same factors affect the interactions among wives and children and the emotional capital spent when husbands precede their wives in death, as was seen when Imam Mohammed died. When the second marriage of Fatimah's mother ended and she remarried soon thereafter, the sudden shift from a monogamous to a polygamous family system was a decisive one for Fatimah:

> I loved my stepfather. He cared for my brother and me as if we were his own kids. And when my two youngest brothers were born, it felt just like one big family. I was sad when they divorced and we left. I know he worked a lot and mom was often alone with us, but I never understood why we couldn't be a family again.[10]

Fatimah's experience mirrors the literature on childhood mental health in that moving into a polygynous environment can challenge a child's sense of trust, confidence, and well-being. Fatimah recalls the stress the new marriage had on her mother, now with four children. Initially, Fatimah just tried to stay out of the way of her mother's new husband, Ghazi. He had sons of his own and they were always around. During the first years of the new marriage, Farah returned her two youngest sons, then toddlers, to their biological father at the direction of her new husband. Farah said Ghazi told her that "if a father is around, he should take responsibility for his own kids." The departure of her siblings made Fatimah question the role of marriage if it means breaking apart families. While she recognized the benefits of her brothers being nurtured by their biological father, she questioned the either/or scenario created by her mother's new husband. She also expressed feeling moments of jealousy; she missed her brothers' father, too, especially since he was the father figure her mother's husband was not. Later, when the family had settled into a routine and Fatimah looked forward to "messing around" with her youngest siblings during their school breaks and summer vacations, Farah delivered more disappointing news. "She told me, 'The boys can visit, but they can't stay as long,'" Fatimah said. It was then, she believes, that her aversion to polygyny was complete.

It is no surprise that Naim's childhood with two and briefly three moms differs significantly from the home life of Fatimah. Even he admits that his family situation was uncommon. Naim grew up in Florida, in a home shared by his two siblings, his father, his mother, and his father's other wife. Unlike their Mormon counterparts, it is uncommon for African American Muslim women living polygyny to share a husband and a house with co-wives. Naim's positive views reflect, at least in part, his father's approach to living polygyny, most notably in that his father perceived his marriage decisions as a family affair. That is, in contrast to many husbands who take other wives, Naim's father gave him advance notice. "He talked to me about it a little bit," Naim says, recalling the conversation at age eight when his father told him he was thinking about taking another wife. "I was like, 'Oh, okay.' I figured it says so in the Qur'an so there's nothing wrong with it." Naim was familiar with his father's bride-to-be, too, having seen her on numerous occasions at their mosque. Nevertheless, when his "other mother," as Naim refers to his father's second wife, moved in, there were a few adjustments to be made:

> It was a little different because just with any new addition to the family whether a cousin or uncle or whatever coming into the house or a guest who kinda stays for an extended period of time, they have to plug their way into the family dynamics. It took a little time trying to get used to her and see how her style was, and she was really nice. . . . [Early on, I learned] "Hey, that's my mom." I don't play stepmom or anything connoting that she's anything less than my mother.[11]

While the parents shared the same residence, each wife had her own bedroom on the upper level, separated by a common bathroom. The children's rooms were in the basement, alongside a makeshift office that his father used. The idea that his two mothers shared a bathroom and had limited privacy did not appear to trouble them. "Everybody shared everything," Naim explained. "They didn't seem to mind. In fact, they are closer on the friendship level with each other than my dad is with either of them."

Being advised of his father's plans makes Naim's experience unusual. While his home life felt less interrupted than it could have been, Naim said his conversations with his father helped him feel part of the decision-making process; Naim came to understand that decisions about family structures are family decisions. His father's approach afforded Naim the opportunity to speak freely with his mother about her feelings without feeling like he was betraying his father. His reflections could translate into suggestions for parents interested in developing strong families.

Leaving behind Survivors, but No Registered Will

The relationships of wives, which can vary from "like sisters" to complicated, difficult, and dismissive, can affect the entire family, especially when the new wife is younger than her husband's adult children, as was the case according to court documents regarding the "Estate of Wallace Mohammed."[12]

If the YouTube video of their marriage ceremony is any indication, Khadijah Siddeeq was a shy, blushing bride when she married her religious leader in 2004. Her father and *wali* led the couple in the exchange of vows and wedding bands at the brief but intimate ceremony held in metropolitan Atlanta.

The heart of the outdoor ceremony was the exchange of vows. The bride and groom were directed by the bride's father and *wali* to stand and repeat their vows once. As the bride stood, she looked radiant. She wore a white gown with an embroidered bodice. A white veil covered her natural curls slightly caressing her shoulders. Her groom wore a black tuxedo and white shirt with a stylish, multicolored *kufi*. As directed, he began his vows first:

> I, Wallace D. Mohammed, accept Khadijah Siddeeq to be my lawful wife in marriage according to Islam, the Qur'an, and the *sunna* of our Prophet and according to the laws of this state and of the United States.[13]

The four-and-a-half-minute video ends with the couple exchanging wedding bands and turning to face the audience and receive their guests. After the wedding, the bride moved from her parents' home in Indianapolis to her husband's residence in Markham, Illinois.

This was the first marriage of Khadijah; Imam Mohammed had been married at least four times. Of those unions, two were to the same woman—Shirley Muhammad—and only hers carried a civilly registered marriage license. Besides Khadijah's and W. D. Mohammed's family members, their wedding guests included a number of the young adults who, along with Khadijah, attended the Mosque Cares Youth Dawah classes taught by Imam Mohammed from 2001 to 2007. One of the students also worked in the ministry office preparing support checks for the imam's former wives. Indeed, the ministry staff and many of his supporters were aware of the responsibility Imam Mohammed assumed to take care of (or maintain) his ex-wives until the women married other men. "The ones to Sister Shirley always included the word 'alimony' in the note area," the office worker would say years later.[14]

The families of Mohammed and Siddeeq differ on many issues relative to the marital status of Imam W. D. Mohammed at the time of his marriage to Khadijah Siddeeq. What neither side disputes is this: Imam Mohammed did not leave behind an enforceable will.[15] Probate court transcripts indicate that Khadijah believed theirs was to be a monogamous marriage between a never-married woman and a divorced man when she and Mohammed first discussed a marriage contract. Members of Mohammed's family maintain a different perspective. They contend that Khadijah and her family were well aware of Mohammed's marital status long before their *nikah* was contracted. As rumors swirled throughout the community about the impending nuptials, women appeared particularly concerned about the propriety of a first-time marriage with a roughly fifty-year age difference. Less attention was directed toward whether Khadijah was about to knowingly choose to live polygyny. Many simply assumed she was not.

In a rare display of personal defensiveness, Imam Mohammed used a Friday congregational lecture to respond to his critics:

> Imam W. D. Mohammed can't marry a girl [of] twenty without being suspected. [You] say, "This is a *khutbah*. You shouldn't be bringing that in." Yes I should. The *khutbah* is for correcting Muslim behavior. And really I feel sorry for you who are hurt because you are not in my house. I'm sorry. Maybe you should have came before she came. Who knows. So I have to defend myself. Yes, and right of self-defense is supported by the law of the land. . . . I get letters from Muslims who [are] saying, "Now I doubt your integrity because you've married a female considerably much younger than himself." That makes a man lose his integrity just because he married a woman younger than himself? I didn't marry an imbecile. I didn't marry a retarded person. I married an exceptional-minded human being, and you should stay out of private business.[16]

Some concerned about the marriage wondered whether the personal decision of their leader might set a precedent for more marriages between senior grooms and young adult brides, especially with so many middle-age women single by circumstance, not by choice. If community members were concerned about the age difference and its potential ramifications, it may come as no surprise that some of Imam Mohammed's family members voiced their unease, according to anonymous sources. At the time of their 2004 *nikah*, Khadijah was nearly three decades younger than her husband's eldest daughter, and the groom was seventy-four. Nevertheless, during the court hearing to determine who would administer her husband's estate, Khadijah testified that she worked with his two eldest daughters and delivered financial support to their mother at her husband's request. During her marriage to their father, Khadijah said she felt she and his eldest children got along until her husband's death in 2008.

Khadijah's situation, according to court transcripts, mirrors the conditions that some women experience living polygyny. After becoming a widow, Khadijah encountered questions from her husband's relatives about her status at the time of Mohammed's death and the form of marriage she had lived for nearly four years. When Khadijah learned of her husband's death, she was in Atlanta attending the *janazah* of her brother. In her absence, a press conference was conducted in the Chicago area in which Mohammed's eldest daughter and family spokesperson, Laila Muhammad, spoke alongside her mother, Shirley Muhammad. When the media accounts of his death named his survivors, his wife was listed as Shirley, not Khadijah. Laila would later mention both.

At Mohammed's *janazah*, female supporters of his ministry stood on hills overlooking the service, mourning their leader and disturbed by what appeared to be confusion among program officials as to who was his wife. Court documents following the probate hearing confirm that Khadijah said she first learned she was living polygyny after the death of her husband.[17] The judge ruled that in the absence of a registered divorce decree from his marriage to Shirley, Khadijah was not his legal widow.[18] Khadijah did not possess legal documents that stated otherwise. The judge did recognize her union with Imam Mohammed, and thus, she was named an heir to the estate. But for some family and community members, Imam Mohammed's marital status was never in doubt. That is, to them, he is survived by two wives.

Laila Mohammed later informed a radio audience that the probate hearing could prove to be an instructive source for legal questions about polygynous marriages in the future. Granted, women in traditional one-husband, one-wife unions could face similar challenges, especially those solemnized in religious-only ceremonies. Still, I agree that how this marriage was treated after the husband's death sheds light on emotional, legal, and maintenance concerns for women living polygyny and the responsibilities of community members to each other.

Emotional Downside of Polygyny

Some of my subjects say their husbands take second wives in secret and inform them only after the ceremony has occurred. Others report learning that their households have become nontraditional family structures from those who witnessed the occasions. If husbands in either scenario precede their wives in death without documenting or updating their final wishes, they can leave their wives at the mercy of adult children, other relatives, or the state, as the case of Imam Mohammed's death indicates. These and other troubling matters that can confront widows whose marriages are not registered and whose husbands do not leave wills help solidify the decision of Imam Khalil Akbar and Imam Oliver Muhammad of North Carolina to refuse to conduct any marriage ceremonies without the documentation required by state law. Both leaders have been asked to perform polygynous unions. Both acknowledge that when they turn away couples, they routinely hear later that the couples have obtained the services of other imams or Muslim males.[19]

The emotional challenges of living polygyny were important to Nasif, Naim's father, as was observing marriage as an act of worship. I was moved by the simplicity, honesty, and forthrightness of this Florida educator who lives in the same dwelling with his two wives. He was surprised to learn that this study revealed few positive experiences of polygyny. Nasif and Kay had been married for twenty years and had three children before they began to have conversations about expanding their family. One day Kay pointed out Charlotte, a never-married family friend, and Nasif says she told him, "The kids love this sister. If anything ever happens to me, I would really love for you to marry her so she can help you take care of the kids."

Eventually, Nasif approached Charlotte, and the three became a family. Charlotte later gave birth to two children. While their living arrangement has produced its share of challenges, Nasif insists that the difference for them is "orientation." Even before Charlotte joined their family, Kay and Nasif researched multiple-wife marriage, studied the Qur'an, prayed together, and talked with others who have had varying degrees of success. "We talked about this together the way you analyze things," he explained. One of the issues Nasif works hardest to dispel has to do with jealousy. When he and Charlotte married religiously, "Kay was there; she participated in the planning," he said. Their choice of housing also was a collaborative decision:

> We were sincere about making [polygyny] work. We talked about the ramifications of not being in the same home and how that would really develop a separate life for each person as if we were doing something wrong. We wanted to live together and grow together as a family.

Given the dynamics of their family as well as their close living quarters, Nasif says he is especially mindful of their personal interactions:

I would never create a situation that would cause someone to become a smoldering bomb of hatred. That's what I call jealousy. . . . Not only are you doing this in front of Allah, Subhanahu Wa Ta'ala, you are hurting two decent people. And it's not the way."[20]

Demographics of Women Living Polygyny

Demographically, women married to polygynous men represent a cross-section of all African American Muslims, those in their twenties and thirties, middle-age women, and members of the Generation of Seniors over the age of sixty. Most are divorced with and without children, and some never before married. A few are widows seeking assistance, but more are independent women who relish their autonomy. Almost all women married to or open to marriage to polygynous men are already Muslims when they contract their marriages. It is the extremely rare woman who enters a polygynous family at the same time she begins her journey to Islam. When she does, she is most likely to be the product of or have experience with a multiple-wife culture. In addition, examples exist of subsequent wives who are older and younger than their husbands' current wives.

It is not uncommon for women living polygyny to be formally educated, with masters or doctorate degrees, while some possess more life experience than formal schooling. Some desire or are willing to conceive more children; others prefer instead to support or help raise grandchildren or live in child-free zones. My research uncovered no instances of underage or forced marriages. Mohassan, from New Jersey, is twice divorced and would welcome a co-wife if the latter were a mother with children. Mohassan would agree to join an established family if the present wife was ill or otherwise unable to function and the circumstances were transparent. By this she means everyone is clear on what is happening.[21] That young, never-married women were interested in sharing husbands and joining established families was one of the more startling findings of this study. Usually young Muslimahs who are native to the United States undergo a conversion in reference to their perceptions about multiple-wife marriage or become Muslim open to the lifestyle. Azra, twenty-four, single, and a resident of Georgia, explains in a written survey response the circumstances under which she would consider living polygyny: "The brother has to be Islamically sane—know what it means to be a servant to Allah and have good intentions." She adds that the practice is good for the community because it means "less divorce, less adultery, and less people hurt."[22]

Regarding Cultural Preferences

The overwhelming majority of African American Muslim men contract marriages to African American Muslim women when they establish polygynous households. A few do select non-Muslim women who may or may not be culturally familiar with Islam. The prevalence of polygyny within African cultures makes African Muslim women attractive to African American Muslim men. It is not unusual for the latter to target the former, as research in the area surrounding the "polygyny mosque" in Texas demonstrates. In other words, the "marriage market" for potential wives is diverse and plentiful for African American men who seek to enter into or expand their polygynous households.[23] Such realities can lead to cultural wars within a single mosque.

In many cases, polygyny does not shift economic resources from men to financially strapped women, my research indicates. Many women who share their husbands either work outside of the home, some of them in family-run businesses, and/or they share responsibilities for all of their husband's children. Thus, material wealth and polygyny are not necessarily related in the experience of African American Muslims.[24] For men and women who perceive their household organization as a direct reflection of the will of Allah for their lives, consciousness of G'd may exceed considerations of material wealth. But then, some women living polygyny are financially stable on their own and more than willing to control their financial affairs. Unlike female Mormons who may believe in the principle but leave its practice to their economically disadvantaged sisters, African American Muslim women who enter into or seek polygynous family lives do so because they are committed to such unions or at least believe they should be. They contend that polygyny is a remedy for this time and this place.[25]

By far, African American Muslim polygynous households feature one wife in each dwelling, though the number of children, length of marriage, and personal preference of each wife can influence the type of accommodations she calls home. Only a handful of husbands with multiple wives house all members of their immediate family in the same dwelling, with wives sharing a common bathroom, kitchen, and living room or caring for themselves and their children on separate floors with private entrances. Polygynous husbands usually retain a room or at least closet space in each of their wives' homes; Omar, while married to two wives, considered acquiring a home of his own in addition to dwellings for his wives. Regardless of whether their wives live together or independently, husbands tend to refer to all family residences as their households. Men living polygyny generally are at least in their thirties, and some are pushing seventy. They are retired, independent businessmen, entrepreneurs, educators, bookstore or health food store owners, religious leaders, national speakers, and salesmen. The size of multiple-wife families varies, too, with most husbands married to two or three wives simultaneously. The rare family includes four wives; most care and support from five to as many as twenty-two children, the majority of them high school age or younger.

Most polygynous husbands reside in the same cities or states as their wives, though some endure periodic commutes across state or national borders. Commuter polygynous marriage can increase the level of stress and jealousy women experience, especially if one wife lives close enough to her husband to see him on a daily or weekly basis. In describing her marriage to Tariq, Lamisha says:

> I see him once a month. I told you I'm a little frustrated because she lives closer [to him], so I think they see each other more often than that. I mean I'm pretty sure they do. I try not to figure it out. I have asked him to tell me if she's going to be there [at his residence], because I kinda want to be busy.[26]

When husbands and wives live separately, the distance between them can also be a benefit, ensuring autonomy, independence, and familiar spaces. As Lamisha explains:

> What's really important to me is if you respect me and you give me my space to grow and be a person and if you respect my work, because my work is important to me. I have things that I want to do and it takes time, and you have to understand that and you have to support that. And he does. He makes me think I'm just the smartest and the most together person in the world and that I can do anything.[27]

Many women who divorce polygynous men obtain religious resolutions due to the absence of legal recognition of their unions. By this I mean they work out (or attempt to agree upon) child support, custody, and any financial arrangements in private. In most cases, neither the local imam nor the community gets involved. While polygynous marriages are often publicly witnessed, divorces routinely are not—nor are they in monogamous marriages unless those involve civil decrees and the jurisdiction requires the court attendance of the petitioners. And unless the soon-to-be divorcee has negotiated and registered in advance an enforceable document, such as a will, there is no entity on earth to compel her husband to comply with his commitments or responsibilities.

My point is that the success of Muslim marriage, in whatever form, and the extent to which women can and do exercise their marital rights are issues directly related to the presence and usefulness of support systems. Perhaps the absence of resources is tied to the lack of a unified body of mosques. Imam Ronald Shaheed expresses the link this way:

We need an "established" Muslim community, and it won't happen until we take the risk, trust each other, and move as a group, towards the destiny outline by our leader, Imam W. Deen Mohammed.[28]

Imam Mohammed neither promoted polygyny nor directed any other leaders to do so. Today, members of his association publicly remain surprised by characterizations of polygyny in reference to him or his father, Elijah Muhammad. Those who do support multiple-wife marriage based in part on their personal and positive experiences of living polygyny acknowledge that the lifestyle is full of challenges but can provide a happy and stable environment for children. They agree, too, that it is not for everyone. Naim asserts that his other mother "added the mutual type of balance" his household needed and influenced its dynamics for the better: "My dad has the ability to solve problems that he did not have before."[29]

Beneficial experiences in childhood do not guarantee a polygynous future, as Naim's marriage demonstrates. Married nearly two years at the time of our interview, Naim explained that his own household formation was a joint decision:

I know right off the bat that if one person doesn't want to do it, that's it, it's over. My wife doesn't want to do it. We had the discussion before marriage. One of the things that was real jumpy with her was she thought I would want polygyny because my dad did. I said, "I'm not down with that, and if you feel really strongly against it, put it in a prenup. I can't fight a clear contract, and I wouldn't do that." I told her, "Do whatever makes you feel safe, but also you have to trust my word about what I plan on doing and not doing."[30]

The emotional attachment Naim had for his mother's co-wife speaks to a closeness and interdependence between women living polygyny that is rare. Its cultivation is more likely, however, when all parties choose to work collaboratively from the start.

I intentionally have focused on the voices of women in this book. Polygyny will continue or vanish within African American Muslim communities depending upon the choices women make. What is equally evident is that the positive examples of multiple-wife marriage are outweighed by those led by men who are financially, spiritually, and/or mentally ill-equipped for such responsibilities and involve women who feel they have no other options. I have no doubt that African American Muslims will continue to wrestle with the presence of and objections to nontraditional family structures like polygyny. Perhaps the choices of the children of polygynous families like Fatimah and Naim signal a shift in perceptions about nontraditional families and the formalization of a single marriage process. When Naim and his wife married, their *nikah* featured an uncommon element. The imam verbalized the contents of their marriage contract. With that simple but surprising gesture, those who witnessed the ceremony took home an important message. Marriage in Islam can and should be a contract supportable by the community. That is, what is known can be enforced, and what can be enforced can be legal.

Afterword

Muslim Womanist Praxis and Polygyny

It's taboo for people to talk about polygamy, at least
in front of the parties involved, because of the assumptions
that the first wife is distraught, that the first marriage is on
the rocks, or that the second wife doesn't care about the first.

Rabi'a, blog post

As a womanist, I routinely ask the "So what?" of my scholarship. That is, I strive to link my intellectual explorations to practical applications that can benefit the communities and subjects I study. This is one way I attempt to give back to those who share their feelings, experiences, and lived realities with me. I wrote *Polygyny* with the hope that the musings within might lead to broader conversations and expanded initiatives about marriage and family life that could educate and empower women like Karimah, with whom I first began to reflect on multiple-wife marriage. I am pleased to say that such reflection is under way. Void of a unified direction that the association of Imam Mohammed is willing to embrace, however, the inequities that I observed will continue. As Mignon Jacobs has discerned, "Relationships define the well-being of a community and reflect its ideologies."[1]

From the start, I have been aware that some women resist becoming Muslim or aligning themselves with the association of Imam Mohammed because of practices like polygyny that they consider to be undesirable.[2] I have been concerned about where and in what manner Muslim women could be situated at the forefront of dialogues that involve them. How, I have wondered, can African American Muslim women bring their experiences of living Islam into the process of theological interpretations and practical applications of them? While I neither condone nor promote polygyny, I do support its decriminalization. I do realize that it is here and practiced by African American Muslims. Thus I feel, as Imam Mohammed has directed, that his community needs to confront it and marriage as a whole to enhance Muslim family life.

Here, I begin to theorize about what a Muslim womanist praxis might begin to look like if the subject were multiple-wife marriage. I have no definitive answers. Still, while these recommendations reside at the reflection stage, they do speak to the findings of this pro-woman, pro-family study.

It should be of no surprise that I am guided by my sources here as well as throughout the study. I take full advantage of a single source—the final interview subject for this book. Rabi'a has been a dear colleague for several years. When she began to home-school her children shortly after the birth of her first son, we drifted apart; our encounters became limited to occasional and chance conversations in the hallways of annual conferences. That said, I always thought she had the perfect academic position, a nice home in a geographical region with great weather, the support of one of the strongest mosque communities in the nation, and a wonderful marriage. I envied her, as did many others. But when we reconnected as publication of this book neared, I was reminded of the real reason I so admired her and continue to do so today. Rabi'a takes her faith seriously and lives it transparently, with a regular mix of vulnerability, honesty, and expectancy. In telephone conversations and email correspondence, we caught up recently. I quickly discovered that Rabi'a gave birth to her third child in 2013; her husband, Waleed, took a second wife two months later. Only now has Rabi'a been ready to talk with me about the experience of living polygyny. She called our conversations therapeutic; I received them as a fitting way to offer a few final thoughts.

Now in their thirties, Rabi'a and Waleed have been married for nine years. This is her first marriage, his second. From the start, Waleed was open about his interest in multiple-wife marriage if the opportunity emerged and if Rabi'a agreed. Like Rabi'a, he was concerned about women in their mosque who desired marriage but were unable to find suitable mates. Rabi'a was convinced that her husband was "the type of person who could do" polygyny, that he was emotionally, physically, spiritually, and financially mature enough to take on the additional responsibility. More important, Rabi'a characterized her husband as one who is faithful to Allah. So, together they studied the authoritative sources of Islam, talked to acquaintances living polygyny, and prayed—a lot, as other couples have done. As they did, Rabi'a reminded Waleed of two of her more earthly preconditions for living polygyny: at least seven years of marriage to her and an annual income of $100,000. Having met both within eight years, Waleed approached Shakirah, a woman Rabi'a agreed would be potentially a good co-wife. Rabi'a was not surprised to learn of Shakirah's first question to Waleed: "What does Rabi'a think?"

My encounters with Rabi'a and other sources for this book have prompted a number of recommendations regarding multiple-wife marriage, especially for five constituencies: mosque communities nationally, those who officiate at *nikah* ceremonies, women about to marry, women who desire to live polygyny, and men who are about to live polygyny and their current spouses.

First, I recommend a widespread process of engagement, dialogue, and education on the forms of marriage permissible in Islam and their application in the secular United States. While the findings of this study reveal a wide array of perceptions, contradictions, and paradoxes, one theme is undeniable: many people live polygyny without the backing of the Qur'an or the tradition of the Prophet, and they do so to the detriment of themselves and others. It is equally evident that no consensus exists among Muslims globally, locally, or within the community of Imam Mohammed on the purpose, benefits, and responsibilities associated with marriage as an institution established by G'd. By this I mean that a Muslim woman from Peoria, Illinois, may encounter different ideas about her marital rights in general or in reference to polygyny specifically if she moves from the Midwest to the South, for example. Furthermore, many imams and religious leaders are divided on the legality of polygyny in the United States and other countries where multiple-wife marriage is prohibited by civil law. For antipolygyny leaders, the equality prescribed by the Qur'an is unobtainable for co-wives in marriages that are unregistered with civil courts. These women do not have access to legal spousal rights in the event of divorce or the deaths of their husbands. Perhaps a series of monthlong events that occur at the same time in every willing mosque and are facilitated by women and men could help dispel the many myths about the single most important framework for family development. Such initiatives about marriage and family life could be incorporated in various forums (Friday congregational prayers, sisters' circles, brothers' classes, Sunday *taleem*, special events, and so forth). Those who say they follow the leadership of Imam Mohammed (and others) would benefit from clarity on a number of crucial issues, like timing, the importance of written marriage contracts, and notice to current wives.

I recommend discussions about children and mental health issues, too, with particular attention devoted to how to Islamically prepare children for marriage and, if necessary, for divorce. A recent focus group for a project on female religious authority reminded me of the urgency of the latter. There, nine African American Muslim women gathered weeks before Ramadan 2014 to respond to a video about Amina Wadud that focused on the woman-led prayer movement. Quickly the discussion turned to scripture and the importance of waiting on Allah for direction in life decisions. Suddenly, a burst from a thirty-eight-year-old woman interrupted the otherwise pleasant discussion, revealing the painful life her mother endured for years after her husband took a second wife. It was clear to all that the experience adversely altered the mother's and daughter's perceptions of themselves and their Creator. "My mother died waiting on Allah," the woman said, emphasizing the word "waiting." This woman did not feel her mother received the necessary care from her community, and she is still wrestling with G'd about the treatment of her mother. Thus, for this woman, her mother's wait extends beyond death.

I suggest an expansion of Imam Mohammed's nine guidelines to require some level of oversight of imams and others who officiate at *nikahs*, regardless of marriage form, and formal instruction on the road to healthy marriage for male and female Muslims. Perhaps some of his leaders who coordinate workshops and forums on family life around the country could take more visible and joint leadership in this endeavor. Already at work are Maryam Muhammad of Charlotte, Imam Faheem Shuaibe of Oakland, Imam Khalil Akbar of Charlotte, Imam Ronald Shaheed of Milwaukee, Munirah Habeel, Imam A. K. Hasan, and Debra Hasan of Los Angeles, and Ndidi Okakpu of Chicago, among others. Endeavors such as the Healthy Marriage Initiative organized by SHARE (Services for Human Advancement and Resource Enhancement) Atlanta add to the mix of opportunities that could be contextualized around the country. Linking these efforts with other activities nationwide might spearhead the formation of a database of contacts and resources by one of these groups that any American Muslim could access. Drawing upon the expertise of female health professionals, sociologists, and theologians could prove useful as well.

Second, I would recommend requiring local mosques and Islamic organizations to keep track of marriage registrations (both civil and religious) of couples affiliated with them, even *nikah*-only unions. In the absence of an ordained member of the clergy, any knowledgeable Muslim can officiate at a wedding; those providing this service have been overwhelmingly male.[3] The lack of transparency in this area has contributed to a number of secret ceremonies. Perhaps the handbook for imams that Imam Rabbani Mubashshir of Chicago has been charged to draft by the Conveners of the Midwest Region will include attention to the roles and responsibilities of female guardians, those who assist in the negotiation of marriage contracts and those who conduct marriage ceremonies.

I certainly am not an advocate for American family law or civil courts, in which petitioners of divorce are required to publicly appear and testify to personal details in the presence of strangers. I must acknowledge, however, that women whose marriages are registered with the state have access to legal judgments that carry enough weight to induce most men to comply. Without communal involvement or enforcement, women living polygyny and divorce in Muslim-minority areas are on their own when they may be most in need of care and protection. Yes, women in Muslim countries can be—and many are—vulnerable, too. But in the United States, a marriage license enables the state to investigate the status of potential spouses. No doubt, this would mean state intrusion, but it could also mean state protection of women and children. For those opposed to civil involvement, a similar process could be developed for religious-only ceremonies. In this study I have discovered that polygyny leaves open the possibility of incredible manipulation; a process of recourse could help ensure gender equality and social justice.

The third recommendation is one I intend for women whose husbands are considering taking additional wives. Rabi'a and other women living polygyny have chosen to exercise their agency by stating in their contracts what type of marriage theirs will be. In addition, Rabi'a and her husband discussed the matter privately and with Shakirah, who was about to enter her second polygynist union. The three also sought advice from knowledgeable and respected community members, marriage therapists, and family law experts. Engaging in such a process could help some women, like those living polygyny of coercion, avoid the pitfalls of unhealthy family dynamics. Rabi'a said she had to learn that "just because he's taken a second wife doesn't mean he doesn't care about you." She had to admit that what she felt distinguished her from all other women, being the only mother of her husband's children while he is married to her, could change one day.

Among the pieces of advice Rabi'a received was this: "Focus inward because this journey is yours, not your husband's, sister's, friend's . . . yours."[4] Even with good advice, however, Rabi'a is quick to acknowledge that living polygyny isn't a simple journey:

> Know that this is potentially a sad situation. . . . To prefer someone over you, you have to have a certain type of relationship with Allah, a certain way of seeing, not the average way. You have to see for the next life. You don't always see through Allah's eyes.
>
> When you're having these apprehensions [that accompany polygyny], it's because your heart is occupied with other than Allah.[5]

Finally, Rabi'a cautions women not to say "yes" or "okay" when they mean "no." It is every woman's Islamic right, she and others say, to choose not to live po-

lygyny even if the wife thinks her husband is approaching the practice according to the dictates of Islam. "Believe that there is something in this for you,"
Rabi'a adds. "If he's a good man and he really loves you, now he's trying to
please you even more."

My fourth recommendation is directed to women who desire to marry and
to live polygyny. Findings in this study suggest that justice and a peaceful existence are more likely when first and potential subsequent wives communicate prior to any multiple-wife marriage. Rabi'a suggests that others do what
Shakirah did: reflect upon the likely journey of the husband's current wife, talk
with her about her feelings, and share one's own. The two women ideally would
explore potential issues such as the likelihood of additional children, managing
family outings and special celebrations, explaining the marriage decision to
others. They would ask questions like "Can he really afford this?" They would
not proceed if the first wife or wives disapprove. The prospective wife would
be mindful, too, that while he is negotiating a new union with her, his current
wife or wives may be renegotiating their contracts. In the end, if women want
for each other what they want for themselves, my subjects say, justice and the
fear of Allah should be their yardstick.

This study reveals the benefits of a fully public *nikah* for second, third, and
fourth wives. On this front, I find the link of acknowledgement to responsibility articulated by Lamisha and Rabi'a instructive. Making vows public, particularly in the presence of a husband's current wife or wives, can add legitimacy to
all his marital decisions, my sources say. But even if they choose not to attend,
nikahs should be conducted with the awareness, if not approval, of all current
spouses.

I acknowledge that this recommendation differs from the qualifications outlined by Imam Mohammed. But he taught his students to have minds of their
own, fully aware that each individual is responsible for her behavior before
Allah. Rabi'a wrote this in her private blog:

When you do something like this, you do it for God. You do it to please
God, to be in God's favor, to receive God's love, to be one of God's favorites.
Because, as the Qur'an states, God loves those who prefer others above
themselves, God loves those who are patient, God loves those who put
their trust in Him, God loves those who carry out the most beautiful acts.

I realized about a month before my husband's wedding that cultivating
a friendship with my co-wife would make things easier for me particularly because we see each other all of the time in our mosque community.

Both of us are active and loved members of the community. We have pretty much the same friends, though our closeness to these friends varies. Since people were going to be watching us, it would be best, I realized, to make those moments in the mosque or other community spaces as comfortable as possible, and forming a friendship with my co-wife would make a difference. And it has!⁶

Obviously for Rabi'a, Shakirah, and others living polygyny of liberation or choice, women who choose their form of marriage and are involved in the selection of subsequent wives position themselves to enhance their marriages and their personal well-being. This means taking "the higher way." Rabi'a has embraced this concept and found the words of one religious leader especially encouraging. She e-mailed them to about a dozen close family members and friends with whom she has shared her "life situation":⁷

Some of the *ulama* say *ahsanahu* means that when Allah calls you to the higher way, you take that way. You don't take the low way, even if it is acceptable. You take the high way. This is the time when Muslims have to rise above their ego, have to rise above their tribalism, rise above their own self identity, rise above their own images of worth that they put up higher than the din [*deen*] sometimes.⁸

Rabi'a says, "My heart was agitated about my life situation" some days, as the other women informants likewise have acknowledged. She says she gains strength in knowing that "this situation is really all about me and my journey to Allah."⁹

The fourth and fifth recommendations are related, but the latter is directed specifically to men. As the strongest examples of living polygyny with any semblance of justice demonstrate, a man who desires to live polygyny must realize that courting or engaging in conversations with prospective wives with the full knowledge of his present wife or wives is the key to an Islamically strong and healthy marriage. It also is important for men to strive to legitimize subsequent unions with the immediate family of their potential wives. Waleed, for example, chose to communicate his rationale first to Rabi'a's family and then to his soon-to-be in-laws:

Rather than being excited, I am rather cautious and concerned, for Rabi'a, for Shakirah and also the impact on my sons. The major reason that more men do not even consider [polygyny] is because it is a serious responsibility; our faith has strong consequences for men who do not treat their wife/wives with fairness and justice. Additionally, there is the financial responsibility that most men would not or could not handle appropriately.

While I realize that polygyny is not the answer for creating healthy relationships in our faith community and beyond, it is one option available to the Muslim community to ensure that women have husbands to support them and children have fathers (stepfathers) to assist in guiding them. Looking back, I wish a courageous brother chose this path with my mother who was single and faithful for the last twenty years of her life.[10]

Interestingly, Waleed's father is a polygynist who took a non-Muslim woman as his second wife but cautioned his son to forgo the practice due to the timing: Waleed approached Shakirah when Rabi'a was pregnant with their third son. He and Shakirah exchanged vows when the youngest son of Waleed and Rabi'a was two months old.

Finally, I recommend the removal of communal acceptance of marriage ceremonies that occur without the knowledge of a husband's current wife or wives. In other words, transparency needs to be woven into the process so that at least the local mosque community is aware of the commencement and conclusion of marriage contracts. This might mean that some men would be encouraged to adjust their timing or discouraged from entering polygyny at all. It may be prudent for them to contemplate the psychological, spiritual, and physical restrictions on their current wives, such as illness and pregnancy, that may limit the options women believe they can exercise. Such reflection might motivate some men to forgo polygyny or to delay taking additional spouses until their current wives are free to fully exert their agency, as Waleed's father encouraged him to do. I would argue further that this is what Nasif, the father of Naim, means by "orientation."

I would characterize the approach of the imam who conducted the *nikah* for Waleed and Shakirah as particularly instructive. Like some other women living polygyny do in this circumstance, Rabi'a chose to attend the event. During the ceremony, the officiating imam announced her agreement before the community and prior to the exchange of vows between Waleed and Shakirah. The imam explained the road to living polygyny he established together with the three of them. His expectations included Rabi'a's presence at one of three premarital counseling sessions he required Waleed and Shakirah to attend. Rabi'a says she encouraged Waleed and Shakirah to make their marriage public and is convinced the officiating imam would not have conducted the wedding without her agreement. Making Waleed's marriage to her co-wife public helped position it on an equal plane with her own, Rabi'a says, and provides space for family members to verbalize their concerns.

As is common with many African American Muslims living polygyny, Rabi'a's extended family included non-Muslims. In fact, her mother, Hanan, also a Muslim, shared the news of her son-in-law's impending marriage, paying particular attention to acknowledge her daughter's role and perspective. Her e-mail read, in part:

> Rabi'a is alright with her husband taking on 2nd wife, even though we know that it will not be an easy path, but God willing, a steeper path where Allah will shower a lot of Blessings and Mercy on them in this world and in the next. Marriage is a very important institution in Al-Islam. Our tradition states that you complete half of your religion through marriage. Each wife will be known publicly and equally as Waleed's wife and not as a mistress. The relationships are honored in the sight of Allah. In most cases, the women have separate households and the man has to equally share his time between the two. This will be the case for them.
>
> Polygyny is not the norm in our religion, but allowed. Allah states through the Qur'an that the man has to be just to all of his wives. If he cannot be just, then he is only allowed one wife. One imam stated that if polygyny is done appropriately it can be a Mercy and a beautiful thing. If it is done inappropriately, it will be a messy thing. All three people involved, Rabi'a, Waleed, and Shakirah are special people of high morals and Muslim character and are good candidates for this situation, God willing. It takes a lot of courage and responsibility. They all want to please Allah and obey Allah. They are looking for the good that Allah has in it for themselves, the families involved, and the community.
>
> We also understand and believe that Allah (God) only wants Good for the believer and we trust in that, and we trust in Him. Our immediate Muslim families (of Rabi'a, Waleed, and Shakirah) have been in many discussions about this upcoming event. There are mixed feelings amongst us as to be expected, but we have tried to honestly address our concerns, doubts, and well wishes openly. This has been therapeutic.[11]

The journey of Rabi'a, Waleed, and Shakirah continues, as do those of many of the sources in this book. Ultimately, the expectations of Qur'anic justice remain whether one enters monogamy or polygyny. Muslim men and women alike must acknowledge that the marriage and divorce processes they embrace in the United States are part of their religious and cultural identities.[12] Together, they have the power, authority, and agency to decide the meaning of these processes for themselves and for their future. My hope is that this book is received as one tool to help foster the good that Allah intends for all of our relationships.

Notes

Preface

1. African American Muslim women who share their husbands rarely play the game of feminine hierarchy. Rather than assign numbers to each other based on years of marriage, they attempt to relate to each other as "co-equals"—at least in theory. One of my female informants characterizes herself as a "polygynist." A second referred to her status and that of her husband's other wife as, simply, "wife." Most others, however, generally use the term "co-wife."

2. I was introduced to the concept of marital multiplicity by Davis in "Regulating Polygamy." Though apt for the focus of this work, "marital multiplicity" is a phrase more common in legal and political theories about adult intimate relationships than in reference to forms of Muslim marriage. Henceforth, "marital multiplicity" in this study will refer to unions with multiple wives.

3. Under Islamic law, husbands are responsible for providing maintenance for their wives and children even if they do not share the same domicile as their wives on a full-time basis. The "law of maintenance" includes supplying food, clothing, and shelter. African American (and other) Muslims living polygyny do not view the wives and children of polygynous husbands as separate family units. Thus it is common practice for husbands to refer to all of the dwellings for which they are responsible as their households, regardless of the amount of time spent there or whether their wives contribute financially to household expenses. For further consideration of the law of maintenance, see Lewis, *Spirit of Islamic Law*.

4. Lepore, "Historians Who Love Too Much," 129.

5. Among other Muslim scholars, Hermansen cites Rahman in the development of a holistic reading of the Qur'an. See his "Introduction: The New Voices of Muslim Women Theologians," 19.

Introduction

1. Like polygyny, *mut'a* marriage is not recognized by U.S. law. Moreover, some cultures require female virgins to obtain permission from their fathers before agreeing to such a contract. Controversy also surrounds this form of Muslim marriage due to

its association with prostitution and as an outlet for male sexual power over women. For an example of the practice among U.S. Muslims, see Walbridge, "Sex and the Single Shi'ite." Interestingly, as of September 2011, Mexico City began to consider legislation that would validate licenses that place a two-year cap on the length of marriage as a way to address the financial and emotional costs associated with divorce. In these "trial" marriages, the union expires after the agreed-upon period unless both parties agree to its continuation. The advances of same-sex marriage globally may add to the prevalence of marital options for Muslims in the future.

2. Brooks, "Problem with Polygamy," 109.

3. Heterosexual monogamy and polygyny are the two most prevalent forms of family structures among Muslims. Though a minority, some Muslim families are headed by lesbian, gay, bisexual, and/or transgendered parents, a reality that is indicative of diverse gender and sexual identities in the global Muslim community.

4. Allied Media Corporation, "Muslim-American Outreach." African Americans account for at least 24 percent of the estimated American Muslim population of six to eight million, according to the study. Granted, not all African American Muslims associate with Imam Mohammed's community, but given the location of the largest "polygynous" regions inhabited by his supporters, one thousand households seems to be a reasonable estimate.

5. Kubayah, interview with author, August 12, 2009.

6. Lepore, "Historians Who Love Too Much," 133.

7. R. Jackson, review of *We Want for Our Sisters What We Want for Ourselves* by Patricia Dixon.

8. Some who use Imam W. D. Mohammed's commentary on the Qur'an and the life of the Prophet to better understand the fundamental teachings of Islam and who self-identify as his followers, students, and supporters live beyond the shores of the United States. In fact, since Imam Mohammed succeeded his father as leader of the Chicago-headquartered Nation of Islam in 1975 and began to steer the movement onto the path of mainstream Islam, his association has become an international one, with thousands of followers in South Africa, Bermuda, and Germany, for example.

9. I distinguish the original Nation of Islam (NOI) founded in Detroit in the early 1930s by W. D. Fard and later headed by the Honorable Elijah Muhammad from the movement of the same name that Minister Louis Farrakhan later organized. The reform measures Imam Mohammed instituted included steering his father's followers onto the path of mainstream Islam and opening membership to people of all races. His movement assumed a number of titles along the way including the World Community of Al-Islam in the West (WCIW), Bilalians, and American Society of Muslims. The adoption of the WCIW name "terminated" the NOI, according to Clegg. Farrakhan, one of the leaders dissatisfied with the changes Imam Mohammed enacted, left the organization within three years of Muhammad's death. By 1979 he began to form a new movement, "sentimentally naming it the Nation of Islam"; Clegg, *Original Man*, 280, 282.

10. W. D. Mohammed routinely identified himself as his own imam, including himself among his followers. On one occasion he informed a gathering at Masjid Malcolm Shabazz that "following him [Imam Mohammed] led me to follow the Qur'an and Muhammad the Prophet."

11. The marital status of these leaders remained contentious after their deaths, an issue I explore in chapters 4, 5, and 6.

12. Lawrence, *The Qur'an*, 163.

13. Harris-Perry, *Sister Citizen*, 5.

14. Banfield, *Black Notes*, 73.

15. S. Jackson, *Islam and the Blackamerican*.

16. Regardless of permission granted, I have changed the names and altered the personal characteristics of most of the living subjects quoted except for religious leaders and other authorities who either do not reside in polygynous households or are not quoted in reference to their personal choices. The exceptions are two of the wives of Imam Mohammed who became public figures due to media coverage and public documents.

17. For a thorough exploration of the scriptural-temporal connection, see Barringer Gordon, *The Mormon Question*.

18. The objectification of Muslim women as victims in need of U.S. liberation was among the arguments First Lady Laura Bush and others used to support the invasions of Afghanistan and Iraq.

19. Results from the 2005 Gallup World Poll, an extensive research study on Islam and perceptions about Muslims, are presented in Esposito and Mogahed, *Who Speaks for Islam?*

20. During the life of Imam Mohammed, those affiliated with his leadership identified themselves in various ways, including as followers, students, and supporters. Of the three labels, "followers" was his least favorite, for he often said that he followed the Qur'an and *sunna* of the Prophet—and his own teachings. Following his death in 2008, a website appeared with the name *Community of Imam W. Deen Mohammed*. Throughout this book, I will intersperse the terms "students," "supporters," and "community" in reference to his leadership base.

21. In this book, a triad is a husband with two wives. It was rare for me to gain permission from each member of a triad to interview them individually or collectively.

22. MARIAM, the Muslim American Research Institute Advocating Marriage, is an organization developed by Faheem Shuaibe, resident imam of Masjidul Waritheen in Oakland, California, and self-described student of Imam Mohammed.

23. Safi, e-mail conversation with author, August 11, 2004.

24. Exploring American Muslim life through the binary of race and birthplace is common among researchers. A Woodrow Wilson study, for example, approached its assessment of Islam in Chicago this way: "Mosque communities are extremely diverse but fall into two general categories of African American or immigrant"; Strum, ed.,

Muslims in the United States, 19. The extent to which such coverage perpetuates the tensions between the factions is worthy of further study.

25. W. D. Mohammed was an international religious leader. Those who follow his leadership and teachings include members of other ethnic groups in the United States and Canada as well as Muslims and non-Muslims who reside outside of North America. Consistent with the teachings of his leader, Imam Faheem Shuaibe used the Friday congressional lecture "Has Faith Entered Your Heart Yet?" to describe Islam as "the perfect way of life," one that provides African American and other Muslims a way to "cultivate our own souls." By making lectures such as this available to online audiences, Imam Shuaibe and others extend the reach of their leader.

26. Foremost among them is Imam Shuaibe. In addition to being an international lecturer and expert on the Qur'an and *hadith*, he regularly facilitates marriage-enrichment workshops through the MARIAM conferences he organizes. I shared facilitation duties with him on one occasion, and I am indebted to him for his insights and counsel on marriage and family issues.

27. For example, in 2014 the president of Kenya signed into law a bill legalizing polygamy. The new legislation gives Kenyan males the right to marry as many wives as they want without the consent of their spouses.

Chapter 1. The Road to Understanding Polygyny

1. At least one dissertation has been devoted to this topic, that of Chanda Green, "Pedagogy of Polygyny." As will become evident, I distinguish between Muslim polygyny and Mormon polygyny.

2. Noteworthy examples include Barringer Gordon, *Mormon Question*; Jacobson, ed., *Modern Polygamy in the United States*; and Bennion, *Polygamy in Primetime*.

3. The FLDS was formed during the 1980s. Interestingly, in the 2013 decision *Brown v. Buhman*, a federal district court in Salt Lake City ruled against the Utah state statute that prohibited polygyny and cohabitation between nonmarried individuals. The judged ruled that the law violated the plantiffs' right to privacy and the free exercise of religion. Technically, the polygyny law remains on the books, however, in that it is still illegal to fraudulently obtain multiple marriage licenses.

4. For the Gallup survey see Newport and Himelfarb, "In U.S., Record-High Say Gay, Lesbian Relations Morally OK." A two-part series that aired May 27–28, 2008, on NPR's *All Things Considered* featured African American Muslims who "quietly engage in polygamy." With interviews conducted by Barbara Bradley Hagerty, NPR's religion correspondent, the series also drew attention to the challenges some husbands experience in their attempts to treat their wives equally. A year earlier, the *San Francisco Chronicle* published Pauline Bartolone's article "For These Muslims, Polygamy Is an Option," an exploration of the practice among African American Muslims. I do acknowledge that some Muslims go beyond the four-wife stipulation established in the Qur'an.

5. Daynes, "Plural Wives and the Nineteenth-Century Mormon Marriage System," 138.

6. Dixon, *We Want for Our Sisters What We Want for Ourselves.*

7. Though not related, the author and I share the common surname Majeed, whose meanings include "worthy of dignity, honor, and respect." Some distributors also include the name of Michelle Saka-El as an author.

8. One blogger has made available a free version of *Polygynous Blessings.* See "cujo-han2: just another Blogdetik.com weblog," http://cujohan2.blogdetik.com/2013/09/19/ mizazeez-polygynous-blessings-musings-of-a-muslim-wife/.

9. Mattu and Maznavi, eds., *Love, InshAllah.*

10. I am especially grateful to my longtime mentor and friend Linda E. Thomas for her assistance in the development of my thinking about Muslim womanism and for introducing me to the works of Dwight Conquergood and D. Soyini Madison and the potential of dialogical performance as a tool of critical ethnography. Her most significant published work for this project is "Womanist Theology, Epistemology, and a New Anthropological Paradigm." I use dialogical performance in chapter 2 to create conversations among subjects.

11. Dixon, *We Want for Our Sisters What We Want for Ourselves,* 269.

12. Karimah, e-mail conversation with author, April 23, 2003.

13. Simmons, "Muslim Women's Experience as a Basis for Theological Interpretation of Islam," 204.

14. Wadud, "The Spirited Voices of Muslim Women in Islamic Reform Movements."

15. Imam Ronald Shaheed, e-mail communication with author, July 7, 2014. Unlike several earlier exchanges, in this one Imam Shaheed shared his dismay with my use of the term "polygyny" to describe the focus of this book. He wrote that "polygyny, literally means, 'many or plural vaginas.' For me, it makes the concept of plural marriages secular and disrespects Islam's 1,400+ year history of uplifting the family and community following the revelation of G'd's word to Prophet Muhammad, the Qur'an." While we agreed to disagree on this and other points, his concern offers additional evidence for the various approaches with which Muslims enter this discussion.

16. Friedman's writings on religious totalitarianism have influenced my theorizing on the subject; "Foreign Affairs." If not the only essay, Waugh and Wannas's is one of the few essays to connect womanist thought to Muslim women and to claim that any form of feminism is at least likely to meet the needs of Muslim women in the United States; "The Rise of a Womanist Movement among Muslim Immigrant Women in Alberta, Canada."

17. Villalon, "Passage to Citizenship and the Nuances of Agency," 552.

18. Wadud says that "waging war with Christian womanist scholars who considered their religious orientation as 'the' religious orientation for womanism" helped to usher her into the feminist camp. Perhaps Muslim womanism will provide her with the motivation to try again; Wadud, interview with author, June 2, 2014. It may come as no surprise that Western feminist scholarship continues to draw attention to and combat studies that represent women solely from a male perspective. For a detailed account of feminism and patriarchy from the perspective of an African American Muslim scholar,

see Simmons, "Muslim Women's Experience as a Basis for Theological Interpretation of Islam."

19. Mahmood, "Feminist Theory, Embodiment, and the Docile Agent," 203.

20. Villalon, "Passage to Citizenship and the Nuances of Agency," 553. Italics mine.

21. Ibid.

22. I distinguish American womanism, as initially espoused by African American Christian scholars, from Africana womanism. For discussion of the latter, see Hudson-Weems, *Africana Womanism*.

23. I incorporate language that Tuppurainen uses to describe feminism; "Challenges Faced by Muslim Women," 11.

24. Ibid., 164. Arndt, "African Gender Trouble and African Womanism," 711.

25. I prefer the term "Muslim feminism" to "Islamic feminism." For me, the latter suggests validation from within divine revelation or a reference to an act, practice, tradition, or structure maintained or suggested by or reflective of the teachings of Islamic authoritative sources. At least one scholar, Jawad, claims the mantle of Muslim feminism for Wadud's hermeneutic; Jawad, "Muslim Feminism."

26. My conceptualization of parallel structures is drawn from the theoretical contributions of Riggs, a first-generation womanist, in her book *Awake, Arise, and Act*.

27. These disparities, too, constitute a topic worthy of examination, but it exceeds the scope of this work.

28. In CNN, "Bush Calls for Ban on Same-Sex Marriages."

29. National Conference of State Legislatures, "Same-Sex Marriage Laws."

30. Pew Research Center and Kohut, *Muslim Americans*, 22.

31. Aisha, in Dettner, "Britain's Part-Time Wives."

32. Thomas, "Womanist Theology, Epistemology, and a New Anthropological Paradigm."

Chapter 2. Agency and Authority in Polygyny

1. Karimah, interviews with author, November 2005.

2. Ibid.

3. Ibid.

4. In addition to copies of some of Wadud's lectures and unpublished works, I rely on her books *Qur'an and Woman* and *Inside the Gender Jihad*.

5. Villalon, "Passage to Citizenship and the Nuances of Agency," 553.

6. McNay, *Gender and Agency*, 5.

7. See, for example, Scott, *Gender and the Politics of History* and "Gender." Also see Norton, *Founding Mothers and Fathers*.

8. Norton articulates a similar trajectory in her decision to transition to gender history from her writing of women's history; "Historically Speaking."

9. For a fuller discussion of harm in the practice, see Calder and Beaman, *Polygamy's Rights and Wrongs*.

10. For this framework I draw from the conceptualization of Conquergood, "Performing as a Moral Act." Like other aspects of performance studies, dialogue embodies culture. In this case, culture represents social and religious ideas, traditions, and institutions and their impacts on African American Muslims as they make sense of their lived realities.

11. My subjects understood that our informal conversations before and after our formal interviews potentially would contribute details for this project.

12. As I indicate in the preface, the dialogical performance is a new way of telling this story of polygyny, one that asks readers to suspend their sense of reality so that, in Madison's words, "coparticipatory performances can be produced"; *Critical Ethnography*, 56.

13. Conquergood, "Performing as a Moral Act," 3.

14. Fine, "Dis-Stance and Other Stances," 19.

15. Madison, *Critical Ethnography*, 192.

16. Ibid., 180.

17. Walker, *In Search of Our Mothers' Gardens*, ix; Cannon, "Response," 96. It is a common practice in womanist scholarship to use roundtables as a tool to add depth, detail, and diverse perspectives to a single issue or question. An example is the *Journal of Feminist Studies in Religion*'s Roundtable Discussion. This 2006 series of essays that responded to Monica Coleman's reflection "Must I Be Womanist?" led to Coleman's edited volume *Ain't I a Womanist Too?* Drawing from the work of Czarniawska in *Narrating the Organization*, I theorize about enacted narrative in terms of performance as a tool to imagine the world of women living polygyny as they see it; Czarniawska, "The Uses of Narrative in Organization Research."

18. I make exceptions to the practice of using pseudonyms in chapters 4–6 when I incorporate the actual names of women whose identities were made public elsewhere.

19. Hall, "The Spectacle of the Other."

20. Page, "Dialogical Principles of Interactive Learning in the Ethnographic Relationship," 164.

21. Hill Collins, "What's in a Name," 9.

22. Rosen, "Breakfast at Spiro's." I credit Czarniawska for pointing me in Rosen's direction with the critique of Rosen's essay that she offers in "Uses of Narrative in Organization Research," 26.

23. Mujerista theology is but one example. See Isasi-Dias, *En la Lucha/In the Struggle*. M. Z. Rosaldo is especially helpful in his insistence on the significance of questions over data; "The Use and Abuse of Anthropology," 390.

24. Isasi-Dias, *En la Lucha/In the Struggle*, 64.

25. Participants in "social performances" are similarly unaware; Madison, *Critical Ethnography*, 171.

26. Ibid., 5.

27. Ibid., 236.

28. Ibid., 6.

29. I recognize that justice can be equally elusive in heterosexual monogamous unions.

30. El Fadl, foreword to *Inside the Gender Jihad*, ix.

31. R. Jones, "Polygyny in Islam," 1. She draws attention to the ways in which "religion is used as a justification for polygyny, but convenience and personal preference are actually indulged" (10). Similarly, Jawad notes, "Many times, a man remarries in his old age and chooses a young bride purely for the sake of feeling younger. So, to legitimize the relationship, he will interpret the Qur'an as he wishes"; "Women and the Question of Polygamy in Islam," 187.

32. Shaikh, "A Tafsir of Praxis," 68.

33. Ibid., 70.

34. Madison, *Critical Ethnography*, 236.

35. Examples include Tevin Campbell's song "Can We Talk?" and a Florida Marriage Preparation series segment titled "Can We Talk? Improving Couples' Communication."

36. Caitlin Gunn, a budding scholar, former religious studies major at Beloit College, and now graduate student, inspired me to consider self-identity through the use of language as a womanist act.

37. Mir-Hosseini, "Towards Gender Equality," 23.

38. Soroush, "The Beauty of Justice," 8.

39. Wadud, *Inside the Gender Jihad*, 191.

40. Bucholtz and Hall, "Language and Identity," 372.

41. While Sawdah is the youngest of my informants, another interviewee complained about the woman her husband is considering as a second wife: a twenty-one-year-old virgin.

42. Bennion, *Polygamy in Primetime*, 146–47.

43. Bucholtz and Hall, "Language and Identity," 370.

44. This is a point I first articulated in Majeed, "Wadud and the Promotion of Experience as Authority," 59.

45. Wadud, *Inside the Gender Jihad*, 5.

46. Wadud, "Islamic Authority."

47. Ibid.

48. Gross, *Feminism and Religion*, 109.

49. Piela, "Claiming Religious Authority," 132.

50. Wadud, unpublished essays in author's possession.

51. In chapter 6 of this volume I conclude with consideration of the creative dimensions of agency as a means of change for the better.

52. Wadud, interview with author, June 2, 2014. Author's notes from worship attendance.

53. Haredy, "Polygamy: Not a Sixth Pillar of Islam!" In this online question-and-answer report, the author uses *hadith* to suggest the validity of regarding multiple-wife marriage as a contextual issue, with its legality to be assessed as obligatory or recommended as permissible, forbidden, or prohibited.

54. An example of a rare communal response to an otherwise private issue involved members of the dialogue. In 2014 the financial stress on Abdul Hameed and his family led others concerned to initiate a nationwide fund-raising effort. The role of polygyny in Abdul Hameed's financial status remains uncertain.

55. Madison, *Critical Ethnography*, 188.

56. At the time of his death, Mohammed was, according to a probate court decision, the husband of two wives. I return to this issue in chapter 6.

57. Shaheed, e-mail conversation with author, December 3, 2002.

Chapter 3. Religious and Experiential Prescriptions

1. Lack of notification is a common complaint of women living polygyny, and the stage at which husbands inform their wives of pending or potential marriages varies. Far from representing the sentiments of one woman, the epigraph that opens this chapter broadly reflects the experience of many of my subjects.

2. Reports of spousal abuse perpetrated by Warren Jeffs, the president of the Fundamentalist Church of Jesus Christ of Latter-Day Saints, and the lengthy legal battles some Malaysian Muslim women have endured to obtain divorces are but two of the numerous examples of the subjugation of women in multiple-wife marriages.

3. These sites also pivot between public and private spaces, as do Muslim women, in situations that characterize African American Muslims differently from the larger African American community. Jawad Syed suggests that Muslim societies (and I would add communities) may be more intentional in their efforts to divide the world or society into gender-segregated spheres using the public-private dichotomy; Syed, "Historical Perspective on Islamic Modesty," 150.

4. Yilmaz, "The Challenge of Post-Modern Legality," 343. Unlike the legal system in the United Kingdom, civil law in the United States does not recognize plural marriages contracted anywhere, even if valid in their countries of origin; Anika Liversage, e-mail conversation with author, December 20–22, 2011. Katharine Charsley and Anika Liversage are coauthors of "Transforming Polygamy."

5. Arat, *Patriarchal Paradox*, 18.

6. Syed, "Historical Perspective on Islamic Modesty," 151. For an interesting though somewhat dated discussion of the gendered application of moral imperatives, see Friedl, "Islam and Tribal Women in a Village in Iran."

7. Though indebted to feminist thought, Barlas is one Muslim scholar who does not identify as a feminist, preferring instead to say, "I am a believer" until "there is greater clarity within the Muslim community about what feminism is"; Barlas, "Interview with Asma Barlas." See also Barlas's "Un-Reading Patriarchal Interpretations" and *Believing Women in Islam* as well as Wadud, *Qur'an and Woman*. Some Muslim scholars contend that Islam was appropriated by patriarchy in the years following the death of the Prophet Muhammad, when misogyny was reasserted; Al-Hibri, "Study in Islamic

Herstory." A notable dissenter, Fatima Mernissi contends that Islam is inherently patriarchal; *Beyond the Veil*.

8. Barlas, *Believing Women in Islam*, 14. Hidayatullah cautions against approaching the Qur'an as a text whose passages never appear to provide obstacles to justice for women; *Feminist Edges of the Qur'an*.

9. I contextualize Bartky's reading of Foucault to specifically address polygyny; Bartky, "Foucault, Femininity, and the Modernization of Patriarchal Power." Similarly, in *Qur'an and Woman*, Wadud points to the importance of considering "*what* the Qur'an says, *how* it says it, what is said *about* the Qur'an, and *who* is doing the saying" as well as "what is left *unsaid*"; xiii, italics in the original.

10. Wadud, "Islam beyond Patriarchy," 101.

11. Wadud, *Qur'an and Woman*, 3. For more on the dynamics of relationships, see Carling, "The Human Dynamics of Migrant Transnationalism."

12. Walby, *Theorizing Patriarchy*.

13. I submit that monogamous marriage also can be driven by patriarchy.

14. Deller Ross, *Women's Human Rights*, 515.

15. Al-Krenawi, "Family Therapy with a Multiparental/Multispousal Family," 67–68.

16. Mitchell, "Power-Control Theory," 11.

17. I use the term "imagined community" with caution, as I recognize that it has come to have a very specific meaning within the study of nationalism. For one of the standard texts on this issue, see Anderson, *Imagined Communities*, which first appeared in 1983. Most proponents of polygyny in my study describe African Americans as "orphans" because of our ancestors' forced separation from land (their African homelands), culture, and identity and because the concept of family did not exist legally for blacks during the slave trade that began in the seventeenth century. In chapter 5 I return to a discussion of the use of "orphans" to characterize African Americans.

18. Rahman, "A Survey of Modernization of Muslim Family Law," 451.

19. Chapman coined the term "man-sharing" as the most accurate characterization of what she observed in African American male-female relationships.

20. Ditz defines the concept as "authority relations in which heads, and not others within households, have the formal right to make final decisions about internal matters"; "Ownership and Obligation," 236. The contextualization of household patriarchy within African American mosques means that women do have freedom to speak for themselves within the mosque and to the larger African American community.

21. Dixon bases her remarks on research conducted among black families in three religious groups in Georgia—African American Muslims, African Hebrew Israelites, and members of the Ausar Auset Society—for her book *We Want for Our Sisters What We Want for Ourselves*.

22. Welchman, ed., *Women's Rights and Islamic Family Law*. Opposition to Law No. 44 of Egypt's 1979 reform effort led to amendments in 1985 that required a woman to establish "material or mental injury" in order to pursue a divorce if her husband took

another wife; Fawzy, "Personal Status Law in Egypt," 38; Zaki, "New Marriage Contract in Egypt." By 2009, legal and religious quarters were embroiled in controversy over the equality of polygyny after the secretary general of the People's Democratic Party sued against demands for the right of women to marry multiple husbands. The official alleged that such demands are both blasphemous and violate the Egyptian criminal code; Al-Baik, "Polyandry Call Is 'Akin To Blasphemy.'"

23. Rashidah, interview with author, July 15, 2005. Ditz explores household organization in the eighteenth century; "Ownership and Obligation."

24. Dixon, *African American Relationships, Marriages, and Families,* 14.

25. Pinderhughes promotes this argument in "African American Marriage in the 20th Century," 270.

26. Kindregan, "Religion, Polygamy, and Non-Traditional Families," 28.

27. Dixon, *African American Relationships, Marriages, and Families,* 15–16.

28. The Morrill Act, passed by Congress in 1862, and the Edmunds Act, enacted in 1882, are sometimes characterized by legal theorists as "morals-based" legislation; Bozzuti, "The Constitutionality of Polygamy Prohibitions after *Lawrence v. Texas.*"

29. Polygyny became an official tenet of the Mormon Church in 1852 and was endorsed by the church for thirty-eight years, until 1890.

30. McClintock, *The Old North Trail,* 188. I am especially indebted to two colleagues and historians who read early drafts of this manuscript: Beatrice McKenzie for guidance on nineteenth-century Indian history and Linda Sturtz for her comments on slavery in the United States.

31. J. Moore, "The Developmental Cycle of Cheyenne Polygyny," 311.

32. Gilles, "Polygamy in Comanche Country," 286.

33. Ibid., 288.

34. See, for example, Butler, "Tennessee Heritage."

35. J. Moore, "The Developmental Cycle of Cheyenne Polygyny," 311.

36. Gibbs and Campbell, "Practicing Polygyny in Black America," 151.

37. Quraishi and Syeed-Miller, "No Altars," 179.

38. Ibid.

39. Estin, "Unofficial Family Law," 449.

40. Quraishi and Syeed-Miller, "No Altars," 181.

41. The term *nikah* has dual meanings for many Muslims. In addition to its use here in reference to written contracts, some Muslims use it in reference to the marriage ceremony.

42. In Britain, Muslims can apply to a Sharia Council to obtain an Islamic divorce.

43. S. Falk Moore, "Law and Social Change," 7.

44. Qur'an 2:187.

45. Barringer Gordon, "A War of Words," 749.

46. As was confirmed during a 2008 hearing of the Senate Judiciary Committee, laws concerning marriage are usually reserved to the states. Multiple-spouse marriages

are illegal in each of the fifty states, though legislation involving sex-same marriage may place in question the finality of legal prohibitions against polygamy.

47. The interpretations my informants gave include these: Polygyny is a man's right; polygyny is a man's right and permitted today; polygyny is a man's right and permitted today, even if it contradicts civil law because religious law supersedes civil law; polygyny is permitted only if the prescribed conditions are met; polygyny is permitted only if the described conditions are met even where the practice contradicts civil law, with the understanding that "orphan" refers to African Americans; polygyny is permitted only if the prescribed conditions are met and the practice is consistent with civil law; and polygyny is not permitted.

48. Sahih Bukhari, vol. 4, Book 53, Hadith No. 342, http://www.sahih-bukhari.com/Pages/Bukhari_4_53.php. A note on usage: The plural of *hadith* is *ahadith*. I have chosen to use a single spelling for all references for the purpose of clarity.

49. Ahmad Hasan, trans., "Marriage (Kitab Al-Nikah)" in *Partial Translation of Sunan Abu-Dawud*.

50. Mudzakir, "The Indonesian Muslim Women's Movement and the Issue of Polygamy," 175. Kennard poses a similar argument; "From Wives of the Prophets to Mothers of the Believers," 53. In "The Pleasure of Our Text," Barlas asserts that "every reading of the Qur'an—even in Arabic—is a function of who reads it, how, and in what contexts."

51. K. Mohammed, "Assessing English Translations of the Qur'an," 58.

52. Sells, *Approaching the Quran*, 22.

53. Blankship, "Murshid al-Qari," 3.

54. Electronic engagement with the Qur'an—via computers, readers, and other devices—is slowly increasing among African American Muslims, especially those who attend communal services during working hours. Nevertheless, holding a bound copy of the Qur'an in one's hand continues to be the preferred practice.

55. Barlas, "The Pleasure of Our Text," italics in the original.

56. Ahmed, *Women and Gender in Islam*, 45; Wadud, *Inside the Gender Jihad*, 133. In the advent of technological advancements such as DNA testing, paternity may soon dissolve as a rationale.

57. Esposito, *Women in Muslim Family Law*, 12. In the 1930s, the region that had encompassed pre-Islamic Arabia became known as the Kingdom of Saudi Arabia under the leadership of King Abdul Aziz Ibn Saud. Today, Saudi Arabia is the largest Arab nation in the Middle East.

58. The business success of Khadijah, the first wife of the Prophet, is a clear indication that some early female Muslims also were financially independent.

59. Hidayatullah, *Feminist Edges of the Qur'an*, 101.

60. In doing so, they read certainty into this verse as a parallel to al-Baqarah 2:117, where the Qur'an states, "When He [Allah] decreeth a matter, He saith to it: 'Be,' and it is.'"

61. "Hadith." *Authentic Tauheed*, n.d., http://www.authentictauheed.com/p/hadith.html (accessed January 27, 2012).

62. The expectation of an ever-present surplus of women is often used to support polygyny as a remedy for the "natural instincts" of men; Mission Islam, "Polygyny Not Polygamy."

63. Jameelah Jones, "Preface: First Edition."

64. Philips and Jones, *Polygamy in Islaam*, 44.

65. I will return to family law matters and their implications for the African American Muslim practice of husband-sharing in chapter 4.

66. Tuwaijri, publisher's note, 7.

67. Philips and Jones, *Polygamy in Islaam*, is available at http://www.islamicbulletin. org/free_downloads/women/polygamy_in_islam.pdf.

68. Philips, "Preface: Third Edition," 9.

69. In Philips, "Polygamy in Islam with Dr. Bilal Philips."

70. Ibid.

71. Ibid.

72. Green, "The Pedagogy of Polygyny." I met Chanda Green on an online listserv, and she agreed to be interviewed. Where I incorporate information she provided as part of a series of interviews and under her Muslim name, her anonymity is retained by the use of a pseudonym.

73. Ibid., 10.

74. Ibid., 140.

75. Ibid., 38. Badawi, *Polygamy in Islamic Law*.

76. Sahih Bukhari, vol. 7, Book 62 (Wedlock, Marriage), Hadith No. 13A, http://sahihbukharihadithcollection.com/book-62-wedlock-marriage-nikah/5816-sahih-bukhari-volume-007-book-062-hadith-number-013a.html (accessed January 31, 2013).

77. See, for example, Yuksel, al-Shaiban, and Schulte-Nafeh, trans., *Quran*.

78. Tucker, *Women, Family, and Gender in Islamic Law*, 68.

79. Rida, "Mohammad Rashid Rida on Muhammad Abdul on Polygamy." Interestingly, Mark Foster Network's *Muhammad Abduh: Wikibook* offers a slightly different assessment in its contention that Abduh opposed polygamy.

80. Yuksel, al-Shaiban, and Schulte-Nafeh, *Quran*, 5. The work opens with congratulatory comments from thirteen scholars including Wadud; 2.

81. Majeed, "Muslim Marriage," 47. Domination in this regard may emerge within a literal or symbolic context. That said, these African American women use polygyny to push back against African American Muslim males who prefer non-Muslim or non–African American Muslim spouses, married African American Muslim women who treat single Muslim women with suspicion and contempt, and non–African Americans who have attempted to eradicate the African American culture.

82. Rabi'a, e-mail conversation with author, July 30, 2014.

83. Majeed, "Muslim Marriage," 46.

84. Wadud, remarks delivered during "Speakers and Leaders: Shaping and Contest-

ing Authority," Inaugural Conference on Islam in America, September 23, 2011, DePaul University, Chicago.

85. In Bradley Hagerty, "Philly's Black Muslims Increasingly Turn to Polygamy."

86. Yilmaz, "The Challenge of Post-Modern Legality and Muslim Legal Pluralism in England," 349.

87. Qaedah, e-mail conversation with author, July 16, 2011.

88. In Heliprin, "Hatch Joins Leavitt in Game of Twister over Polygamy Issues."

89. Pinderhughes considers slavery's instigation of black maleness in her essay "African American Marriage in the 20th Century."

90. Glenn, "Identity Crisis," 5.

91. K. Ali, *Sexual Ethics in Islam*, 55.

Chapter 4. Legalities and Emotional Well-Being

1. Divorces among Muslims in the United States and Canada have increased substantially in the past twenty-five years, according to findings of a four-year study conducted by the Institute for Social Policy and Understanding (ISPU). The study also found that one in seven American Muslim women identified polygyny as the major reason for the end of their marriages; Macfarlane, *Understanding Trends in American Muslim Divorce and Marriage*, 5, 23.

2. Martha, interview with author, July 10, 2012. Because Martha pursued the dissolution of her marriage as a *khul* (divorce initiated by a wife), she would be required to return any portion of her *mahr* already received under some schools of Islamic jurisprudence in return for her release from the marriage. That a husband has not fulfilled his *mahr* obligations is not an uncommon reality for some Muslim women regardless of their form of marriage. Nevertheless, securing a divorce in the absence of an Islamic court or arbitration system can be a far less involved procedure than Muslims face in Muslim-minority environments or in Muslim-minority regions where religious courts handle personal status matters. In Muslim-majority countries, a woman may take her divorce request to a family court judge who may decide in her favor even without her husband's consent.

3. When they married, neither Rashidah nor Medinah negotiated any financial compensation (*mahr*, life insurance policy, will, and so forth) to protect them in case of divorce or the death of their husband.

4. This line of reasoning does not overlook the thousands of divorced American Muslim and other women for whom the justice system in the United States has not brought justice.

5. The ISPU report recommends that religious and community leaders in North American mosques discourage the use of the *nikah* for polygyny; Macfarlane, *Understanding Trends in American Muslim Divorce and Marriage*, 39.

6. Martha's state is one of fifteen U.S. states where primary jurisdiction over family law matters resides with district courts.

7. I am appreciative of Aminah McCloud and her insistence that an exploration of polygyny is wholly inadequate without reference to the physical and mental landscapes women living polygyny traverse. I briefly explore the issue in this chapter and in chapter 6.

8. As indicated in chapter 2, I distinguish the movement whose architect and leader was Elijah Muhammad until his son W. D. Mohammed succeeded him in 1975 from the contemporary organization of the same name headed by Louis Farrakhan, who recovered the Nation of Islam (NOI) name for his group.

9. By "legal wife" I mean Clara Muhammad was the only woman whose marriage to Elijah Muhammad was registered with civil authorities. I recognize that women who marry religiously only assert the legality of their unions by the highest authority there is: Allah.

10. Quraishi and Syeed-Miller, "No Altars," 183; El Fadl, *Speaking in God's Name*.

11. Bennion, *Polygamy in Primetime*.

12. Esposito, *Islam*, 75.

13. Although some scholars who read early drafts of this chapter disagreed with the word selection, I use *tafsir* and "commentary" interchangeably when speaking of Imam Mohammed's interpretation on the permissibility and warnings the Qur'an gives on multiple-wife marriage. I base my choice on a meaning of *tafsir* as the science of interpretation that "lifts the curtain" of or "makes clear" the meaning of the Qur'an and the insistence of the religious leaders in the association of Imam Mohammed that these definitions most accurately reflect the outcome of his interpretations. I also recognize that *tafsir* (*tafaseer*) are written and open for comment from other scholars. Most of Imam Mohammed's teachings on polygyny are audio or video recordings of lectures to his association. I am among the first to place them in writing and make them available for scholarly analysis.

14. Most American Muslims rarely use such labels, preferring instead to identify themselves only as Muslims.

15. In K. Moore, *Unfamiliar Abode*, inside front jacket.

16. Ibid., 14.

17. An-Na'im, *Islam and the Secular State*, 35. Ghana, a country Malcolm X visited on behalf of Elijah Muhammad in 1959, also considered banning polygyny after that nation gained independence in 1957; *Afro-American*, "Ghana Tells Plans to Outlaw Polygamy."

18. K. Moore, *Unfamiliar Abode*, 24.

19. Ibid., 130.

20. Mir-Hosseini, "Islamic Law and Feminism," 37.

21. The respect afforded Muhammad and the invitation extended to him to perform *ummrah* helped legitimate the NOI as a Muslim organization at a time when most global Muslims discounted the NOI leader and his followers.

22. This is based on an English translation of the 2004 Moroccan Family Code (Moudawana) provided by Global Rights.

23. Polygyny has been a "bar" to U.S. immigration since 1891. By bar, I mean the Immigration and Naturalization Act (INA) stipulates that multiple-wife marriage is grounds for inadmissibility for the purpose of immigration. Women may not immigrate to the United States as co-wives, nor may men with multiple spouses even if some of the wives reside outside of the country. Even so, as Smearman has observed, "the polygamy ground of inadmissibility (the polygamy bar)" points to the gender inequality inherent in multiple-wife marriage; Smearman, "Second Wives' Club," 383, 388. Smearman in this article gives in-depth consideration to multiple-wife marriage and immigration law. Anecdotal evidence indicates that some men and women living polygyny have successfully gained entrance to the United States.

24. In Kern, "Britain," http://www.gatestoneinstitute.org/3234/muslim-polygamists-welfare-benefits.

25. Section 293 of the Criminal Code of Canada, 2011 BCSC 1588. While hearing affidavits about the practice of polygyny in other regions, the court was presented evidence that a minority of Muslims in the United States may be living in polygyny even though multiple-wife marriage is illegal throughout North America.

26. I was among a number of scholars invited to provide affidavits on multiple-wife marriage.

27. Muhammad-Ali, *Evolution of the Nation*, 57.

28. In appendix C and under the subhead "Elijah Muhammad's Concubines," Clegg identifies seven women who gave birth to thirteen children—eight girls and five boys—between 1960 and 1967; *Original Man*, 453. Some of my sources said they believe Elijah Muhammad was "married" to at least nine women other than Clara Muhammad and fathered as many as fifteen children in addition to the eight born to Clara.

29. Laila Muhammad, interview with author, June 22, 2012.

30. This is the subtitle of a recent book on the teachings of the NOI leader by one of his followers; P. Muhammad, *Messenger Elijah Muhammad*.

31. Farrakhan, "Rising above Emotion into the Thinking of God." In chapter 6 of the present volume, Rabi'a, whose family dynamics offer a model of living polygyny successfully, likewise points to the importance of developing a different, more divinely focused sight.

32. Muhammad-Ali, *Evolution of the Nation*, 57–58.

33. Laila Muhammad, interview with author, June 22, 2012. I did not see nor do I possess copies of the letters. My claim about Mohammed's characterization of his father's family relations is based on this interview, though conversations with some of his officials who say Elijah Muhammad practiced polygyny add further weight to the possibility.

34. Ibid.

35. One critic of the actions of Elijah Muhammad is quick to distinguish his behavior from that of the Prophet Muhammad. The Qur'anic injunction directs men to marry and assume responsibility for offspring. To Janice, Elijah's lack of public validation of these relationships as marriages during his lifetime leads her to conclude that

he left behind "a bunch of baby-mamas," which the Prophet did not; Janice, interview with the author, August 2, 2012.

36. E. Muhammad, *Message to the Blackman*, 228. This book was originally published in 1965.

37. My research did not uncover any physical health issues related to the practice of polygyny among African American Muslims. Anecdotal reports do, however, mention a number of health professionals who treat African American and other Muslim women living polygyny for clinometer, a precursor to HIV, and for STDs.

38. Clegg, *Original Man*, 185–86.

39. In Farrakhan, "What Malcolm Did Not Tell You!!!" Part 2.

40. In Farrakhan, "What Malcolm Did Not Tell You!!!" Part 1.

41. Clegg, e-mail message to author, June 21, 2012. Evanzz corroborates Clegg's slightly earlier analysis of their subject's private life. In addition to research they conducted independently, both authors base their claims about the personal side of Muhammad on files obtained from the Federal Bureau of Investigation through the Freedom of Information Act and from Malcolm X and Alex Haley's *Autobiography of Malcolm X*.

42. Clegg, e-mail to author, June 21, 2012.

43. Also known as Hebrew Israelites, the group was organized by Chicagoan Ben Ammi Ben Israel (formerly Ben Carter) and was officially recognized by Israel in 2003. For some Black Hebrew women, polygyny permits self-development, and women may participate in the selection of their husbands' additional wives. "A woman can do everything here but be a man, there are no limits," said one. "We made the decision together about the other wife. If I'm separated because of menstrual activity, somebody has to care for him. Why not someone who's a part of the family? This life style affords me time for self-development. I don't have to be all things for everyone"; in Ferhinard, "Polygamy among the Blackamerikkan Jews Who Migrated to Israel."

44. Gardell, *In the Name of Elijah Muhammad*, 76. Gardell's work was one of three biographies to focus exclusively or partially on Elijah Muhammad in the 1990s.

45. Clegg suggests that such early transitions to mainstream Islamic rituals represented a response to pressure from Sunni and other "orthodox" Muslims and to Elijah Muhammad's desire to legitimate his movement in the eyes of global Muslims; "Message from the Wilderness of North America."

46. Malcolm X and Haley, *Autobiography of Malcolm X*, 345.

47. Frantz and Pulley, "Harlem Church Is Outpost of Empire." Prior to organizing the International Peace Mission movement in the 1930s, Father Divine was known by two other names: George Baker and the Reverend Major Jealous Divine. "The Marriage of Father and Mother Divine" video produced by the Father Divine Project depicts the community's celebration of what would have been the fiftieth anniversary of his marriage to Mother Divine (the former Edna Rose Ritchings). Mother Divine appears in the 1996 video. Bishop Charles Emmanuel Grace, known to his followers as Sweet Daddy

Grace, sowed an entrepreneurial spirit into the souls of his members with charismatic preaching. Followers sold toothpaste and other products much as Elijah Muhammad's NOI members would later peddle bean pies. Grace promised black people salvation and upward mobility; followers accepted his self-proclaimed divinity. Daddy Grace died in 1960. A YouTube video promotes the accomplishments of both Father Divine and Daddy Grace; "Father Divine and Daddy Grace," video posted to YouTube by Ashli Edwards, November 19, 2013, https://www.youtube.com/watch?v=6Iwgzza01wA.

48. Faheem Shuaibe, interview with author, June 19, 2012.

49. Laila Muhammad, interview with author, June 22, 2012. She contends that two of her uncles took multiple wives after her father, W. D. Mohammed, assumed the leadership of the NOI in 1975.

50. Farrakhan, "What Malcolm Did Not Tell You!!!" Parts 1 and 2.

51. Mohammed recalled this conversation with his mother during our interview, November 13, 1997.

52. Elizabeth, written response to survey, September 5, 2003.

53. Karimah, interview with author, February 10, 2005.

54. Al-Alawi et al., *Guide to Shariah Law and Islamist Ideology in Western Europe.*

55. Zuhara, interview with author, July 12, 2012.

Chapter 5. Imam Mohammed's Commentary on Polygyny

1. I am grateful to a former research assistant, Caitlin Gunn, for her assistance with Lamisha's interview of June 22, 2012.

2. K. Ali, "Polygyny," 505.

3. Mohammed (primary sources), "Excerpts from Imam Mohammed's Talk to Sisters Only Meeting in Detroit in 1995."

4. Imam Mohammed's approval of this marriage demonstrated, in my view, that he attached a legal significance to the religious ceremony even though it was not recognized as a civil marriage by law. That is, for him, when G'd has made an act permissible, religious law may supersede secular law even though those involved must be prepared to address any civil consequences. Granted, Mohammed was neither a civil judge nor an official with legal authority, but it was not uncommon for his followers to attribute such weight to his teachings.

5. This is a common approach exhibited by at least two of my sources who successfully live polygyny, including Lamisha, whose epigraph begins this chapter.

6. Imam Mohammad and Khadijah Siddeeq were married in 2004. Controversy surrounding her legal status at the time of his death is explored in Chapter 6. To many observers, the increased acceptance of same-sex marriage has set up polygyny to be "the next marriage fight." See, for example, Skojec, "Polygamy: The Next Marriage Fight," and Kennan, "Legalize Polygamy! No, I'm Kidding."

7. Givens, "Mormons Change References to Blacks, Polygamy."

8. The *Muslim Journal*, the weekly newspaper associated with the ministry of Imam Mohammed, is available electronically at http://muslimjournal.net/.

9. Shachar has examined the issue of public accommodation and recognition of family law matters in "Privatizing Diversity."

10. Bano, "In Pursuit of Religious and Legal Diversity," 300.

11. Martha, interviews with author, June 10, 2005–June 10, 2012. I devote more space to Martha's experience for two key reasons. One, her journey symbolizes what most of my respondents say they endured. Two, Martha was extremely open with me, sharing details of her divorce proceedings as well as some of the materials that were executed on her behalf. Her experiences shed further light on the realities of my subjects.

12. In the United States, couples may solemnize their marriages through civil or religious ceremonies after they have obtained licenses. Following a ceremony, the license must be filed with the clerk of the relevant county or state.

13. Martha, Rashidah, and Medinah entered marriages in a state that does not recognize common-law unions other than those that are valid in another state. Thus, only Martha's marital rights would be recognized in court unless Rashidah or Medinah could present other acceptable documents, such as a valid will.

14. Some Americans obtain civil or religious marriages and/or enter into publicly witnessed covenants that declare their unions to their communities.

15. The requirements for a civil, or legal, divorce vary per state and, in some regions, per county in the United States.

16. Some African American Muslim women choose not to register their marriages with the state, even when the woman is the sole wife of her husband.

17. It is unclear whether Jewish tribunals have received or would consider cases of multiple-wife marriage. Jewish law does not prohibit multiple-wife marriage, though the practice is rare; Silberberg, "Does Jewish Law Forbid Polygamy?" At least one Orthodox Jew has established the *Orthodox Jewish Pro Polygamy Page*, http://emeslyaakov.com/.

18. In an address approximately in 1987, W. D. Mohammed recalled comments he made about polygyny "eight, nine, or ten years" earlier; "Al-Islam in America Today," tape recording.

19. Ibid.

20. Ibid.

21. W. D. Muhammad, *The Man and the WoMan in Islam*, 19. The author changed the spelling of his surname to Mohammed years after the publication of this pamphlet.

22. Ibid., 21.

23. Imam Ronald Shaheed, e-mail conversation with author, July 5, 2012.

24. See Majeed, "Clara Evans Muhammad: Pioneering Social Activism in the Original Nation of Islam" and "Clara Evans Muhammad."

25. My research suggests that few women are aware of or comfortable with exercising the full range of options open to them.

26. Geertz, *Interpretation of Cultures*, 52. I am indebted to Benjamin Berger for his astute analysis of Geertz as well as the inspiration to couch Mohammed's language within the matrix of a cultural system; Berger, "Polygamy and the Predicament of Contemporary Criminal Law."

27. For Mohammed, many of the considerations he raises go beyond polygyny and are important regardless of form of marriage.

28. As stated earlier, I use the actual names of women whose identities were made public in documents and proceedings.

29. The status of Khadijah Siddeeq-Mohammed at the time of her husband's death remains mired in controversy. Imam Shaheed, who reviewed a draft of this chapter, wrote that "regardless to what the Illinois probate court said, by the law of Qur'an, Imam Mohammed was divorced from (not married to) Shirley Muhammad and had not lived with her in a conjugal relationship for over 30 years"; Shaheed, e-mail conversation with author, July 5, 2012.

30. Omar, interview with author, February 19, 2006.

31. Omar, interview with author, July 4, 2012.

32. Mohammed, "Speeches to the Men and Women of the American Society of Muslims: Sisters Meeting," Chicago. Some could read his statement as a contradiction of his defense against those who questioned his marriage to a much younger woman.

33. Aadila, interview with author, March 22, 2006. In African American Muslim communities, it is a common practice for women and men to refer to each other as "sister" and "brother." For many, this is one way to retain modesty in interactions with members of the opposite sex to whom one is not related.

34. Ibid.

35. Mohammed, "Speeches to the Men and Women of the American Society of Muslims: Sisters Meeting," Detroit.

36. Serck, "Polygamy in Islam." The Muslim Council of Britain is a "Muslim umbrella body" for more than five hundred civic, charitable, and educational entities in the region; Muslim Council of Britain, http://www.mcb.org.uk/index.php.

37. Z. Hasan, "Polygamy, Slavery, and Qur'anic Sexual Ethics." Kecia Ali argues in her encyclopedia reference "Polygyny" that "premodern Muslim scholars took it for granted that polygamy was permissible"; 505. Many subsequent jurists and others treated the assumption as the norm.

38. K. Ali, *Sexual Ethics and Islam*, 156–57.

39. Mohammed, "Speeches to the Men and Women of the American Society of Muslims: Brothers Only Meeting," Atlanta.

40. Ibid. At least one polygynist Muslim husband has been convicted of bigamy in the United Kingdom. See Serck, "Polygamy in Islam." See also BBC News Berkshire, "Bigamy Slough Councillor Pervez Choudhry Must Wear Tag."

41. Omar, interview with author, February 9, 2006.

42. Naeema, interview with author, October 19, 2006.

43. Ibid.

Chapter 6. Mental Health and Living Polygyny

1. This story represents those told to me in separate interviews by two women who were raised in a small community. I have chosen to combine them and alter some details to protect their privacy.

2. Elbedour et al., "The Effect of Polygamous Marital Structure on Behavioral, Emotional, and Academic Adjustment in Children," 268.

3. Ibid.

4. Interviews with the children of informants living polygyny were conducted, for the most part, during 2003–2008, a period in which the national economy was more stable. What impact the higher rates of unemployment and home foreclosures may have had on the behavior of children raised in nontraditional family structures like polygyny is an interesting research question.

5. I have chosen not to reveal the identity of one professional because her current client base includes women living polygyny.

6. Marsha, interview with author, August 11, 2003.

7. I use the first name of this resident imam and chaplain to distinguish him from his religious leader, W. D. Mohammed. In doing so I also recognize that it is not uncommon for some imams like Oliver to prefer going on a first-name basis to avoid formalities.

8. Imam Oliver Muhammad, interview with author, August 2, 2003. As noted earlier, it is acceptable for African American and other Muslims to refer to each other with the family labels of "brother" and "sister," and some refer to their imams as "brother imam."

9. Whether the stepfather formally adopts the children of his wife differs by family, as does the family names children use. If, for example, the biological father retains primary custody, his children often retain their father's name. The name issue can be especially confusing when the mother's last name differs from that of her husband and her children—a practice that is not uncommon.

10. Fatimah, interview with author, November 10, 2005.

11. Naim, interview with author, March 12, 2006.

12. Cook County, IL, Probate File 2008 P 6374 (microfilm PR090472806). Copy in possession of author. A transcript of the September 28, 2009, hearing before Cook County probate Judge Henry A. Budzinski was made available to members of the community of Imam Mohammed. The page on siddeeq.com from which I accessed the document is no longer active. Interestingly, a Henry Budzinski was the probate judge who ruled on the 1986 case involving the twenty-two children of Elijah Muhammad.

13. "Wedding of Imam W D Mohammed and Khadijah Siddeeq," video posted to YouTube by Muhammad Siddeeq, September 17, 2008, https://www.youtube.com/

watch?v=1vJtCZau-eM&index=18&list=PLgz448Jf3lv9GsMtXQRk_DCCFI7aKvYh3 (accessed February 23, 2009). In this clip the thinking of Imam Mohammed is evident as he began his marriage. Regardless of whether he was or was not becoming a polygynist, it is clear that he believed his marriage to Khadijah to be "lawful," as do all Muslims who exchange vows in solely religious ceremonies.

14. Gwen, interview with author, July 6, 2014.

15. According to his eldest child, Imam Mohammed created a will in 1987 that identified his then spouse, Shirley Mohammed (the spelling in court documents), as his wife. That will was never updated or registered; L. Muhammad, "The Estate of Warith Deen Mohammed," interview.

16. W. D. Mohammed, "Imam Mohammed Defends His Marriage in Jumah."

17. The "Khadijah Siddeeq Probate Court Hearing," as the case was publicized on her family's website, began in the downtown Chicago courtroom of Judge Budzinski on May 11, 2009. Regardless of whether court documents or her recollection best represent the events, the experiences of Khadijah Siddeeq-Mohammed offer the strongest evidence of the need for a paper trail to document religious marriages and divorces alike to best position women to protect themselves and their rights.

18. Shirley Mohammed testified that she had not lived with Imam Mohammed for at least twenty years. Witness testimony, "In the Matter of: Estate of Wallace Mohammed," September 28, 2009, 35. Document in author's possession acquired from "Family Siddeeq" site, http://siddeeq.com. Link no longer active.

19. In Islam, the officiant at a religious marriage ceremony is not required to be the resident imam or religious leader. For the vast majority of Muslims, however, the common expectation is that the officiant is male.

20. Nasif, interview with author, March 9, 2006.

21. Mohassan, interview with author, March 22, 2006.

22. Azra, written response to survey, August 29, 2009.

23. The term "marriage market" is taken from Daynes, "Plural Wives and the Nineteenth-Century Mormon Marriage System."

24. Some members of Imam Mohammed's community link a family's reliance on a wife's employment to the husband's fitness for polygyny. For example, during a stock-and options-trading workshop on August 2, 2014, at the Ephraim Bahar Cultural Center in Chicago, investment expert and presenter Fuad Akbar offered the following unsolicited advice regarding polygyny: "You can't have a second wife if you have her on welfare. The first qualification is that you are taking care of the first wife. That means you don't have her working. If you want a second wife, why is the first wife working?"

25. Daynes, "Plural Wives and the Nineteenth-Century Mormon Marriage System," 199.

26. Lamisha, interview with author, June 22, 2012.

27. Ibid.

28. Shaheed, e-mail conversation with author, July 9, 2012.

29. Naim, interview with author, March 12, 2006.

30. Ibid.

Afterword

1. Jacobs, *Gender, Power, and Persuasion*, 15.

2. See Gibson and Karim, *Women of the Nation*, 190.

3. Scholar and activist Kecia Ali, among other women, was asked and consented to officiate at a *nikah* in 2005. She records her reflections of the experience in "A Woman Officiates at a Muslim Wedding."

4. Rabi'a, e-mail conversation with author, July 17, 2014.

5. Rabi'a, interview with author, July 18, 2014.

6. Rabi'a, blog post used with permission. This is a private site for which either a link sent by the author or a password is needed. Those with access to the blog are Rabi'a's family and friends who are aware of her household arrangement.

7. In an earlier e-mail Rabi'a refers to Eckhart Tolle's use of the phrase "to distinguish between our life and the situations that come up in life (so we don't identify our essence with a temporary situation)"; Rabi'a, e-mail conversation with author, July 18, 2014.

8. Rabi'a, e-mail reflection shared with author, July 28, 2014.

9. Rabi'a, e-mail conversation with author, July 21, 2014.

10. Waleed, e-mail shared with author, July 17, 2014. Waleed gave permission for Rabi'a to share with me the e-mail he sent to the family of his fiancée on the eve of their wedding.

11. Hanan, e-mail message shared with author, July 18, 2014.

12. For a fuller discussion on marriage and divorce in the West, see Macfarlane, *Islamic Divorce in North America*.

Glossary

alhamdu-lillah. Appreciation, thankfulness, and/or praise for Allah.

Allah. The Qur'anic term for the one G'd worshipped by adherents of the three Abrahamic traditions—Judaism, Christianity, and Islam.

As Salaam Alaikum. Translated as "The peace of God be upon you"—a common greeting shared between Muslims.

asbab al-nuzul. The occasion of revelation.

athan. The Muslim call to prayer made fives times daily.

ayat. Plural of *aya*, meaning verses of the Qur'an.

deen. Religion.

du'a. Supplication.

exegesis. Interpretation.

fiqh. Jurisprudence.

G'd. An alternative spelling of "God" used by some Jews and Muslims as a reminder that human speech concerning the names for the genderless Creator are ambiguous and inadequate.

hadith. Reports of sayings and actions of the Prophet.

Hajj. The pilgrimage to Mecca every able-bodied Muslim is required to perform at least once.

halal. Permissible or religiously acceptable according to Islamic law, often used in reference to food or behavior.

haram. Not permissible, unhealthy, un-Islamic.

ijma. Consensus among Muslim scholars and/or the collective decision reached by Muslims.

ijtihad. Independent reasoning to arrive at a legal decision.

istikara **prayer**. A supplication for guidance in major decisions.

janazah. Funeral service.

jannah. Heaven or paradise.

jihad. Struggle against the lower inclinations of the self or the soul; also defense from external threats of injustice.

jum'ah. Friday congregational prayer service.

khalifah. Vicegerent of Allah on earth, responsible for advancement of justice.

khutbah. Lecture delivered as part of the Friday congregational prayer service.

khul. Wife-initiated divorce.

kufi. Skullcap worn by many Muslim men.

mahr **or dower**. Money, materials, or other agreed-upon gifts a groom promises to give to the bride as a condition of their marriage contract. Some or all of the dower may be delayed.

masjid **or mosque**. The physical building in which Islamic worship and religious education is conducted. Plural *masaasjid*.

Muslimah. Female Muslim.

mut'a. Union between a man (married or unmarried) and an unmarried woman for a specified period of time and involving an exact sum of money.

nikah. Marriage contract.

qiyas. Analogy.

Qur'an. The divine revelation given to humanity through the Prophet Muhammad. It is the highest authority in Islam.

revert. An individual who chooses Islam as a return to the religion of his or her ancestors.

salat. Required prayer offered at stated times five times daily.

Subhanahu Wa Ta'ala. Translated as "Glory to Him, the Exalted" or "All Praise Is Due to G'd" to glorify Allah when mentioning the name of the Creator; sometimes abbreviated "SWT" following the name of G'd in written form.

sunna. The path or life example of Prophet Muhammad transmitted through the Qur'an, his companions, and early leaders.

Sunni. A follower of the traditions or way (*sunna*) of the Prophet.

sura. Chapter of the Qur'an.

tafsir. Commentary of the Qur'an.

taleem. A lecture delivered by male and female speakers as the central focus of Sunday-afternoon programs among by African American Muslims.

taqwa. Piety, reverence for Allah, G'd-consciousness.

ulama. Scholars and theologians of Islam.

ummah. Community of believers, often used in reference to the global and/or a local Islamic community.

Ummrah. The lesser pilgrimage, in contrast to the Hajj.

wali. Derived from the Arabic word that means "protector" or "helper" and used to refer to the male relative, family friend, parental figure, or religious leader with (or sometimes through) whom a female Muslim contracts a marriage.

zina. Unlawful sexual relations between Muslim individuals who are not married to each other.

Bibliography

Primary Sources

*Pseudonyms used for confidentiality

*Aadila. Interview with author, March 22, 2006.

*Abdul Hameed. Interview with author, August 14 and 29, 2009.

Abdullah, Imam Yahya. Author notes from marital workshop, August 5, 2006, Charlotte, NC.

*Agnes. Interview with author, November 10, 2005.

*Ahmed. Interview with author, July 1–2, 2009.

Akbar, Fuad. Author's notes from Stock and Options Trading Workshop presented by Akbar, August 2, 2014.

Akbar, Imam Khalil. Interview with author, January 8, 2006, and July 29, 2009.

*Azra. Written response to survey, August 29, 2009.

*Amaya. Interview with author, October 17, 2006.

*Brenda. Interview with author, July 31, 2009.

Clegg, Claude Andrew III. E-mail conversation with author, June 20, 2012.

*Elizabeth. Written response to survey, September 5, 2003.

*Fatimah. Interview with author, June 1 and November 10, 2005.

*Gwen. Interview with author, July 6, 2014.

*Hanan. E-mail message to family shared with author, July 18, 2014.

Hasan, Imam A. K. Interview with author, June 6, 2012.

*Jamillah. Interview with author, August 14, 2009.

*Janice. Interview with author, August 2, 2012.

Karim, Jamillah. E-mail conversations with author, July 17, 18, 20, and 21, 2014; interviews with author, July 18 and 20, 2014.

*Karimah. E-mail conversation with author, April 23, 2003; interviews with author, February 10–November 16, 2005.

*Kubayah. Interview with author, August 12, 2009.

*Lamisha. Interviews with author, March 3, 2008–June 20, 2012; with author and Caitlin Gunn, June 22, 2012.

*Lanita. Interview with author, July 16, 2005.

*Latifah. Interview with author, July 14, 2005.

*Lisa. Interview with author, July 1–2, 2009.

Liversage, Anika. E-mail conversation with author, December 20–22, 2011.

*Marsha. Interview with author, August 11, 2003.

*Martha. Interviews with author, June 10, 2005–June 10, 2012.

Mohammed, Imam W. D. Interview with author, November 13, 1997.

———. "Excerpts from Imam Mohammed's Talk to Sisters Only Meeting in Detroit in 1995," in Imam Ronald Shaheed, e-mail message to author, December 1, 2002.

*Mohassan. Interview with author, March 22, 2006.

Muhammad, Laila. Interview with author, June, 20–22, 2012.

Muhammad, Imam Oliver. Interviews with author, August 2–3, 2003; June 7, 2009.

*Naeema. Interview with author, October 19, 2006.

*Naim. Interview with author, March 12, 2006.

*Nasif. Interview with author, March 9, 2006.

*Nissa. Interview with author, August 14, 2009.

*Omar. Interview with author, February 9, 2006, and July 4, 2012.

*Qaedah. E-mail conversations with author, July 6–August 7, 2011.

*Rabi'a. Interview with author, July 18, 2014; e-mail conversations with author, July 17–August 3, 2014.

*Rashad. Interview with author, October 17, 2006.

Rashidah. Interview with author, July 15, 2005.

Saahir, Imam Mikal. Interview with author, June 11, 2009.

Safi, Louay M. E-mail conversation with author, August 11, 2004.

*Salimah. Interview with author, August 14, 20014.

*Sawdah. Interview with author, March 31, 2007.

Shaheed, Imam Ronald. Interview with author, July 5, 2012; e-mail conversations with author, December 1, 2, and 3, 2002; May 5, 2011; July 5 and 9, 2012; July 7–9, 2014.

*Shakirah. Interview with author, June 7, 2005.

Shuaibe, Imam Faheem. Interview with author, June 19, 2012.

Wadud, Amina. Interview with author, June 2, 2014.

*Waleed. E-mail shared with author, July 17, 2014.

*Walladah. E-mail conversations with author, July 16–August 7, 2011.

*Zuhara. Interview with author, July 11, 2012.

Secondary Sources

Afro-American. "Ghana Tells Plans to Outlaw Polygamy." May 26, 1962, 12. http://news.google.com/newspapers?nid=2211&dat=19620526&id=fNMmAAAAIBAJ&sjid=n AIGAAAAIBAJ&pg=5958,2323337.

Ahmed, Leila. *Women and Gender in Islam.* New Haven, CT: Yale University Press, 1992.

Al-Alawi, Irfan, Stephen Suleuman Schwartz, Kamal Hasani, Veli Sirin, Daut Dauti, and Qanta Ahmed. *A Guide to Shariah Law and Islamist Ideology in Western Europe 2007–2009*. Washington, DC: Center for Islamic Pluralism, 2009.

Al Andalusia, Shariffa Carlo. "The Second Wife." In *Islam. The Modern Religion*. http://www.themodernreligion.com/women/w_polysecond.htm (accessed November 13, 2012).

Al-Baik, Duraid. "Polyandry Call Is 'Akin to Blasphemy.'" *Gulf News*, December 23, 2009. http://gulfnews.com/news/region/polyandry-call-is-akin-to-blasphemy-1.556934 (accessed November 11, 2014).

Al-Hibri, Azizah. "Study in Islamic Herstory, or How Did We Ever Get into This Mess." *Women's Studies International Forum* 5, no. 2 (1982): 207–19.

Ali, Kecia. "Polygyny." In *The Qur'an: An Encyclopedia*, edited by Oliver Leaman, 505–6. London: Routledge, 2006.

———. *Sexual Ethics in Islam: Feminist Reflections on Qur'an, Hadith, and Jurisprudence*. Oxford, England: Oneworld, 2006.

———. "A Woman Officiates at a Muslim Wedding." *PakiBarbie*, April 2, 2005. http://pakibarbie.blogspot.com/2005/04/woman-officiates-at-muslim-wedding.html (accessed September 23, 2011).

Ali, Yusuf. *The Quran: Text, Translation, and Commentary*. Beltsville, MD: Amana, 1997.

Al-Krenawi, Alean. "Family Therapy with a Multiparental/Multispousal Family." *Family Process* 37, no. 1 (March 1998): 65–81.

Allied Media Corporation. "Muslim American Outreach." 2010. http://www.allied-media.com/muslim_americans/muslim_american_demographics.html (accessed May 23, 2011).

Anderson, Benedict. *Imagined Communities: Reflections on the Origin and Spread of Nationalism*. London: Verso, 1983.

An-Na'im, Abdullahi Ahmed. *Islam and the Secular State: Negotiating the Future of Shari'a*. Cambridge: Harvard University Press, 2008.

Arat, Yesm. *The Patriarchal Paradox: Women Politicians in Turkey*. Cranbury, NJ: Associated University Presses, 1989.

Arndt, Susan. "African Gender Trouble and African Womanism: An Interview with Chikwenye Ogunyemi and Wanjira Muthoni." *Signs* 25, no. 3 (Spring 2000): 709–26.

Badawi, Jamal A. *Polygamy in Islamic Law*. Islamic Research Foundation International, n.d. http://www.irfi.org/articles/articles_251_300/polygamy_in_islamic_law.htm.

Banfield, William C. *Black Notes: Essays of a Musician Writing in a Post-Album Age*. Lanham, MD: Scarecrow Press, 2004.

Bano, Samia. "In Pursuit of Religious and Legal Diversity: A Response to the Archbishop of Canterbury and the 'Sharia Debate' in Britain." *Ecclesiastical Law Society* 10 (2008): 283–309.

Barazangi, Nimat Hafez. *Women's Identity and the Qur'an: A New Reading*. Gainesville: University Press of Florida, 2004.

Barlas, Asma. *Believing Women in Islam: Unreading Patriarchal Interpretations of the Qur'an*. Austin: University of Texas Press, 2002.

———. "Interview with Asma Barlas: 'It Is the Right of Every Muslim to Interpret the Quran for Themselves.'" Liberal Islam Network, 2005; republished by Muslims for Progressive Values, January 11, 2007, at http://www.mpvusa.org/uploads/Interview-with_Asma_Barlas.pdf (accessed February 20, 2012)

———. "The Pleasure of Our Text: Re-Reading the Qur'an." Presentation to the Interchurch Conference on Women in Religion in the 21st Century, New York, October 18, 2006.

———. "Un-Reading Patriarchal Interpretations of the Qur'an: Beyond the Binaries of Tradition and Modernity." Paper presented at the Association of Muslim Social Scientists Conference on Islam, Toronto, November 4, 2006.

Barringer Gordon, Sarah. *The Mormon Question: Polygamy and Constitutional Conflict in Nineteenth Century America*. Chapel Hill: University of North Carolina Press, 2002.

———. "A War of Words: Revelation and Storytelling in the Campaign against Mormon Polygamy." *Chicago-Kent Law Review* 78 (2003): 747–57.

Bartky, Sandra Lee. "Foucault, Femininity, and the Modernization of Patriarchal Power." In *Feminism and Foucault*, edited by Irene Diamond and Lee Quinby, 64–82. Boston: Northeastern University Press, 1998.

Bartolone, Pauline. "For These Muslims, Polygamy Is an Option." *San Francisco Chronicle*, August 5, 2007.

BBC News Berkshire. "Bigamy Slough Councillor Pervez Choudhry Must Wear Tag." May 18, 2012. http://www.bbc.com/news/uk-england-berkshire-18116577 (accessed June 16, 2012).

Bennion, Janet. *Polygamy in Primetime: Media, Gender, and Politics in Mormon Fundamentalism*. Lebanon, MA: Brandeis University Press, 2012.

Berger, Benjamin. "Polygamy and the Predicament of Contemporary Criminal Law." *Comparative Research in Law and Political Economy*. Research Paper no. 36 (2012). http://digitalcommons.osgoode.yorku.ca/cgi/viewcontent.cgi?article=1012&context=clpe (accessed January 10, 2013).

Besant, Ann. *The Life and Teachings of the Prophet Muhammad*. Adyar, India: The Theosophical Society, 1932.

Blankship, Khalid. "Murshid al-Qari: A Reader's Guide to Classical Muslim Religious Literature in English." Personal copy of unpublished manuscript.

Blassingame, John W. *The Slave Community: Plantation Life in the Antebellum South*. New York: Oxford University Press, 1979.

Bonar, Daphne L. "Possibilities of Agency: The Impact of the Work of Natalie Zemon Davis." Bachelor of arts thesis, Concordia University, 1991. summit.sfu.ca/system/files/iritems1/5735/b15249633.pdf (accessed June 3, 2008).

Bozzuti, Joseph. "The Constitutionality of Polygamy Prohibitions after *Lawrence v. Texas*: Is Scalia a Punchline or a Prophet?" *Catholic Lawyer* 43 (2004): 409–22.

Bradley Hagerty, Barbara. "Philly's Black Muslims Increasingly Turn to Polygamy." *All Things Considered*, National Public Radio, May 28, 2008. http://www.npr.org/templates/story/story.php?storyId=90886407 (accessed June 3, 2008).

———. "Some Muslims in the U.S. Quietly Engage in Polygamy." *All Things Considered*, National Public Radio, May 27, 2008. http://www.npr.org/templates/story/story.php?storyId=90857818 (accessed June 3, 2008).

Brooks, Thom. "The Problem with Polygamy." *Philosophical Topics* 37, no. 1 (Spring 2009): 190–22.

Bucholtz, Mary, and Kira Hall. "Language and Identity." In *A Companion to Linguistic Anthropology*, edited by Alessandro Duranti, 268–94. Oxford, England: Basil Blackwell, 2004.

Butler, Francelia. "Tennessee Heritage." *Parabola* 7, no. 3 (1982): 26–33.

Calder, Gillian, and Lori G. Beaman. *Polygamy's Rights and Wrongs: Perspectives on Harm, Family, and Law*. Vancouver, Canada: University of British Columbia Press, 2013.

Cannon, Katie G. "Response." *Journal of Feminist Studies in Religion* 22, no. 1 (2006): 96–98.

Carling, Jorgen. "The Human Dynamics of Migrant Transnationalism." *Ethnic and Racial Studies* 31, no. 8 (November 2008): 1452–77.

Chapman, Audrey. *Man-Sharing: Dilemma of Choice, a Radical New Way of Relating to Men in Your Life*. New York: William Morrow, 1986.

Charsley, Katharine, and Anika Liversage. "Transforming Polygamy: Migration, Transnationalism, and Multiple Marriages among Muslim Minorities." *Global Networks* 13, no. 1 (January 2013): 60–78.

Clegg, Claude Andrew III. "Message from the Wilderness of North America: Elijah Muhammad and the Nation of Islam, c. 1960." *Journal for MultiMedia History* 1, no. 1 (Fall 1998). http://www.albany.edu/jmmh/vol1no1/elijahmuhammad.html (accessed May 23, 2007).

———. *An Original Man: The Life and Times of Elijah Muhammad*. New York: St. Martin's Griffin, 1997.

CNN. "Bush Calls for Ban on Same-Sex Marriages." February 25, 2004. http://www.cnn.com/2004/ALLPOLITICS/02/24/elec04.prez.bush.marriage/ (accessed March 1, 2004).

Coleman, Monica, ed. *Ain't I a Womanist Too? Third Wave Womanist Religious Thought (Innovations)*. Minneapolis, MN: Fortress Press, 2013.

Conquergood, Dwight. "Performing as a Moral Act: Ethical Dimensions of the Ethnography of Performance." *Literature in Performance* 5, no. 2 (1985): 1–13.

Czarniawska, Barbara. *Narrating the Organization: Dramas of Institutional Identity*. Chicago: University of Chicago Press, 1997.

———. "The Uses of Narrative in Organization Research." GRI Report 5. Gothenburg, Sweden: Gothenburg Research Institute, 2000. https://gupea.ub.gu.se/bitstream/2077/2997/1/GRI-rapport-2000-5.pdf (accessed March 3, 2004).

Dannin, Robert. *Black Pilgrimage to Islam*. New York: Oxford University Press, 2002.

Davis, Adrienne D. "Regulating Polygamy: Intimacy, Default Rules, and Bargaining For Equality." *Columbia Law Review* 110, no. 8 (2010): 1955–2046.

Daynes, Katherine M. "Plural Wives and the Nineteenth-Century Mormon Marriage System: Manti, Utah, 1849–1910." PhD diss., Indiana University, 1991.

Deller Ross, Susan. *Women's Human Rights: The International and Comparative Law Casebook*. Philadelphia: University of Pennsylvania Press, 2009.

Demosthenes. *Demosthenes, with an English Translation by Norman W. DeWitt, PhD, and Norman J. DeWitt, PhD*. Cambridge: Harvard University Press, 1949.

Dettner, Jamie. "Britain's Part-Time Wives." *Daily Beast*, August 5, 2013. http://www.the-dailybeast.com/witw/articles/2013/08/05/britain-s-muslim-communities-see-rise-in-multiple-marriages-as-career-women-seek-part-time-husbands.html (accessed November 11, 2014).

Ditz, Toby L. "Ownership and Obligation: Inheritance and Patriarchal Households in Connecticut, 1750–1820." *William and Mary Quarterly* 47, no. 2 (April 1990): 235–65.

Dixon, Patricia. *African American Relationships, Marriages, and Families: An Introduction*. New York: Taylor and Francis, 2007.

———. *We Want for Our Sisters What We Want for Ourselves, Polygyny-Copartnering: A Relationship, Marriage, and Family Alternative*. Decatur, GA: Oji, 2002.

Elbedour, Salman, Anthony J. Onwuegbuzie, Corin Caridine, and Hasan Abu-Saad. "The Effect of Polygamous Marital Structure on Behavioral, Emotional, and Academic Adjustment in Children: A Comprehensive Review of the Literature." *Clinical Child and Family Psychology Review* 5, no. 4 (December 2002): 255–71.

El Fadl, Khaled Abou. Foreword to *Inside the Gender Jihad: Women's Reform in Islam*, by Amina Wadud. London: Oneworld, 2006.

———. *Speaking in God's Name: Islamic Law, Authority and Women*. Oxford, England: Oneworld, 2001.

Esposito, John L. *Islam*. Oxford, England: Oxford University Press, 1988.

———. *Women in Muslim Family Law*. 2nd ed. Syracuse, NY: Syracuse University Press, 2001.

Esposito, John L., and Dalia Mogahed. *Who Speaks for Islam? What a Billion Muslims Really Think*. New York: Gallup Press, 2007.

Estin, Anne Laquer. "Unofficial Family Law." *Iowa Law Review* 94, no. 2 (February 2009): 449–80.

Evanzz, Karl. In *The Messenger: The Rise and Fall of Elijah Muhammad*. New York: Vintage, 1999.

Falk Moore, Sally. "Law and Social Change: The Semi-Autonomous Social Field as an Appropriate Subject of Study." *Law and Society Review* 7, no. 4 (Summer, 1973): 719–46.

Farrakhan, Louis. "Rising above Emotion into the Thinking of God." In *The Nation of Islam Study Course*. Muhammad University of Islam, Chicago, 2011. http://v1.noi.org/study/docs/sg18_pt1_week_31_fri.pdf (accessed June 20, 2011).

———. "What Malcolm Did Not Tell You!!! The Wives Speak." Part 1. YouTube video, posted by Rodney Muhammad, November 14, 2009. https://www.youtube.com/watch?v=7KCni7e8eLY (accessed July 23, 2013).

———. "What Malcolm Did Not Tell You!!! The Wives Speak." Part 2. YouTube video, posted by Rodney Muhammad, November 14, 2009. https://www.youtube.com/watch?v=TxIfkQNMGzk (accessed July 23, 2013).

Father Divine Project. "The Marriage of Father and Mother Divine." 1996. Video. Posted at YouTube by Will Luers, May 22, 2007, https://www.youtube.com/watch?v=SGLEPCdQT9U.

Fawzy, Essam. "Personal Status Law in Egypt: An Historical Overview." In *Women's Rights and Islamic Family Law*, edited by Lynn Welchman, 30–44. London: Zed Books, 2004.

Ferhinard, Pamela. "Polygamy among the Blackamerikkan Jews Who Migrated to Israel." *Miami Herald*, December 6, 1991.

Fine, M. "Dis-Stance and Other Stances: Negotiations of Power inside Feminist Research." In *Power and Method: Political Activism and Educational Research*, edited by Andrew Gitlin, 13–55. New York: Routledge, 1994.

Franklin, John Hope. *From Slavery to Freedom*. New York: Knopf, 1967.

Frantz, Douglas, and Brett Pulley. "Harlem Church Is Outpost of Empire; Hose of Prayer Built Wide Holdings on Devotion to Sweet Daddy Grace." *New York Times*, December 17, 1995. http://www.nytimes.com/1995/12/17/nyregion/harlem-church-outpost-empire-house-prayer-built-wide-holdings-devotion-sweet.html.

Friedl, Erica. "Islam and Tribal Women in a Village in Iran." In *Unspoken Worlds: Women's Religious Lives in Non-Western Cultures*, edited by N. A. Falk and R. M. Gross, 157–67. San Francisco: Harper and Row, 1980.

Friedman, Thomas. "Foreign Affairs: The Real War." *New York Times*, November 27, 2001.

Gardell, Mattias. *In the Name of Elijah Muhammad: Louis Farrakhan and the Nation of Islam*. Durham, NC: Duke University Press, 1996.

Geertz, Clifford. *The Interpretation of Cultures*. New York: Basic, 1973.

Gibbs, Tyson, and Judith Campbell. "Practicing Polygyny in Black America: Challenging Definition, Legal and Social Considerations for the African American Community." *Western Journal of Black Studies* 23, no. 3 (1999): 144–53.

Gibson, Dawn-Marie, and Jamillah Karim. *Women of the Nation: Between Black Protest and Sunni Islam*. New York: New York University Press, 2014.

Gilles, Albert Sr. "Polygamy in Comanche Country." *Southwest Review* 51, no. 3 (1966): 286–97.

Givens, Terryl. "Mormons Change References to Blacks, Polygamy." Interview with Jacki Lyden. *All Things Considered*, National Public Radio, March 17, 2013. http://www.npr.org/2013/03/17/174559275/mormons-change-references-to-blacks-polygamy (accessed May 23, 2013).

Glenn, Madison. "Identity Crisis: Oversimplifying Negotiation Strategies of American Muslim Women." Unpublished final paper for Religious Studies 210 course, Women and Gender in Islam, Beloit College, in possession of author.

Global Rights. (Unofficial English translation of) The Moroccan Family Code (Moudawana) of February 5, 2004. Human Rights Education Associates. http://www.hrea.org/moudawana.html.

Green, Chanda. "The Pedagogy of Polygyny: A Narrative Inquiry into the Lives of American Born African American Muslim Women." PhD diss., University of St. Thomas, 2011.

Gross, Rita M. *Feminism and Religion: An Introduction*. Boston: Beacon Press, 1996.

Hall, Stuart. "The Spectacle of the Other." In *Representations: Cultural Representations and Signifying Practices*, edited by Stuart Hall, 223–91. London: Sage, 1987.

Hammer, Julianne. "Gender Justice in a Prayer: American Muslim Women's Exegesis, Authority, and Leadership." *Hawwa: Journal of Women of the Middle East and the Islamic World* 8 (2010): 26–54.

Haredy, Mohsen, "Polygamy: Not a Sixth Pillar of Islam!" *Onislam*, June 27, 2014. http://www.onislam.net/english/ask-about-islam/society-and-family/social-life/457613-polygamy-not-a-sixth-pillar-of-islam.html.

Harris-Perry, Melissa V. *Sister Citizen: Shame, Stereotypes, and Black Women in America*. New Haven, CT: Yale University Press, 2011.

Hasan, Ahmad, trans. *Partial Translation of Sunan Abu-Dawud*. Center for Muslim-Jewish Engagement, University of Southern California, n.d. http://www.usc.edu/org/cmje/religious-texts/hadith/abudawud/ (accessed January 27, 2012).

Hasan, Zeeshan. "Polygamy, Slavery, and Qur'anic Sexual Ethics." *Star Weekend Magazine [Bangladesh]*, August 30, 1996.

Heliprin, John. "Hatch Joins Leavitt in Game of Twister over Polygamy Issues." *Salt Lake Tribune*, August 29, 1998.

Hermansen, Marcia. "Introduction: The New Voices of Muslim Women Theologians." In *Muslima Theology: The Voices of Muslim Women Theologians*, edited by Ednan Aslan, Marcia Hermansen, and Elif Medeni, 11–34. New York: Peter Lang, 2013.

Hidayatullah, Aysha A. *Feminist Edges of the Qur'an*. Oxford, England: Oxford University Press, 2014.

Hill Collins, Patricia. "What's in a Name? Womanism, Black Feminism, and Beyond." *Black Scholar* 26, no. 1 (Winter/Spring, 1996): 9–17.

Hirsch, Susan F. *Asserting Male Authority, Recreating Female Experience: Gendered Discourse in Costal Kenyan Muslim Courts*. Chicago: American Bar Association, 1990.

Hudson-Weems, Clenora. *Africana Womanism: Reclaiming Ourselves*. New York: Bedford, 2004.

Isasi-Dias, Ada Maria. *En la Lucha/In the Struggle: Elaborating a Mujerista Theology*. Minneapolis, MN: Fortress Press, 2004.

Jackson, Raphael. Review of *We Want for Our Sisters What We Want for Ourselves*, by

Patricia Dixon. In *People with Voices*, September 30, 2011. http://peoplewithvoices. com/2011/09/30/book-review-we-want-for-our-sisters-what-we-want-for-ourselves/.

Jackson, Sherman. *Islam and the Blackamerican: Looking toward the Third Resurrection.* New York: Oxford University Press, 2011.

Jacobs, Mignon R. *Gender, Power, and Persuasion: The Genesis Narrative and Contemporary Portraits.* Grand Rapids, MI: Baker Academics, 2007.

Jacobson, Cardell D., ed. *Modern Polygamy in the United States: Historical, Cultural, and Legal Issues.* New York: Oxford University Press, 2011.

Jawad, H. A. "Women and Polygamy in Islam." *Islamic Quarterly* 35, no. 3:181–190.

———. "Women and the Question of Polygamy in Islam." In *The Rights of Women in Islam: An Authentic Approach,* by Haifaa A. Jawad, 41–51. London: Palgrave Macmillan, 1998.

Jawad, Haifaa. "Muslim Feminism: A Case Study of Amina Wadud's 'Quran and Woman.'" *Islamic Studies* 42, no. 1 (Spring 2003): 107–25.

Jones, Jameelah. "Preface: First Edition [1985]." In *Polygamy In Islaam,* by Abu Ameenah Bilal Philips and Jameelah Jones, iii. Riyadh: International Islamic Publishing House, 1998.

Jones, Joy. "'Marriage Is for White People.'" *Washington Post,* March 26, 2006.

Jones, Rachel. "Polygyny in Islam." *Macalester Islam Journal* 1, no. 1 (2006): 61–79.

Kennan, Jillian. "Legalize Polygamy! No, I'm Kidding." *Slate.com,* April 15, 2013. http:// www.slate.com/articles/double_x/doublex/2013/04/legalize_polygamy_marriage_ equality_for_all.html (accessed June, 10, 2013).

Kennard, Lauren S. "From Wives of the Prophets to Mothers of the Believers: The Polygamous Wives of Muhammad and Joseph Smith." Master's thesis, Claremont Graduate University, 2011.

Kern, Soeren. "Britain: Muslim Polygamists to Get More Welfare Benefits." Gatestone Institute, August 1, 2012. http://www.gatestoneinstitute.org/3234/muslim-polygamists-welfare-benefits (accessed June 12, 2013).

Kindregan, Charles P., Jr. "Religion, Polygamy, and Non-Traditional Families: Disparate Views on the Evolution of Marriage in History and in the Debate over Same-Sex Unions." *Suffolk University Law Review* 41, no. 1 (2007–8): 19–48.

Lawrence, Bruce. *The Qur'an: A Biography.* London: Atlantic Monthly Press, 2006.

Lepore, Jill. "Historians Who Love Too Much: Reflections on Microhistory and Biography." *Journal of American History* 88, no. 1 (2001): 129–44.

Lewis, Bernard G. *The Spirit of Islamic Law.* Athens: University of Georgia Press, 1998.

Macfarlane, Julie. *Islamic Divorce in North America: A Shari'a Path in a Secular Society.* Oxford, England: Oxford University Press, 2012.

———. *Understanding Trends in American Muslim Divorce and Marriage: A Discussion Guide for Families and Communities.* Institute for Social Policy and Understanding, January 5, 2012. http://www.ispu.org/getreports/35/2399/publications.aspx (accessed March 3, 2012).

Madison, D. Soyini. *Critical Ethnography: Methods, Ethics, and Performance.* London: Sage, 2011.

Mahmood, Saba. "Feminist Theory, Embodiment, and the Docile Agent: Some Reflections on the Egyptian Islamic Revival." *Cultural Anthropology* 16, no. 2 (2001): 202–36.

———. "Women's Agency within Feminist Historiography." *Journal of Religion* 84, no. 4 (October 2004): 573–79.

Majeed, D. Hadayai S. *Emerging Victorious: A Dialogue on Polygamy/Polygyny in America.* Augusta, GA: Morris, 1997.

Majeed, Debra. "Clara Evans Muhammad." In *Encyclopedia of Women and Religion in North America,* edited by Rosemary Skinner Keller and Rosemary Radford Ruether, 746–52. Bloomington: Indiana University Press, 2005.

———. "Clara Evans Muhammad: Pioneering Social Activism in the Original Nation of Islam." *Union Seminary Quarterly Review* 57, no. 3–4 (2003): 746–52.

———. "Muslim Marriage: A Womanist Perspective on Troubling U.S. Traditions." In *Ain't I a Womanist Too?* edited by Monica A. Coleman, 35–48. Minneapolis, MN: Fortress Press, 2012.

———. "Wadud and the Promotion of Experience as Authority." In *A Jihad for Justice: Honoring the Life and Work of Amina Wadud,* edited by Kecia Ali, Julianne Hammer, and Laury Silvers, 59–62. Akron, OH: 48HrBooks, 2012.

Malcolm X and Alex Haley. *The Autobiography of Malcolm X.* New York: First Ballantine, 1992.

Mark Foster Network. *Muhammad Abduh: Wikibook.* 2013. www.markfoster.net/struc/ Muhammad_Abduh.pdf (accessed July 25, 2014).

Mattu, Ayesha, and Nura Maznavi, eds. *Love, InshAllah: The Secret Love Lives of American Muslim Women.* Berkeley, CA: Soft Skull Press, 2012.

McClintock, Walter. *The Old North Trail.* London: Macmillan, 1910.

McNay, Lois. *Gender and Agency: Reconfiguring the Subject in Feminist and Social Theory.* Cambridge, England: Polity, 2000.

Mernissi, Fatima. *Beyond the Veil: Male-Female Dynamics in Modern Muslim Society.* Bloomington: Indiana University Press, 1987.

Mir-Hosseini, Ziba. "Islamic Law and Feminism: The Story of a Relationship." *Yearbook of Islamic and Middle Eastern Law* 9 (2004): 32–42.

———. "Towards Gender Equality: Muslim Family Laws and the Shari'ah." In *WANTED: Equality and Justice in the Muslim Family,* edited by Zainah Anwar, 23–64. Selangor, Malaysia: Musawah: An Initiative of Sisters of Islam, 2009. http://www.musawah. org/sites/default/files/WANTED-EN-2edition_0.pdf (accessed April 2, 2010).

Mission Islam. "Polygyny Not Polygamy." Derived from *Polygamy in Islaam,* by Philips and Jones. http://www.missionislam.com/family/polygamy.htm (accessed January 27, 2012).

Mitchell, Jessica Nicole. "Power-Control Theory: An Examination of Private and Public Patriarchy." Master's thesis, University of South Florida, 2009.

MizAzeez. *Polygynous Blessings: Musings of a Muslim Wife.* Raleigh, NC: Lulu Press, 2007.

Mohammed, Khaleel. "Assessing English Translations of the Qur'an." *Middle East Quarterly* 12, no. 2 (Spring 2005): 58–71.

Mohammed, Warith Deen. "Al-Islam in America Today." Tape recording, date unknown.

——. "Imam Mohammed Defends His Marriage in Jumah." YouTube video posted by Muhammad Siddeeq, September 25, 2008. https://www.youtube.com/watch?v=vHL KZ4kHExY&list=PLgz448Jf3lv9GsMtXQRk_DCCFI7aKvYh3&index=19 (accessed March 23, 2009).

——. "Speeches to the Men and Women of the American Society of Muslims: Brothers Only Meeting," Atlanta, May 17, 2003.

——. "Speeches to the Men and Women of the American Society of Muslims: Sisters Meeting," Chicago, March 8, 2003.

——. "Speeches to the Men and Women of the American Society of Muslims: Sisters Meeting," Detroit, 1995.

——. "Speeches to the Men and Women of the American Society of Muslims: Sisters Meeting," San Francisco, June 7, 2003.

Moore, John H. "The Developmental Cycle of Cheyenne Polygyny." *American Indian Quarterly* 15, no. 3, (Summer 1991): 311–28.

Moore, Kathleen. *The Unfamiliar Abode: Islamic Law in the United States and Britain.* Oxford, England: Oxford University Press, 2010.

Mosher, Aisha. "A Wife's Prerogative." *Abdulmateenkhan.com.* http://www.abdulmateenkhan.com/mail_archive/2002/November/Religious/AWifesPerogative.htm (accessed June 2, 2003).

Moxley Rouse, Carolyn. *Engaged Surrender: African American Muslim Women.* Oakland: University of California Press, 2004.

Mudzakir, Ro'fah. "The Indonesian Muslim Women's Movement and the Issue of Polygamy: The 'Aisyiyah Interpretation of Qur'an 4:3 and 3:129." In *Approaches to the Qur'an in Contemporary Indonesia,* edited by Abdullah Saeed, 175–92. New York: Oxford University Press, 2005.

Muhammad, Elijah. *Message to the Blackman.* Hampton, VA: United Brothers Communications Systems, 1992. Originally published 1965.

Muhammad, Laila. "The Estate of Warith Deen Mohammed." Interview by Thomas Abul-Salaam. *Blogtalkradio,* September 16, 2011. http://www.blogtalkradio.com/americanmuslim360/2011/09/16/laila-mohammed-the-estate-of-imam-warith-deen-mohammed (accessed September 25, 2011).

Muhammad, Princetta. *Messenger Elijah Muhammad: The Crowning Glory of the Blackman and Woman in America.* Oklahoma City: CreateSpace, 2011.

Muhammad, W. Deen. *The Man and the WoMan in Islam.* Chicago: The Hon. Elijah Muhammad Mosque #2, 1976.

Muhammad-Ali, Jesus. *The Evolution of the Nation: The Story of the Honorable Elijah Muhammad.* Birmingham, AL: JMA, 2002.

National Conference of State Legislatures. "Same-Sex Marriage Laws." November 13, 2014. http://www.ncsl.org/research/human-services/same-sex-marriage-laws.aspx#1 (accessed November 16,2014).

Newport, Frank, and Igor Himelfarb. "In U.S., Record-High Say Gay, Lesbian Relations Morally Ok." Gallup.com, May 20, 2013. http://www.gallup.com/poll/162689/record-high-say-gay-lesbian-relations-morally.aspx (accessed June 1, 2013).

Norton, Mary Beth. *Founding Mothers and Fathers: Gendered Power and the Forming of American Society*. New York: Vintage, 1997.

———. "Historically Speaking: An Interview with Mary Beth Norton." Interview by Ben Barker-Benfield, *Journal for MultiMedia History* 3 (2000). http://www.albany.edu/jmmh/vol3/norton/norton.html (accessed June 3, 2001).

Nurmilla, Nina. *Women, Islam, and Everyday Life: Renegotiating Polygamy in Indonesia*. London: Routledge, 2009.

Page, Helan. E. "Dialogical Principles of Interactive Learning in the Ethnographic Relationship." *Journal of Anthropological Research* 44, no. 2 (Summer 1988): 163–81.

Patterson, Orlando. *Rituals of Blood: Consequences of Slavery in Two American Centuries*. New York: Basic, 1998.

Pew Research Center and Andrew Kohut. *Muslim Americans: Middle Class and Mostly Mainstream*. Washington, DC: Pew Research Center, 2007.

Philips, Abu Ameenah Bilal. "Preface: Third Edition." In *Polygamy in Islaam*, by Abu Ameenah Bilal Philips and Jameelah Jones, i–ii. Riyadh: International Islamic Publishing House, 1998.

Philips, Abu Ameenah Bilal, and Jameelah Jones. *Polygamy in Islaam*. Riyadh: International Islamic Publishing House, 1998. Originally published 1985; also republished 2005 at http://www.islamicbulletin.org/free_downloads/women/polygamy_in_islam.pdf (accessed November 15, 2014).

Philips, Bilal. "Polygamy in Islam with Dr. Bilal Philips." Interview, *Deen Show*, Muslim Video.com, 2010. http://www.muslimvideo.com/tv/watch/122e98cfb9c6487f8438/Polygamy-in-Islam-with-Dr.-Bilal-Philips-on-TheDeenShow (accessed November 23, 2011).

Phillips, Layli. "Womanism: on Its Own." In *The Womanist Reader*, edited by Layli Phillips, xix–lv. New York: Routledge, 2006.

Piela, Anna. "Claiming Religious Authority: Muslim Women and New Media." In *Media, Religion, and Gender: Key Issues and New Challenges*, edited by Mia Lövheim, 125–40. London: Routledge, 2013.

Pinderhughes, Elaine B. "African American Marriage in the 20th Century." *Family Process* 41, no. 2 (June 2002): 269–82.

Quraishi, Asifa, and Najeeba Syeed-Miller. "No Altars: A Survey of Islamic Family Law in the United States." In *Women's Rights and Islamic Family Law: Perspectives on Reform*, edited by Lynn Welchman, 177–217. London: Zed Books, 2004.

Rahman, Fazlur. "A Survey of Modernization of Muslim Family Law." *International Journal of Middle East Studies* 11, no. 4 (July 1980): 451–65.

Rida, Mohammad Rashid. "Mohammad Rashid Rida on Muhammad Abdul on Polygamy." *Megalextoria* archive. http://www.megalextoria.com/usenet-archive/news128f1/b175/soc/religion/islam/00000488.html (accessed June 3, 2013).

Riggs, Marcia I. *Awake, Arise, and Act: A Womanist Call for Black Liberation.* Cleveland, OH: Pilgrim Press, 1994.

Rosaldo, M. Z. "The Use and Abuse of Anthropology: Reflections on Feminism and Cross-Cultural Understanding." *Signs* 5, no. 3 (Spring 1980): 389–417.

Rosen, Michael. "Breakfast at Spiro's: Dramaturgy and Dominance." *Journal of Management* 11, no. 2 (Summer 1985): 31–48.

Rosenwasser, David, and Jill Stephen. *Writing Analytically.* 6th ed. Boston: Wadsworth, 2011.

Saeed, Abdullah, ed. *Approaches to the Qur'an in Contemporary Indonesia.* New York: Oxford University Press, 2005.

Scott, Joan Wallace. *Gender and the Politics of History.* New York: Columbia University Press, 1988.

———. "Gender: A Useful Category of Historical Analysis." *American Historical Review* 91 (1986): 1053–75.

Sells, Michael. *Approaching the Quran.* Ashland, OR: White Cloud Press, 2005.

Serck, Linda. "Polygamy in Islam: The Women Victims of Multiple Marriage." *BBC News Berkshire*, May 31, 2012. http://www.bbc.com/news/uk-england-berkshire-18252958 (accessed June 2, 2012).

Shachar, Ayelet. "Privatizing Diversity: A Cautionary Tale from Religious Arbitration in Family Law." *Theoretical Inquiries in Law* 9 (2008): 573–607.

Shaikh, Sa'diyya. "A Tafsir of Praxis: Gender, Marital Violence, and Resistance in a South African Muslim Community." In *Violence against Women in Contemporary World Religions: Roots and Cures*, edited by Daniel C. Maguire and Sa'diyya Shaikh, 66–89. Cleveland, OH: Pilgrim Press, 2007.

Shuaibe, Imam Faheem. "Has Faith Entered Your Heart Yet?" Jumu'ah lecture. *Blogtalkradio*, August 24, 2012. http://www.blogtalkradio.com/faheem-shuaibe/2012/08/24/live-jumuah-from-masjidul-waritheen.

Silberberg, Naftali. "Does Jewish Law Forbid Polygamy?" Chabad.org, n.d. http://www.chabad.org/library/article_cdo/aid/558598/jewish/Does-Jewish-Law-Forbid-Polygamy.htm (accessed June 10, 2013).

Simmons, Gwendolyn Zoharah. "Muslim Women's Experience as a Basis for Theological Interpretation of Islam." In *Muslims in the United States: Identity, Influence, Innovation*, edited by Philippa Strum, 203–12. Washington, DC: Woodrow Wilson International Center for Scholars, 2005. http://www.wilsoncenter.org/sites/default/files/Muslim_Thought_final.pdf (accessed December 1, 2005).

Sisters in Islam. *Islam and Polygamy.* Kuala Lumpur, Malaysia: 2002

Skojec, Steve. "Polygamy: The Next Marriage Fight." *CatholicVote.org.* http://www.catholicvote.org/polygamy-the-next-marriage-fight/ (accessed July 1, 2013).

Smearman, Claire A. "Second Wives' Club: Mapping the Impact of Polygamy in U.S. Immigration Law." *Berkeley Journal of International Law* 27, no. 2 (2009): 382–447.

Soroush, Abdolkarim. "The Beauty of Justice." *CSD Bulletin* 14, nos. 1 and 2 (Summer 2007): 8–12.

Strum, Philippa, ed. *Muslims in the United States: Identity, Influence, Innovation.* Washington, DC: Woodrow Wilson International Center for Scholars, 2005. http://www.wilsoncenter.org/sites/default/files/Muslim_Thought_final.pdf (accessed Dec. 1, 2005).

Syed, Jawad. "An Historical Perspective on Islamic Modesty and Its Implications for Female Employment." *Equality, Diversity, and Inclusion: An International Journal* 29, no. 2 (2010): 150–66.

Thomas, Linda E. "Womanist Theology, Epistemology, and a New Anthropological Paradigm." *Cross Currents* 48, no. 4 (1998): 488–99.

Tucker, Judith E. *Women, Family, and Gender in Islamic Law.* Cambridge, England: Cambridge University Press, 2008.

Tuppurainen, Anne Johanna. "Challenges Faced by Muslim Women: An Evaluation of the Writings of Leila Ahmed, Elizabeth Fernea, Fatima Mernissi, and Amina Wadud." PhD diss., University of South Africa, 2010.

Tuwaijri, Muhammad ibn 'Abdul-Muhsin al-. Publisher's note in *Polygamy in Islaam*, by Abu Ameenah Bilal Philips and Jameelah Jones, 7–8. Riyadh, Saudi Arabia: International Islamic Publishing House, 2005.

Van Doorn-Harder, Pieternella. *Women Shaping Islam: Reading the Qur'an in Indonesia.* Champaign: University of Illinois Press, 2006.

Villalon, Roberta. "Passage to Citizenship and the Nuances of Agency: Latina Battered Immigrants." *Women's Studies International Forum* 33 (2010): 552–60.

Wadud, Amina. *Inside the Gender Jihad: Women's Reform in Islam.* London: Oneworld, 2006.

———. "Islam beyond Patriarchy: Through Gender Inclusive Qur'anic Analysis." In *WANTED: Equality and Justice in the Muslim Family*, edited by Zainah Anwar, 95–112. Selangor, Malaysia: Musawah: An Initiative of Sisters of Islam, 2009. http://www.musawah.org/sites/default/files/WANTED-EN-2edition_0.pdf (accessed April 2, 2010).

———. "Islamic Authority." Draft of presentation to the International Congress on Islamic Feminism, Barcelona, September 24, 2008. Copy in author's possession.

———. *Qur'an and Woman: Rereading the Sacred Text from a Woman's Perspective.* New York: Oxford University Press, 1999.

———. "The Spirited Voices of Muslim Women in Islamic Reform Movements." Presentation at the Islam, Democracy, and Gender Rights Symposium, University of Sydney, April 28, 2011.

Walbridge, Linda S. *Sex and the Single Shi'ite: Mut'a Marriage in an American Lebanese Shi'ite Community*. Dakar, Senegal: Women Living under Muslim Laws, 1997.

Walby, Sylvia. *Theorizing Patriarchy*. Oxford, England: Basil Blackwell, 1991.

Walker, Alice. *In Search of Our Mothers' Gardens: Womanist Prose*. San Diego, CA: Harcourt Brace Jovanovic, 1983.

Waugh, Earl H., and Jenny Wannas. "The Rise of a Womanist Movement among Muslim Immigrant Women in Alberta, Canada." *Studies in Contemporary Islam* 5, nos. 1–2 (Spring–Fall, 2003): 5–36.

Welchman, Lynn, ed. *Women's Rights and Islamic Family Law: Perspectives on Reform*. London: Zed Books, 2004.

Yilmaz, Ihsan. "The Challenge of Post-Modern Legality and Muslim Legal Pluralism in England." *Journal of Ethnic and Migration Studies* 28, no. 2 (2002): 343–54.

Yuksel, Edip, Layth Saleh al-Shaiban, and Martha Schulte-Nafeh, trans. *Quran: A Reformist Translation*. Torrington, CT: Rainbow Press, 2007.

Zaki, Hind Ahmed. "The New Marriage Contract in Egypt: Religious Reframing and the Hazards of Reform." Prepared for the American Anthropological Association Annual Meeting, November 19, 2010. https://www.academia.edu/2132743/The_New_Marriage_Contract_in_Egypt_Religious_Reframing_and_the_Hazards_of_Reform (accessed November 11, 2014).

Index

Page numbers in italics indicate a table

Debra Majeed is professor of religious studies at Beloit College. A religious historian, Majeed has made the interconnection of religion, gender, and culture central to her life's work. She has published in *CrossCurrents, Journal of Feminist Studies in Religion*, and *Teaching Theology and Religion*, among a host of other journals, as well as in the *Encyclopedia of Religious Freedom*, the *Encyclopedia of Women and Religion in America*, and the *Encyclopedia of Women in Islamic Cultures*. She also has served as a resource for several media groups including the *Washington Post* and has appeared on NPR's *News and Notes*. She is married and lives in Beloit, Wisconsin.

CPSIA information can be obtained
at www.ICGtesting.com
Printed in the USA
BVHW072034010319
541595BV00001B/58/P

9 780813 054063